A CONFLICT OF VISIONS

A CONFLICT OF VISIONS

*Ideological Origins of
Political Struggles*

THOMAS SOWELL

BASIC
BOOKS

A Member of the Perseus Books Group

Published by Basic Books,
A Member of the Perseus Books Group

Designed by Heather Hutchison

Library of Congress Cataloging-in-Publication Data

Sowell, Thomas, 1930-
    A conflict of visions : ideological origins of political struggles / Thomas
Sowell.
        p. cm.
    Includes index.
    ISBN 0-465-08142-8
    1. Social values. 2. Ideology. 3. Visions. I. Title.
HM681 .S69 2002
303.3'72--dc21

                                                                    2001043787

02 03 04 / 10 9 8 7 6 5 4 3 2 1

To my wife Mary, with love

Every man, wherever he goes, is encompassed by a cloud of comforting convictions, which move with him like flies on a summer day.

—Bertrand Russell[1]

CONTENTS

PREFACE

A conflict of visions differs from a conflict between contending interests. When interests are at stake, the parties directly affected usually understand clearly what the issue is and what they individually stand to gain or lose. The general public may not understand—and indeed may be confused precisely because of the propaganda of the contending parties. But such public confusion is the direct consequence of the clarity of the interested parties themselves. However, when there is a conflict of visions, those most powerfully affected by a particular vision may be the least aware of its underlying assumptions— or the least interested in stopping to examine such theoretical questions when there are urgent "practical" issues to be confronted, crusades to be launched, or values to be defended at all costs.

Yet visions are not mere emotional drives. On the contrary, they have a remarkable logical consistency, even if those devoted to these visions have seldom investigated that logic. Nor are visions confined to zealots and ideologues. We all have visions. They are the silent shapers of our thoughts.

Visions may be moral, political, economic, religious, or social. In these or other realms, we sacrifice for our visions and sometimes, if need be, face ruin rather than betray them. Where visions conflict irreconcilably, whole societies may be torn apart. Conflicts of interests dominate the short run, but conflicts of visions dominate history.

We will do almost anything for our visions, except think about them. The purpose of this book is to think about them.

Thomas Sowell
The Hoover Institution
Stanford University

PART I: PATTERNS

Chapter 1

THE ROLE OF VISIONS

One of the curious things about political opinions is how often the same people line up on opposite sides of different issues. The issues themselves may have no intrinsic connection with each other. They may range from military spending to drug laws to monetary policy to education. Yet the same familiar faces can be found glaring at each other from opposite sides of the political fence, again and again. It happens too often to be coincidence and it is too uncontrolled to be a plot. A closer look at the arguments on both sides often shows that they are reasoning from fundamentally different premises. These different premises—often implicit—are what provide the consistency behind the repeated opposition of individuals and groups on numerous, unrelated issues. They have different visions of how the world works.

It would be good to be able to say that we should dispense with visions entirely, and deal only with reality. But that may be the most utopian vision of all. Reality is far too complex to be comprehended by any given mind. Visions are like maps that guide us through a tangle of bewildering complexities. Like maps, visions have to leave out many concrete features in order to enable us to focus on a few key paths to our goals. Visions are indispensable—but dangerous, precisely to the extent that we confuse them with reality itself. What has been deliberately neglected may not in fact turn out to be negligible in its effect on the results. That has to be tested against evidence.

A vision has been described as a "pre-analytic cognitive act."[1] It is what we sense or feel *before* we have constructed any systematic reasoning that could be called a theory, much less deduced any specific consequences as hypotheses to be tested against evidence. A vision is our sense of how the world works. For example, primitive man's sense of why leaves move may have been that some spirit moves them, and his sense of why tides rise or volcanoes erupt may have run along similar lines. Newton had a very different vision of how the world works and Einstein still another. For social phenomena, Rousseau had a very different vision of human causation from that of Edmund Burke.

Visions are the foundations on which theories are built. The final structure depends not only on the foundation, but also on how carefully and consistently the framework of theory is constructed and how well buttressed it is with hard facts. Visions are very subjective, but well-constructed theories have clear implications, and facts can test and measure their objective validity. The world learned at Hiroshima that Einstein's vision of physics was not *just* Einstein's vision.

Logic is an essential ingredient in the process of turning a vision into a theory, just as empirical evidence is then essential for determining the validity of that theory. But it is the initial vision which is crucial for our glimpse of insight into the way the world works. In Pareto's words:

> Logic is useful for proof but almost never for making discoveries. A man receives certain impressions; under their influence he states—without being able to say either how or why, and if he attempts to do so he deceives himself—a proposition, which can be verified experimentally. . . .[2]

Visions are all, to some extent, simplistic—though that is a term usually reserved for other people's visions, not our own. The ever-changing kaleidoscope of raw reality would defeat the human mind by its complexity, except for the mind's ability to abstract, to pick out parts and think of them as the whole. This is nowhere more necessary than in social visions and social theory, dealing with the complex and often subconscious interactions of millions of human beings.

No matter what vision we build on, it will never account for "every sparrow's fall." Social visions especially must leave many important phenomena unexplained, or explained only in *ad hoc* fashion, or by inconsistent assumptions that derive from more than one vision. The purest vision may not be the basis of the most impressive theories, much less the most valid ones. Yet purer visions may be more revealing as to unspoken premises than are the more complex theories. For purposes of understanding the role of visions, William Godwin's *Enquiry Concerning Political Justice*

(1793) may tell us more than Marx's *Capital*. Indeed, we may understand more of Marx's *Capital* after we have seen how similar premises worked out in the simpler model of William Godwin. Likewise, the vision of social causation underlying the theories of the Physiocrats was in its essentials very much like the vision elaborated in a more complex and sophisticated way by Adam Smith and still later (and still more so) by Milton Friedman.

A vision, as the term is used here, is not a dream, a hope, a prophecy, or a moral imperative, though any of these things may ultimately derive from some particular vision. Here a vision is a sense of *causation*. It is more like a hunch or a "gut feeling" than it is like an exercise in logic or factual verification. These things come later, and feed on the raw material provided by the vision. *If* causation proceeds as our vision conceives it to, *then* certain other consequences follow, and theory is the working out of what those consequences are. Evidence is fact that discriminates between one theory and another. Facts do not "speak for themselves." They speak for or against competing theories. Facts divorced from theory or visions are mere isolated curiosities.

Theories can be devastated by facts but they can never be proved to be correct by facts. Ultimately there are as many visions as there are human beings, if not more, and more than one vision may be consistent with a given fact. Facts force us to discard some theories—or else to torture our minds trying to reconcile the irreconcilable—but they can never put the final imprimatur of ultimate truth on a given theory. What empirical verification can do is to reveal which of the competing theories currently being considered is more consistent with what is known factually. Some other theory may come along tomorrow that is still more consistent with the facts, or explains those facts with fewer, clearer, or more manageable assumptions—or covers both this and other empirical phenomena hitherto explained by a separate theory.

Social visions are important in a number of ways. The most obvious is that policies based on a certain vision of the world have consequences that spread through society and reverberate across the years, or even across generations or centuries. Visions set the agenda for both thought and action. Visions fill in the necessarily large gaps in individual knowledge. Thus, for example, an individual may act in one way in some area in which he has great knowledge, but in just the opposite way elsewhere, where he is relying on a vision he has never tested empirically. A doctor may be a conservative on medical issues and a liberal on social and political issues, or vice versa.

The political battles of the day are a potpourri of special interests, mass emotions, personality clashes, corruption, and numerous other factors. Yet the enduring historic trends have a certain consistency that reflects certain visions. Often special interests prevail to the extent that they can mobilize support from the general public's responsiveness to visions which can be invoked for or against a given policy. From the standpoint of personal motivation, ideas may be simply the chips with which special interests, demagogues, and opportunists of various sorts play the political game. But from a broader perspective of history, these individuals and organizations can be viewed as simply carriers of ideas, much as bees inadvertently carry pollen—playing a vital role in the grand scheme of nature while pursuing a much narrower individual purpose.

The role of rationally articulated ideas may be quite modest in its effect on a given election, a legislative vote, or an action of a head of state. Yet the atmosphere in which such decisions take place may be dominated by a particular vision—or by a particular conflict of visions. Where intellectuals have played a role in history, it has not been so much by whispering words of advice into the ears of political overlords as by contributing to the vast and powerful currents of conceptions and misconceptions that sweep human action along. The effects of visions do not depend upon their being articulated, or even on decision-makers' being aware of them. "Practical" decision-makers often disdain theories and visions, being too busy to examine the ultimate basis on which they are acting. However, the object here will be precisely to examine the underlying social visions whose conflicts have shaped our times and may well shape times to come.

Chapter 2

CONSTRAINED AND UNCONSTRAINED VISIONS

At the core of every moral code there is a picture of human nature, a map of the universe, and a version of history. To human nature (of the sort conceived), in a universe (of the kind imagined), after a history (so understood), the rules of the code apply.

—Walter Lippman[1]

Social visions differ in their basic conceptions of the nature of man. A creature from another planet who sought information about human beings from reading William Godwin's *Enquiry Concerning Political Justice* in 1793 would hardly recognize man, as he appears there, as the same being who was described in *The Federalist Papers* just five years earlier. The contrast would be only slightly less if he compared man as he appeared in Thomas Paine and in Edmund Burke, or today in John Kenneth Galbraith and in Friedrich A. Hayek. Even the speculative pre-history of man as a wild creature in nature differs drastically between the free, innocent being conceived by Jean-Jacques Rousseau and the brutal participant in the bloody war of each against all conceived by Thomas Hobbes.

The capacities and limitations of man are implicitly seen in radically different terms by those whose explicit philosophical, political, or social theories are built on different visions. Man's moral and mental natures are seen so differently that their respective concepts of knowledge and of institutions necessarily differ as well. Social causation itself is conceived differently, both as to mechanics and results. Time and its ancillary phenomena—traditions, contracts, economic speculation, for example—are also viewed quite differently in theories based on different visions. The abstractions which are part of all theories tend to be viewed as more real by followers of some visions than by followers of opposing visions. Finally, those who believe in some visions view themselves in a very different moral role from the way the followers of other visions view themselves. The ramifications of these conflicting visions extend into economic, judicial, military, philosophical, and political decisions.

Rather than attempt the impossible task of following all these ramifications in each of the myriad of social visions, the discussion here will group these visions into two broad categories—the constrained vision and the unconstrained vision. These will be abstractions of convenience, recognizing that there are degrees in both visions, that a continuum has been dichotomized, that in the real world there are often elements of each inconsistently grafted on to the other, and innumerable combinations and permutations. With all these caveats, it is now possible to turn to an outline of the two visions, and specifics on the nature of man, the nature of knowledge, and the nature of social processes, as seen in constrained and unconstrained visions.

THE NATURE OF MAN

The Constrained Vision

Adam Smith provided a picture of man which may help make concrete the nature of a constrained vision. Writing as a philosopher in 1759, nearly twenty years before he became famous as an economist, Smith said in his *Theory of Moral Sentiments*:

> Let us suppose that the great empire of China, with all its myriads of inhabitants, was suddenly swallowed up by an earthquake, and let us consider how a man of humanity in Europe, who had no sort of connection with that part of the world, would react upon receiving intelligence of this dreadful calamity. He would, I imagine, first of all express very strongly his sorrow for the misfortune of that unhappy people, he would make many melancholy reflections upon the precariousness of human life, and the vanity of all the labours of man, which could thus be annihilated in a moment. He would, too, perhaps, if he was a man of speculation, enter into many reasonings concerning the effects which this disaster might produce upon the commerce of Europe, and the trade and business of the world in

general. And when all this fine philosophy was over, when all these humane sentiments had been once fairly expressed, he would pursue his business or his pleasure, take his repose or his diversion, with the same ease and tranquility as if no such accident had happened. The most frivolous disaster which could befall himself would occasion a more real disturbance. If he was to lose his little finger tomorrow, he would not sleep to-night; but, provided he never saw them, he would snore with the most profound security over the ruin of a hundred million of his brethren. . . .[2]

The moral limitations of man in general, and his egocentricity in particular, were neither lamented by Smith nor regarded as things to be changed. They were treated as inherent facts of life, the basic constraint in his vision. The fundamental moral and social challenge was to make the best of the possibilities which existed within that constraint, rather than dissipate energies in an attempt to change human nature—an attempt that Smith treated as both vain and pointless. For example, if it were somehow possible to make the European feel poignantly the full pain of those who suffered in China, this state of mind would be "perfectly useless," according to Smith, except to make him "miserable,"[3] without being of any benefit to the Chinese. Smith said: "Nature, it seems, when she loaded us with our own sorrows, thought that they were enough, and therefore did not command us to take any further share in those of others, than what was necessary to prompt us to relieve them."[4]

Instead of regarding man's nature as something that could or should be changed, Smith attempted to determine how the moral and social benefits desired could be produced in the most efficient way, *within* that constraint. Smith approached the production and distribution of moral behavior in much the same way he would later approach the production and distribution of material goods. Although he was a professor of moral philosophy, his thought processes were already those of an economist. However, the constrained vision is by no means limited to economists. Smith's contemporary in politics, Edmund Burke, perhaps best summarized the constrained vision from a political perspective when he spoke of "a radical infirmity in all human contrivances,"[5] an infirmity inherent in the fundamental nature of things. Similar views were expressed by Alexander Hamilton in *The Federalist Papers*:

> It is the lot of all human institutions, even those of the most perfect kind, to have defects as well as excellencies—ill as well as good propensities. This results from the imperfection of the Institutor, Man.[6]

Clearly, a society cannot function humanely, if at all, when each person acts as if his little finger is more important than the lives of a hundred million other human beings. But the crucial word here is *act*. We cannot "prefer ourselves so shamelessly and blindly to others" when we act, Smith said,[7] even if that is the spontaneous or natural inclination of our feelings. In practice, people on many occasions "sacrifice their own interests to the greater interests of others," according to Smith,[8] but this was due to such intervening factors as devotion to moral principles, to concepts of honor and nobility, rather than to loving one's neighbor as one-self.[9]

Through such artificial devices, man could be persuaded to do for his own self-image or inner needs what he would not do for the good of his fellow man. In short, such concepts were seen by Smith as the most efficient way to get the moral job done at the lowest psychic cost. Despite the fact that this was a moral question, Smith's answer was essentially economic—a system of moral incentives, a set of *trade-offs* rather than a real *solution* by changing man. One of the hallmarks of the constrained vision is that it deals in trade-offs rather than solutions.

In his classic work, *The Wealth of Nations*, Smith went further. Economic benefits to society were largely unintended by individuals, but emerged systematically from the interactions of the marketplace, under the pressures of competition and the incentives of individual gain.[10] Moral sentiments were necessary only for shaping the general framework of laws within which this systemic process could go on.

This was yet another way in which man, with all the limitations conceived by Smith, could be induced to produce benefits for others, for reasons ultimately reducible to self-interest. It was not an atomistic theory that individual self-interests added up to the interest of society. On the contrary, the functioning of the economy and society required each individual to do things for other people; it was simply the *motivation* behind these acts—whether moral of economic—which was ultimately self-centered. In both his moral and his economic analyses, Smith relied on incentives rather than dispositions to get the job done.

The Unconstrained Vision

Perhaps no other eighteenth-century book presents such a contrast to the vision of man in Adam Smith as William Godwin's *Enquiry Concerning Political Justice*, a work as remarkable for its fate as its contents. An immediate success upon its publication in England in 1793, within a decade it encountered the chilling effect of British hostile reactions to ideas popularly associated with the French Revolution, especially after France became an enemy in war. By the time two decades of warfare between the two countries were ended at Waterloo, Godwin and his work had been relegated to the periphery of intellectual life, and he was subsequently best known for his influence on Shelley. Yet no work on the eighteenth-century "age of reason" so clearly, so consistently, and so systematically elaborated the unconstrained vision of man as did Godwin's treatise.

Where in Adam Smith moral and socially beneficial behavior could be evoked from man only by incentives, in William Godwin man's understanding and disposition were capable of intentionally creating social benefits. Godwin regarded the *intention* to benefit others as being "of the essence of virtue,"[11] and virtue in turn as being the road to human happiness. Unintentional social benefits were treated by Godwin as scarcely worthy of notice.[12] His was the unconstrained vision of human nature, in which man was capable of directly feeling other people's needs as more important than his own, and therefore of consistently acting impartially, even when his own interests or those of his family were involved.[13] This was not meant as an empirical generalization about the way most people currently behaved. It was meant as a statement of the underlying nature of human potential.

Conceding current egocentric behavior did not imply that it was a permanent feature of human nature, as human nature was conceived in the unconstrained vision. Godwin said: "Men are capable, no doubt, of preferring an inferior interest of their own to a superior interest of others; but this preference arises from a combination of circumstances and is not the necessary and invariable law of our nature."[14] Godwin referred to "men as they hereafter may be made,"[15] in contrast to Burke's view: "We cannot change the Nature of things and of men—but must act upon them the best we can."[16]

Socially contrived incentives were disdained by Godwin as unworthy and unnecessary expedients, when it was possible to achieve directly what Smith's incentives were designed to achieve indirectly: "If a thousand men are to be benefited, I ought to recollect that I am only an atom in the comparison, and to reason accordingly."[17] Unlike Smith, who regarded human selfishness as a given, Godwin regarded it as being promoted by the very system of rewards used to cope with it. The real solution toward which efforts should be bent was to have people do what is right because it is right, not because of psychic or economic payments—that is, not because someone "has annexed to it a great weight of self interest."[18]

Having an unconstrained vision of the yet untapped moral potential of human beings, Godwin was not preoccupied like Smith with what is the most immediately effective incentive under the current state of things. The real goal was the long-run development of a higher sense of social duty. To the extent that immediately effective incentives retarded that long-run development, their benefits were illusory. The "hope of reward" and "fear of punishment" were, in Godwin's vision, "wrong in themselves" and "inimical to the improvement of the mind."[19] In this, Godwin was seconded by another contemporary exemplar of the unconstrained vision, the Marquis de Condorcet, who rejected the whole idea of "turning prejudices and vices to good account rather than trying to dispel or repress them." Such "mistakes" Condorcet traced to his adversaries' vision of human nature—their confusing "the natural man" and his potential with existing man, "corrupted by prejudices, artificial passions and social customs."[20]

TRADE-OFFS VERSUS SOLUTIONS

Prudence—the careful weighing of trade-offs—is seen in very different terms within the constrained and the unconstrained visions. In the constrained vision, where trade-offs are all that we can hope for, prudence is among the highest duties. Edmund Burke called it "the first of all virtues."[21] "Nothing is good," Burke said, "but in proportion and with reference"[22] in short, as a trade-off. By contrast, in the unconstrained vision, where moral improvement has no fixed limit, prudence is of a lower order of importance. Godwin had little use for "those moralists"—quite conceivably meaning Smith— "who think only of stimulating men to good deeds by considerations of frigid prudence and mercenary self-interests," instead of seeking to stimulate the "generous and magnanimous sentiment of our natures."[23]

Implicit in the unconstrained vision is the motion that the potential is very different from the actual, and that means exist to improve human nature toward its potential, or that such means can be evolved or discovered, so that man will do the right thing for the right reason, rather than for ulterior psychic or economic rewards. Condorcet expressed a similar vision when he declared that man can eventually "fulfill by a natural inclination the same duties which today cost him effort and sacrifice."[24] Thus a solution can supersede mere trade-offs.

Man is, in short, "perfectible"—meaning continually improvable rather than capable of actually reaching absolute perfection. "We can come nearer and nearer," according to Godwin,[25] though one "cannot prescribe limits" to this process.[26] It is sufficient for his purpose that men are "eminently capable of justice and virtue,"[27] not only isolated individuals, but "the whole species."[28] Efforts must be made to "wake the sleeping virtues of mankind."[29] Rewarding existing behavior patterns was seen as antithetical to this goal.

Here, too, Condorcet reached similar conclusions. The "perfectibility of man," he said, was "truly indefinite."[30] "The progress of the human mind" was a recurring theme in Condorcet.[31] He acknowledged that there were "limits of man's intelligence,"[32] that no one believed it possible for man to know "all the facts of nature" or to "attain the ultimate means of precision" in their measurement or analysis.[33] But while there was ultimately a limit to man's mental capability, according to Condorcet, no one could specify what it was. He was indignant that Locke "dared to set a limit to human understanding."[34] As a devotee of mathematics, Condorcet conceived perfectibility as a never-ending asymptotic approach to a mathematical limit.[35]

While use of the word "perfectibility" has faded away over the centuries, the concept has survived, largely intact, to the present time. The notion that "the human being is highly plastic material"[36] is still central among many contemporary thinkers who share the unconstrained vision. The concept of "solution" remains central to this vision. A solution is achieved when it is no longer necessary to make a trade-off, even if the development of that solution entailed costs now past. The goal of achieving a solution is in fact what justifies the initial sacrifices or transitional conditions which might otherwise be considered unacceptable. Condorcet, for example, anticipated the eventual "reconciliation, the identification, of the interests of each with the interests of all"—at which point, "the path of virtue is no longer arduous."[37] Man could act under the influence of a socially beneficial disposition, rather than simply in response to ulterior incentives.

SOCIAL MORALITY AND SOCIAL CAUSATION

Human actions were dichotomized by Godwin into the beneficial and the harmful, and each of these in turn was dichotomized into the intentional and the unintentional. The intentional creation of benefits was called "virtue,"[38] the intentional creation of harm was "vice"[39] and the unintentional creation of harm was "negligence," a sub-species of vice.[40] These definitions can be represented schematically:

	Beneficial	Harmful
Intentional	Virtue	Vice
Unintentional		Negligence

The missing category was unintentional benefit. It was precisely this missing category in Godwin that was central to Adam Smith's whole vision, particularly as it unfolded in his classic work *The Wealth of Nations.* The economic benefits to society produced by the capitalist, were, according to Smith, "no part of his intention."[41] The capitalist's intentions were characterized by Smith as "mean rapacity"[42] and capitalists as a group were referred to as people who "seldom meet together, even for merriment or diversion, but the conversation ends in a conspiracy against the public, or in some contrivance to raise prices."[43] Yet, despite his repeatedly negative depictions of capitalists,[44] unrivaled among economists until Karl Marx, Adam Smith nevertheless became the patron saint of *laissez-faire* capitalism. Intentions, which were crucial in the unconstrained vision of Godwin, were irrelevant in the constrained vision of Smith. What mattered to Smith were the systemic characteristics of a competitive economy, which produced social benefits from unsavory individual intentions.

While Adam Smith and William Godwin have been cited as especially clear and straightforward writers espousing opposing visions, each is part of a vast tradition that continues powerful and contending for domination today. Even among their contemporaries, Smith and Godwin each had many intellectual compatriots with similar visions, differently expressed and differing in details and degree. Edmund Burke's *Reflections on the Revolution in France* in 1790 was perhaps the most ringing polemical application of the constrained vision. Thomas Paine's equally polemical reply, *The Rights of Man* (1791), anticipated in many ways the more systematic unfolding of the unconstrained vision by Godwin two years later.

Godwin credited Rousseau with being "the first to teach that the imperfections of government were the only perennial source of the vices of mankind."[45] Rousseau was certainly the most famous of those who argued on the basis of a human nature not inherently constrained to its existing limitations, but narrowed and corrupted by social institutions—a vision also found in Condorcet and in Baron D'Holbach, among others of that era. In the nineteenth century, John Stuart Mill said that the "present wretched education" and "wretched social arrangements" were "the only real hindrance" to attaining general happiness among human beings.[46] Mill's most ringing rhetoric reflected the unconstrained vision, though his eclecticism in many areas caused him to include devastating provisos more consonant with the constrained vision.[47]

Much of nineteenth-century socialism and twentieth-century liberalism builds upon these foundations, modified and varying in degree, and applied to areas as disparate as education, war, and criminal justice. Marxism, as we shall see, was a special hybrid, applying a constrained vision to much of the past and an unconstrained vision to much of the future.

When Harold Laski said that "dissatisfaction" was an "expression of serious ill in the body politic,"[48] he was expressing the essence of the unconstrained vision, in which neither man nor nature have such inherent constraints as to disappoint our hopes, so that existing institutions, traditions, or rulers must be responsible for dissatisfaction. Conversely, when Malthus attributed human misery to "laws inherent in the nature of man, and absolutely independent of all human regulations,"[49] he was expressing one of the most extreme forms of the constrained vision, encompassing inherent constraints in both nature and man.

Godwin's reply to Malthus, not surprisingly, applied the *unconstrained* vision to both nature and man: "Men are born into the world, in every country where the cultivation of the earth is practised, with the natural faculty in each man of producing more food than he can consume, a faculty which cannot be controlled but by the injurious exclusions of human institution."[50] Given the unconstrained possibilities of man and nature, poverty or other sources of dissatisfaction could only be a result of evil intentions or blindness to solutions readily achievable by changing existing institutions.

By contrast, Burke considered complaints about our times and rulers to be part of "the general infirmities of human nature," and that "true political sagacity" was required to separate these from real indicators of a special malaise.[51] Hobbes went even further, arguing that it was precisely when men are "at ease" that they are most troublesome politically.[52]

The constraints of nature are themselves important largely through the constraints of human nature. The inherent natural constraint of the need for food, for example, becomes a practical social problem only insofar as human beings multiply to the point where subsistence becomes difficult. Thus this central constraint of nature in Malthus becomes socially important only because of Malthus' highly constrained vision of *human* nature, which he saw as inevitably behaving in such a way as to populate the earth to that point. But Godwin, who readily conceded the natural constraint, had a very different vision of human nature, which would not needlessly overpopulate. Therefore, the possibility of a geometrical increase in people was of no concern to Godwin because "possible men do not eat, though real men do."[53]

Malthus, on the other hand, saw overpopulation not as an abstract possibility in the future but as a concrete reality already manifested. According to Malthus, "the period when the number of men surpass their means of subsistence has long since arrived ... has existed ever since we have had any histories of mankind, does exist at present, and will for ever continue to exist."[54] It would be hard to conceive of a more absolute statement of a constrained vision. Where Malthus and Godwin differed was not over a natural fact—the need for food— but over behavioral theories based on very different visions of human nature. Most followers of the unconstrained vision likewise acknowledge death, for example, as an inherent constraint of nature (though Godwin and Condorcet did not rule out an eventual conquest of death), but simply do not treat this as a constraint on the social development of mankind.

The great evils of the world—war, poverty, and crime, for example—are seen in completely different terms by those with the constrained and the unconstrained visions. If human options are not inherently constrained, then the presence of such repugnant and disastrous phenomena virtually cries out for explanation—and for solutions. But if the limitations and passions of man himself are at the heart of these painful phenomena, then what requires explanation are the ways in which they have been avoided or minimized. While believers in the unconstrained vision seek the special causes of war, poverty, and crime, believers in the constrained vision seek the special causes of peace, wealth, or a law-abiding society. In the unconstrained vision, there are no intractable reasons for social evils and therefore no reason why they cannot be solved, with sufficient moral commitment. But in the constrained vision, whatever artifices or strategies restrain or ameliorate inherent human evils will themselves have costs, some in the form of other social ills created by these civilizing institutions, so that all that is possible is a prudent trade-off.

The two great revolutions in the eighteenth century—in France and in America—can be viewed as applications of these differing visions, though with all the reservations necessary whenever the flesh and blood of complex historical events are compared to skeletal theoretical models. The underlying premises of the French Revolution more clearly reflected the unconstrained vision of man which prevailed among its leaders. The intellectual foundations of the American Revolution were more mixed, including men like Thomas Paine and Thomas Jefferson, whose thinking was similar in many ways to that in France, but also including as a dominant influence on the Constitution, the classic constrained vision of man expressed in *The Federalist Papers*. Where

Robespierre looked forward to the end of revolutionary bloodshed, "when all people will have become equally devoted to their country and its laws,"[55] Alexander Hamilton in *The Federalist Papers* regarded the idea of individual actions "unbiased by considerations not connected with the public good" as a prospect "more ardently to be wished than seriously to be expected."[56] Robespierre sought a solution, Hamilton a trade-off.

The Constitution of the United States, with its elaborate checks and balances, clearly reflected the view that no one was ever to be completely trusted with power. This was in sharp contrast to the French Revolution, which gave sweeping powers, including the power of life and death, to those who spoke in the name of "the people," expressing the Rousseauean "general will." Even when bitterly disappointed with particular leaders, who were then deposed and executed, believers in this vision did not substantially change their political systems or beliefs, viewing the evil as localized in individuals who had betrayed the revolution.

The writers of *The Federalist Papers* were quite conscious of the vision of man that underlay the Constitution of checks and balances which they espoused:

> It may be a reflection on human nature that such devices should be necessary to control the abuses of government. But what is government itself but the greatest of all reflections on human nature.[57]

To the Federalists, the evil was inherent in man, and institutions were simply ways of trying to cope with it. Adam Smith likewise saw government as "an imperfect remedy" for the deficiency of "wisdom and virtue" in man.[58] *The Federalist Papers* said:

> Why has government been instituted at all? Because the passions of men will not confirm to the dictates of reason and justice without constraint.[59]

To those without this constrained vision of man, the whole elaborate system of constitutional checks and balances was a needless complication and impediment. Condorcet condemned such "counterweights" for creating an "overcomplicated" political machine "to weigh upon the people."[60] He saw no need for society to be "jostled between opposing powers"[61] or held back by the "inertia" of constitutional checks and balances.[62]

The constrained vision is a tragic vision of the human condition. The unconstrained vision is a moral vision of human intentions, which are viewed as ultimately decisive. The unconstrained vision promotes pursuit of the highest ideals and the best solutions. By contrast, the constrained vision sees the best as the enemy of the good—a vain attempt to reach the unattainable being seen as not only futile but often counterproductive, while the same efforts could have produced a viable and beneficial trade-off. Adam Smith applied this reasoning not only to economics but also to morality and politics: The prudent reformer, according to Smith, will respect "the confirmed habits and prejudices of the people," and when he cannot establish what is right, "he will not disdain to ameliorate the wrong." His goal is not to create the ideal but to "establish the best that the people can bear."[63]

But Condorcet, expressing the unconstrained vision, rejected any notion that laws should "change with the temperature and adapt to the forms of government, to the practices that superstition has consecrated, and even to the stupidities adopted by each people. . . ."[64] Thus he found the French Revolution superior to the American Revolution, for "the principles from which the constitution and laws of France were derived were purer" and allowed "the people to exercise their sovereign right" without constraint.[65] Related to this is the question whether the institutions of one society can be transferred to another, or particular blueprints for better societies be applied to very different countries. Jeremy Bentham was noted for producing both specific reforms and general principles intended to apply in very different societies. Yet to Hamilton, "What may be good at Philadelphia may be bad at Paris and ridiculous at Petersburgh."[66] Each of these conclusions is consistent with the respective vision from which it came.

While the constrained vision sees human nature as essentially unchanged across the ages and around the world, the particular cultural expressions of human needs peculiar to specific societies are not seen as being readily and beneficially changeable by forcible intervention. By contrast, those with the unconstrained vision tend to view human nature as beneficially changeable and social customs as expendable holdovers from the past.

Ideals are weighed against the cost of achieving them, in the constrained vision. But in the unconstrained vision, every closer approximation to the ideal should be preferred. Costs are regrettable, but by no means decisive. Thomas Jefferson's reply to those who turned against the French Revolution, because of the innocent people it had killed, exemplified this point:

> My own affections have been deeply wounded by some of the martyrs to this cause, but rather than it should have failed, I would have seen half the earth desolated.[67]

Belief in the irrelevance of process costs in the pursuit of social justice could hardly have been expressed more clearly or categorically. Yet, in the end, Jefferson too turned against the French Revolution, as its human cost increased beyond what he could continue to accept. Jefferson was not completely or irrevocably committed to the unconstrained vision.

The relative importance of process costs has continued, over the centuries, to distinguish the constrained and the unconstrained visions. Modern defenders of legal technicalities which allow criminals to escape punishment who declare, "That is the price we pay for freedom," or defenders of revolutions who say, "You can't make omelettes without breaking eggs," are contemporary exemplars of an unconstrained vision which has historically treated process costs as secondary. At the other end of the philosophical spectrum are those who in essence repeat Adam Smith's view of process costs: "The peace and order of society is of more importance than even the relief of the miserable."[68] The continuing battle between ideals and the costs of achieving them is only one part of the ongoing conflict of visions.

SUMMARY AND IMPLICATIONS

Visions rest ultimately on some sense of the nature of man—not simply his existing practices but his ultimate potential and ultimate limitations. Those who see the potentialities of human nature as extending far beyond what is currently manifested have a social vision quite different from those who see human beings as tragically limited creatures whose selfish and dangerous impulses can be contained only by social contrivances which themselves produce unhappy side effects. William Godwin and Adam Smith are two of the clearest and most consistent exemplars of these respective social visions— the unconstrained and the constrained. Yet they are neither the first nor the last in these two long traditions of social thought.

When Rousseau said that man "is born free" but "is everywhere in chains,"[69] he expressed the essence of the unconstrained vision, in which the fundamental problem is not nature or man but institutions. According to Rousseau, "men are not naturally enemies."[70] The diametrically opposite vision was presented in Hobbes' *Leviathan*, where the armed power of political institutions was all that prevented the war of each against all[71] that would otherwise exist among men in their natural state, where life would be "solitary, poore, nasty, brutish, and short."[72] While the unconstrained vision of Condorcet led him to seek a society in which man's "natural inclination" would coincide with the social good,[73] Hayek's constrained vision led to the conclusion that the "indispensable rules of the free society require from us much that is unpleasant"[74]; that is, man's nature inherently could not coincide with the social good but must be deliberately subordinated to it, despite the unpleasantness this entailed.

Given the wider capabilities of man in the unconstrained vision, the intentions which guide those capabilities are especially important. Words and concepts which revolve around intention—"sincerity," "commitment," "dedication"—have been central to the unconstrained vision for centuries, and the policies sought by this vision have often been described in terms of their intended goals: "Liberty, equality, fraternity," "ending the exploitation of man by man," or "social justice," for example. But in the constrained vision, where man's ability to directly consummate his intentions is very limited, intentions mean far less. Burke referred to "the Beneficial effects of human faults" and to "the ill consequences attending the most undoubted Virtues."[75] Adam Smith's entire economic doctrine of *laissez-faire* implicitly assumed the same lack of correspondence between intention and effect, for the systemic benefits of capitalism were no part of the intention of capitalists.

In the constrained vision, social processes are described not in terms of intentions or ultimate goals, but in terms of the systemic characteristics deemed necessary to contribute to those goals—"property rights," "free enterprise," or "strict construction" of the Constitution, for example. It is not merely that there are different goals in the two visions but, more fundamentally, that the goals relate to different things. The unconstrained vision speaks directly in terms of desired results, the constrained vision in terms of process characteristics considered conducive to desired results, but not directly or without many unhappy side effects, which are accepted as part of a trade-off.

With all the complex differences among social thinkers as of a given time, and still more so over time, it is nevertheless possible to recognize certain key assumptions about human nature and about social causation which permit some to be grouped together as belonging to the constrained vision and others as belonging to the unconstrained vision. Although these groupings do not encompass all social theorists, they cover many important figures and enduring ideological conflicts of the past two centuries.

Running through the tradition of the unconstrained vision is the conviction that foolish or immoral choices explain the evils of the world—and that wiser or more moral and humane social policies are the solution. William Godwin's elaboration of this unconstrained vision in his *Enquiry Concerning Political Justice* drew upon and systematized such ideas found among numerous eighteenth-century thinkers—Jean-Jacques Rousseau, Voltaire, Condorcet, Thomas Paine, and D'Holbach being notable examples. This general approach was carried forth in the nineteenth century, in their very different ways, by Saint-Simon, Robert Owen, and by George Bernard Shaw and other Fabians. Its twentieth-century echoes are found in political theorists such as Harold Laski, in economists like Thorstein Veblen and John Kenneth Galbraith, and in the law with a whole school of advocates of judicial activism, epitomized by Ronald Dworkin in theory and Earl Warren in practice.

By contrast, the constrained vision sees the evils of the world as deriving from the limited and unhappy choices available, given the inherent moral and intellectual limitations of human beings. For amelioration of these evils and the promotion of progress, they rely on the systemic characteristics of certain social processes such as moral traditions, the marketplace, or families. They conceive of these processes as evolved rather than designed—and rely on these general patterns of social interaction rather than on specific policy designed to directly produce particular results for particular individuals and groups. This constrained view of human capacities found in Adam Smith is also found in a long series of other social thinkers, ranging from Thomas Hobbes in the seventeenth century, through Edmund Burke and the authors of *The Federalist Papers* among Smith's contemporaries, through such twentieth-century figures as Oliver Wendell Holmes in law, Milton Friedman in economics, and Friedrich A. Hayek in general social theory.

Not all social thinkers fit this schematic dichotomy. John Stuart Mill and Karl Marx, for example, do not fit, for very different reasons, as will be noted in Chapter 5. Others take midway positions between the two visions, or convert from one to the other. However, the conflict of visions is no less real because everyone has not chosen sides or irrevocably committed themselves.

Despite necessary caveats, it remains an important and remarkable phenomenon that how human nature is conceived at the outset is highly correlated with the whole conception of knowledge, morality, power, time, rationality, war, freedom, and law which defines a social vision. These correlations will be explored in the chapters that follow.

Because various beliefs, theories, and systems of social thought are spread across a continuum (perhaps even a multi-dimensional continuum), it might in one sense be more appropriate to refer to *less* constrained visions and *more* constrained visions instead of the dichotomy used here. However, the dichotomy is not only more convenient but also captures an important distinction. Virtually no one believes that man is 100 percent unconstrained and virtually no one believes that man is 100 percent constrained. What puts a given thinker in the tradition of one vision rather than the other is not simply whether he refers more to man's constraints or to his untapped potential but whether, or to what extent, constraints are built into the very structure and operation of a particular theory. Those whose theories incorporate these constraints as a central feature have a constrained vision; those whose theories do not make these constraints an integral or central part of the analysis have an unconstrained vision. Every vision, by definition, leaves something out—indeed, leaves *most* things out. The dichotomy between constrained and unconstrained visions is based on whether or not inherent limitations of man are among the key elements included in the vision.

The dichotomy is justified in yet another sense. These different ways of conceiving man and the world lead not merely to *different* conclusions but to sharply divergent, often diametrically opposed, conclusions on issues ranging from justice to war. There are not merely differences of visions but conflicts of visions.

Chapter 3

VISIONS OF KNOWLEDGE AND REASON

The constrained and the unconstrained visions tend to differ in their very definition of knowledge, as well as in their conceptions of its quantity, concentration, or dispersal, and its role in the social process. Reason likewise takes on entirely different meanings in the two visions.

THE MOBILIZATION OF KNOWLEDGE

The Constrained Vision

In the constrained vision, any individual's own knowledge alone is grossly inadequate for social decision-making, and often even for his own personal decisions. A complex society and its progress are therefore possible only because of numerous social arrangements which transmit and coordinate knowledge from a tremendous range of contemporaries, as well as from the even more vast numbers of those from generations past. Knowledge as conceived in the constrained vision is predominantly *experience*—transmitted socially in largely inarticulate forms, from prices which indicate costs, scarcities, and preferences, to traditions which evolve from the day-to-day experiences of millions in each generation, winnowing out in Darwinian competition what works from what does not work. Friedrich A. Hayek expressed this view when he said:

> The growth of knowledge and the growth of civilization are the same only if we interpret knowledge to include all the human adaptations to environment in which past experience has been incorporated. Not all knowledge in this sense is part of our intellect, nor is our intellect the whole of our knowledge. Our habits and skills, our emotional attitudes, our tools, and our institutions—all are in this sense adaptations to past experience which have grown up by selective elimination of less suitable conduct. They are as much an indispensable foundation of successful action as is our conscious knowledge.[1]

In this vision, it is not simply that individuals rationally choose what works from what does not work, but also—and more fundamentally—that the competition of institutions and whole societies leads to a general survival of more effective collections of cultural traits, even if neither the winners nor the losers rationally understand what was better or worse about one set or the other. Values which may be effective at the tribal level will tend to be overwhelmed by values that permit or promote the functioning of larger aggregations of people. From this perspective, "man has certainly more often learnt to do the right thing without comprehending why it was the right thing, and he still is better served by custom than understanding." There is thus *"more 'intelligence' incorporated in the system of rules of conduct than in man's thoughts about his surroundings."*[2]

Knowledge is thus the social experience of the many, as embodied in behavior, sentiments, and habits, rather than the specially articulated *reason* of the few, however talented or gifted those few might be. When knowledge is conceived as social experience rather than solitary excogitation, then "a very small part is gained in the closet," according to Hamilton.[3]

In Burke's words: "We are afraid to put men to live and trade each on his own private stock of reason; because we suspect that this stock in each man is small, and that the individuals would do better to avail themselves of the general bank and capital of nations and of ages."[4] By reason, Burke did not mean simply the written words of notable individuals but the whole experience of peoples, summarized in the feelings, formalities, and even prejudices embodied in their culture and behavior. These cultural distillations of knowledge were not considered infallible or immutable—which would have been a solution instead of a trade-off—but rather as a tested body of experience that worked, and which was to be changed only after the most circumspect, and perhaps even reluctant, examination. We should attend to the defects of the social order, according to Burke, with the same trepidation with which we would tend the wounds of our father.[5] They are not to be ignored, but neither are they a mandate for experiment or hasty inspiration. With no examination whatever, there would be no evolutionary process, and therefore, in this vision, no basis for the confidence in tradition and enduring institutions which was the hallmark of Burke, and to varying degrees of other believers in a constrained vision.

The trade-off perspective of the constrained vision treats defects as inevitable, and therefore not in themselves reason for change, unless their magnitudes merit the inevitable costs entailed by change. "Preserving my principles unshaken," Burke said, "I reserve my activity for rational endeavours."[6] On another occasion, he said: "I must bear with infirmities until they fester into crimes."[7] This was not a mere verbal patina on apathetic drift, as shown by Burke's own relentless prosecution of Warren Hastings for alleged misconduct in his governance of India, or Burke's unpopular stand in Parliament for freeing the rebellious American colonies, or his anti-slavery proposals.[8] Adam Smith likewise urged the freeing of the American colonies—and other colonies as well—in addition to suggesting a number of domestic reforms and being opposed to slavery.[9] In America, the men who wrote *The Federalist Papers*—Alexander Hamilton, James Madison, and John Jay—first came to public notice as leaders in the revolt against British rule. The constrained vision was not synonymous with (or camouflage for) acceptance of the status quo.

The Unconstrained Vision

The unconstrained vision had no such limited view of human knowledge or of its application through reason. It was the eighteenth-century exemplars of the unconstrained vision who created "the age of reason," as expressed in the title of Thomas Paine's famous book of that era. Reason was as paramount in their vision as experience was in the constrained vision. According to Godwin, experience was greatly overrated—"unreasonably magnified," in his words—compared to reason or to "the general power of a cultivated mind."[10] Therefore the wisdom of the ages was seen by Godwin as largely the illusions of the ignorant. The age of a belief or practice did not exempt it from the crucial test of validation in specifically articulated terms. In Godwin's words, "we must bring everything to the standard of reason." He added:

> Nothing must be sustained, because it is ancient, because we have been accustomed to regard it as sacred, or because it has been unusual to bring its validity into question.[11]

Similarly, according to Condorcet, "everything that bears the imprint of time must inspire distrust more than respect."[12] It was "only by mediation," Condorcet said, "that we can arrive at any general truths in the science of man."[13]

Given the ability of a "cultivated mind" to apply reason directly to the facts at hand, there was no necessity to defer to the unarticulated systemic processes of the constrained vision, as expressed in the collective wisdom derived from the past. "The pretense of collective wisdom is the most palpable of all impostures," according to Godwin.[14] Validation was not to be indirect, collective, and systemic but direct, individual, and intentional. Articulated rationality was to be the mode of validation, not general acceptance based on pragmatic experience. According to Godwin, "persons of narrow views and observation" readily accept whatever happens to prevail in their society.[15] Therefore, this cannot be the method by which to decide issues.

Implicit in the unconstrained vision is a profound inequality between the conclusions of "persons of narrow views" and those with "cultivated" minds. From this it follows that progress involves raising the level of the former to that of the latter. According to Godwin:

> Real intellectual improvement demands, that mind should, as speedily as possible, be advanced to the height of knowledge already existing among the enlightened members of the community, and start from thence in pursuit of further acquisitions.[16]

Also implicit in the unconstrained vision is the view that the relevant comparison is between the beliefs of one sort of person and another—between x and y, rather than between (1) systemic processes working through successive generations of individuals a through x, as expressed through the living generation x, versus (2) the articulated rationality of y in isolation. The rejection of the concept of collective wisdom leaves individual comparisons as the standard of judgment. Since the experiences of a through w no longer count, the issue reduces to the articulated rationality of x versus that of y. Therefore, the unconstrained vision necessarily favors the "cultivated mind" y, while the constrained vision necessarily favors the views expressed through x, seen as representative of the unarticulated experience of many others (*a* through *w*). The two visions thus lead to opposite conclusions as to which opinion should prevail, and why.

Burke clearly saw himself in the role of *x* rather than *y*:

> I give you opinions which have been accepted amongst us, from very early times to this moment, with a continued and general approbation, and which indeed are so worked into my mind, that I am unable to distinguish what I have learned from others from the results of my own meditations.[17]

The kind of knowledge or understanding referred to by Burke was conceived as a common fund in which he participated. That of Godwin was the knowledge or understanding of "cultivated minds"—a knowledge which, by its nature, was concentrated in a few rather than dispersed among the many. The very meaning of knowledge was also different, which is why it was distributed so differently in the two visions. In the constrained vision, where knowledge was a multiplicity of experience too complex for explicit articulation, it was distilled over the generations in cultural processes and traits so deeply embedded as to be virtually unconscious reflexes—widely shared. This was, in Burke's words, "wisdom without reflection."[18]

Wisdom *without reflection* was a concept utterly foreign to the unconstrained vision, in which human beings have both the capacity, and the obligation to exercise explicit reason on all issues. "Reason," according to Godwin, "is the proper instrument, and the sufficient instrument for regulating the actions of mankind."[19] Passions and biases may exist, but "if we employ our rational faculties, we cannot fail of thus conquering our erroneous propensities."[20]

Given that explicitly articulated knowledge is special and concentrated, in the unconstrained vision, the best conduct of social activities depends upon the special knowledge of the few being used to guide the actions of the many. What is needed is to infuse "just views of society" into "the liberally educated and reflecting members" of society, who in turn will be "to the people guides and instructors," according to Godwin.[21] This idea was by no means peculiar to Godwin but rather has been a central and enduring theme of the unconstrained vision. Along with it has often gone a vision of intellectuals as disinterested advisors. Voltaire declared, "the philosophers having no particular interest to defend, can only speak up in favor of reason and the public interest."[22] Condorcet likewise referred to "truly enlightened philosophers, strangers to ambition."[23] Rousseau considered it "the best and most natural arrangement for the wisest to govern the multitude."[24] Even if nonintellectuals run the actual machinery of government, according to D'Alembert, "the greatest happiness of a nation is realized when those who govern agree with those who instruct it."[25]

These eighteenth-century themes were repeated, with at least equal vigor, by John Stuart Mill in the nineteenth century. To Mill a special role was reserved for "the most cultivated intellects in the country,"[26] for "thinking minds,"[27] for "the best and the wisest,"[28] for "the really superior intellects and characters."[29] Much could be accomplished "if the superior spirits would but join with each other,"[30] if the universities would send forth "a succession of minds, not the creatures of their age, but capable of being its improvers and regenerators."[31] Similar prescriptions remain common today. In short, the special role of "thinking people" or of "the brightest and the best" has for centuries been a central theme of the unconstrained vision.

For those with the constrained vision, however, a special role for intellectuals in the running of society has long been seen as a grave danger. In Burke's words:

> Happy if learning, not debauched by ambition, had been satisfied to continue the instructor and not aspired to be the master.[32]

John Randolph was likewise repelled by the idea of "professors in a university turned statesmen."[33] In a similar vein, Hobbes regarded universities as places where fashionable but insignificant words flourished[34] and added that "there is nothing so absurd, but may be found in the books of Philosophers."[35]

The central danger, as seen by those with the constrained vision, is the intellectuals' narrow conception of what constitutes knowledge and wisdom. They are, in Burke's words, "endeavouring to confine the reputation of sense, learning, and taste to themselves or their following," and are capable of "carrying the intolerance of the tongue and of the pen into a persecution" of others.[36] Adam Smith spoke of the doctrinaire "man of system" who is "wise in his own conceit" and who "seems to imagine that he can arrange the different members of a great society with as much ease as the hand arranges the different pieces upon a chess-board."[37] The whole notion of a philosopher-king was abhorrent to Smith, who declared that "of all political speculators sovereign princes are by far the most dangerous."[38]

The superiority of experts within a narrow slice of the vast spectrum of human understanding was not denied. What was denied was that this expertise conferred a general superiority which should supersede more widely dispersed kinds of knowledge. "It may be admitted that, as far as scientific knowledge is concerned, a body of suitably chosen experts may be in the best position to command all the best knowledge available," according to Hayek. But, he added, with respect to other kinds of knowledge, "practically every individual has some advantage over all others because he possesses unique information of which beneficial use might be made, but of which use can be made only if the decisions depending on it are left to him or are made with his active cooperation."[39] With knowledge conceived of as both fragmented and widely dispersed, systemic coordination among the many supersedes the special wisdom of the few.

Nor was this systemic coordination to be planned or imposed by the wise few. It was an evolved *natural* order, in the phrase of one of the eighteenth-century Physiocrats,[40] the group who coined the expression *laissez-faire*. The same kind of reasoning was found in Adam Smith, the most famous exponent of this doctrine:

> The statesman who should attempt to direct people in what manner they ought to employ their capitals, would not only load himself with a most unnecessary

attention, but assume an authority which could safely be trusted, not only to no single person, but to no council or senate whatever, and which would nowhere be so dangerous as in the hands of a man who had folly and presumption enough to fancy himself fit to exercise it.[41]

The marketplace was only one of a number of evolved systemic processes for making decisions. The family, languages, and traditions are other examples, among many. Believers in the constrained vision rely heavily on such processes to make better decisions than any given individual could make, however talented or knowledgeable compared to other individuals.

In short, starting from different conceptions of how much a given individual can know and understand, the constrained and the unconstrained visions arrive at opposite conclusions as to whether the best social decisions are to be made by those with the most individual knowledge of a special kind or by systemic processes that mobilize and coordinate knowledge scattered among the many, in individually unimpressive amounts.

ARTICULATED VERSUS SYSTEMIC RATIONALITY

The power of specifically articulated rationality is central to the unconstrained vision. The power of unarticulated social processes to mobilize and coordinate knowledge is central to the constrained vision.

In the unconstrained vision, to act without "explicit reason" is to act on "prepossession and prejudice."[42] According to Godwin: "Discussion is the path that leads to discovery and demonstration."[43] "Accuracy of language is the indispensable prerequisite of sound knowledge,"[44] in Godwin's vision, where knowledge is synonymous with articulated rationality. Virtue is promoted when men must "avow their actions, and assign the reasons upon which they are founded."[45] If we could "render the plain dictates of justice level to every capacity," according to Godwin, "we may expect the whole species to become reasonable and virtuous."[46] To Condorcet as well, the task is to "render common to almost every man those principles of strict and unsullied justice."[47]

Reason has at least two very different meanings. One is a cause-and-effect meaning: There is a reason why water expands when it freezes into ice, even though most of us who are not physicists do not know what that reason is—and at one time, no one knew the reason. The other meaning of reason is articulated specification of causation or logic: When it is demanded that individuals or society justify their actions before the bar of reason, this is what is meant. The more constrained one's vision of human capabilities and potential, the greater the difference between these two meanings. Everything may have a cause and yet human beings may be unable to specify what it is. Since no theory is *literally* unconstrained entirely, there is always some awareness of the difference between the two meanings of reason.

Conversely, no theory is so constrained that man can understand nothing, which would imply a total lack of overlap between the two meanings of reason. But at the more unconstrained end of the spectrum, the overlap between the two concepts is considered to be so great that to say that a reason exists is virtually to say that we can specify it. At the very least, our decision-making must proceed on the basis of those reasons which we can specify. But, at the more constrained end of the spectrum, knowledge and reasons unknown to any given individual must be brought to bear on many decisions, through social processes in which articulated rationality plays at best a subordinate role.

Classical and neo-classical economics, especially of the Austrian school, exemplify this constrained vision of systemic rationality, in which individual articulation means little. In an uncontrolled market, as seen in this vision, changing prices, wages, and interest rates adjust the economy to shifting demands, technological changes, and evolving skills—without any of the actors in this drama knowing or caring how his individual responses affect the whole. It can be analyzed as a general process of interaction with its own characteristic patterns and results—otherwise there would be no Austrian economics—but cannot be specified in such concrete detail as to make it feasible for any individual or group to plan or control the actual process. The rationality in it is systemic, not individual—and such individual rationality as may exist is largely incidental, so that the much-vexed question as to just how rational man is has little relevance in this vision.[48]

A similar difference between individual and systemic rationality can be found in religious doctrines in which (1) the Deity is conceived to act directly to affect natural and human phenomena, versus (2) those in which a Providential systemic process makes life possible and beneficent without requiring Divine superintendence of details.[49]

What both the secular and the religious versions of systemic processes have in common is that the wisdom of the individual human actor is not the wisdom of the drama. Conversely, there are both secular and religious versions of individual rationality, the religious version being one in which the Deity directly decides on individual events, from daily weather changes to deaths of individuals. Fundamentalist religion is the most pervasive vision of central planning, though many fundamentalists may oppose human central planning as a usurpation or "playing God." This is consistent with the fundamentalist vision of an unconstrained God and a highly constrained man.

Law

The two visions conflict in law, as well as in economics and religion. Oliver Wendell Holmes expressed the systemic concept when he declared: "The life of the law has not been logic: it has been experience."[50] Articulation was not essential to decision-making, for "many honorable and sensible judgments" express "an intuition of experience which outruns analysis and sums up many unnamed and tangled impressions; impressions which may lie beneath consciousness without losing their worth."[51] Law incorporates the experience that reflects "not only our own lives but the lives of all men that have been," according to Holmes.[52] It is a "fallacy" to conceive of law as purely a process of articulated logic, for while "it is true in the broadest sense that the law is a logical development," it is not "worked out like mathematics from general axioms of conduct."[53] In short, the logic of the law's development is a systemic logic:

The development of our law has gone on for nearly a thousand years, like the development of a planet, each generation taking the next step, mind, like matter, simply obeying a law of spontaneous growth."[54]

John Stuart Mill, however, objected that laws are made, not evolved. What those with the constrained vision characterized as a spontaneous order evolving from history was merely "the fortuitous concourse of atoms in ages of barbarism," according to Mill.[55] He said:

The laws of Moses, those of Mahomet, were made, and did not grow; they had, it is true, the direct sanction of religious faith; but the laws of Lycurgus, the laws of Solon, were *made*, and were as durable as any laws which *grew* have hitherto been found.[56]

To look at legal precedents was, in Mill's view, to make an "absurd sacrifice of present ends to antiquated means."[57]

Yet, as in other areas, Mill's assertions were modified, if not repealed, by his provisos. Those who "make" law have, according to Mill, taken into account "what the people will bear" and that is a function of their "ancient habits" or of their "durable and strenuous convictions, without which the whole system of laws would become inoperative." The "acquiescence of mankind" thus "depends upon the preservation of something like continuity of existence in institutions" representing "those innumerable compromises between adverse interests and expectations, without which no government could be carried on a year, and with difficulty even for a week."[58] With these provisos included, Mill's position is not very far from that to which it seems at first to be the very opposite, namely that "all the famous early law-givers," as Hayek put it, "did not intend to create new law but merely to state what law was and had always been."[59] That is, it was "largely the articulation of previously existing practice," according to Hayek.[60]

Many modern writers on law represent the unconstrained vision much more unambiguously than Mill. For example, Ronald Dworkin dismisses "the silly faith that ethics as well as economics moves by an invisible hand, so that individual rights and the general good will coalesce, and law based on principle will move the nation to a frictionless utopia where everyone is better off than he was before."[61]

These different visions applied to the law lead to opposite conclusions regarding judicial activism. The unconstrained vision, as applied by Dworkin, calls for "an activist court" to read its own meanings into the words of the Constitution.[62] In this he is by no means alone, either in his conclusions or in the methods used to reach them. His call for "a fusion of constitutional law and moral theory,"[63] for "fresh moral insight,"[64] has been one among many.[65]

Oliver Wendell Holmes' conception of the law left no such room for judicial activism:

> It is dangerous to tie down legislatures too closely by judicial constrictions not necessarily arising from the words of the constitution.[66]

Nor was it merely the words but rather the original meanings of those words that were to be adhered to. He refused to declare unconstitutional under the Fourteenth Amendment "methods of taxation which were well known when that Amendment was adopted."[67] He later spoke of "the more than anxiety that I feel at the ever-increasing scope given to the Fourteenth Amendment."[68] In yet another case he saw "no reason for reading into the Sherman Act more than we find there."[69]

As in other clashes between the two visions, the issue is posed very differently by each side. Those with the unconstrained vision, favoring articulated rationality see the issue as one between two sets of contemporaries, x and y, while those with a constrained vision, favoring systemic processes, see the issue as being between the experience of successive generations, represented by group x in today's generation, versus the articulated rationality of their contemporary opponents, group y.

Insofar as those with the unconstrained vision acknowledge prior generations, they see the issue as being between some given prior generation—say generation h—and the current generation's group y. This is dismissed as a conflict between the living and the dead, in which the dead have no right to rule beyond the grave.[70] From this perspective, we must use "our own reasoned and revocable will, not some idealized ancestral compulsion"[71] to advance. Alternatively, the conditions of prior times are deemed irrelevant, or less relevant, than current views based on current conditions. Chief Justice Earl Warren, for example, spoke of contemporary circumstances "far beyond the wisdom of even the wisest of the Founding Fathers."[72]

But when Oliver Wendell Holmes characterized the law as summarizing "not only our own lives but the lives of all men that have been," he clearly rejected any notion that the clash was between opposing groups in one generation, or even between one contemporary group and one past group, such as "the Founding Fathers." Rather, the clash was conceived as being between two whole processes, one of historical experience over many generations versus the articulated rationality of one contemporary school of thought. Neither Holmes nor others who argued for systemic processes seriously contest the claims of intellectual and/or moral superiority which are central to the articulated rationality and "social justice" of those with the unconstrained vision. With the constrained vision, the issue is not whether one individual or group is wiser than another but whether systemic experience is wiser than both.

Yet those who argue for deliberate lawmaking through judicial activism do so not on the basis of having a democratic majority, even in the given generation, but rather of having an intellectually and morally superior process for decision-making. When Dworkin dismissed the opposing process as a "silly faith," "a pessimistic theory of human nature,"[73] "the curious philosophy of Edmund Burke,"[74] and "the chaotic and unprincipled development of history,"[75] this was a prelude to asserting a superiority competent to override a democratic majority of contemporaries, quite aside from dismissing prior generations. For Dworkin, "a more equal society is a better society even if its citizens prefer inequality."[76]

Social Policy

The two visions entail very different views of the relationship between members of the existing society. The unconstrained vision has tended historically toward creating more equalized economic and social conditions in society, even if the means chosen imply great inequality in the right to decide such issues and choose such means. Clearly, only very unequal intellectual and moral standing could justify having equality imposed, whether the people want it or not, as Dworkin suggests, and only very unequal power would make it possible. It is consistent for the unconstrained vision to promote equalitarian ends by unequalitarian means, given the great differences between those whom Mill called "the wisest and best" and those who have not yet reached that intellectual and moral level.

Conversely, those with the constrained vision have tended to be less concerned with promoting economic and social equality, but more concerned with the dangers of an inequality of power, producing an articulate ruling elite of rationalists. In Hayek's words:

> The most dangerous stage in the growth of civilization may well be that in which man has come to regard all these beliefs as superstitions and refuses to accept or to submit to anything which he does not rationally understand. The rationalist whose reason is not sufficient to teach him those limitations of the power of conscious reason, and who despises all the institutions and customs which have not been consciously designed, would thus become the destroyer of the civilization built upon them.[77]

The clash over judicial activism reflects a much more general clash over the best way to contribute to the social good. In the unconstrained vision, wise and conscientious individuals should strive to shape the best outcomes in particular issues that come within their jurisdiction. In the constrained vision, the inherent limitations of individuals mean that each individual's best contribution to society is to adhere to the special duties of his institutional role, and let systemic processes determine outcomes. By contrast, the unconstrained vision was exemplified in Chief Justice Earl Warren's interruption of lawyers unfolding complex legal principles to ask: "But is it *right*? Is it *good*?" In the constrained vision, that was neither his business nor within his competence, for the specialist's superiority exists only within a narrow range of skills—in this instance, determining how the written law applied to the case at hand. Burke said, "I revere men in the functions which belong to them"[78] but not beyond.

Just as the unconstrained vision urges judicial activism on judges, it urges "social responsibility" upon businessmen—that they should hire, invest, donate, and otherwise conduct their businesses with an eye to producing specific benefits to society at large. The socially responsible businessman should, for example, hire the disadvantaged, invest in things that seem most needed by society rather than those most profitable to his firm, and turn part of the proceeds over to charitable and cultural activities, rather than pay all the proceeds out to the stockholders or plow them back into the business.

The constrained vision sees such things as outside the competence of businessmen, given the wider ramifications of such decisions in a complex systemic process. According to the constrained vision of human knowledge, what is within the businessman's competence is the running of his particular firm so as to promote its prosperity, within the law. It is the systemic effect of competition, rather than the individual intentions of businessmen, which this vision relies on to produce social benefit. According to Adam Smith, it is when the businessman "intends only his own gain" that he contributes—via the process of competition—to promote the social good "more effectually than when he really intends to promote it." Smith added: "I have never known much good done by those who affected to trade for the public good."[79]

The writings of those with the constrained vision abound with examples of counterproductive consequences of well-intentioned policies. But to those with the unconstrained vision, this is simply seizing upon isolated mistakes that are correctable, in order to resist tendencies that are socially beneficial on the whole. However, to those with the constrained vision, these mistakes are not happenstances, but symptoms of what to expect when the inherent limitations of individuals are ignored and systemic processes for coping with these limitations are deranged by specific tinkering.

Sincerity Versus Fidelity

Because of conflicting visions of how much knowledge a given individual can have, and how effective that knowledge can be in deciding complex social issues, the two visions attach widely differing importance to sincerity and fidelity. Where the wise and conscientious individual is conceived to be competent to shape socially beneficial outcomes directly, then his sincerity and dedication to the common good are crucial. Godwin's whole purpose was to strengthen the individual's "sincerity, fortitude, and justice."[80] The "importance of general sincerity"[81] was a recurring theme in Godwin, and has remained so over the centuries among others with the unconstrained vision. Sincerity tends to "liberate,"[82] according to Godwin, and to "bring every other virtue in its train."[83] While conceding that everyone is insincere at some time or other,[84] Godwin nevertheless urged "a general and unalterable sincerity"[85] as a powerful ideal, capable of producing profound social benefits.

Sincerity holds no such place of honor in the constrained vision. Those with this vision often readily concede sincerity to their adversaries, treating it as an individual virtue of minor social benefit—and sometimes as a major aggravating factor, when people persist in socially counterproductive ideals. What is morally central to the constrained vision is *fidelity* to duty in one's role in life. There, within the sphere of his competence, the individual can make the greatest contribution to the social good by serving the great systemic process which decides the actual outcomes. This is an entirely different conception of duty from that of the unconstrained vision, where one's duty is direct beneficence to mankind.[86] But in the constrained vision, the individual wielding social decision-making power lacks the competence to continually make *ad hoc* determinations of what specifically is good for mankind, however sincere he may be.

In the constrained vision, the businessman's moral duty is fidelity to the stockholders, who have entrusted their savings to him, not sincere pursuit of the public good through charitable donations or investment or hiring decisions which compromise that trust. Similarly, the judge's moral duty is to faithfully carry out the law he was sworn to uphold, not sincerely change that law to produce better results as he sees them. Within this vision, a scholar's moral duty is to faithfully promote the intellectual process among his students and readers, not lead them to specific conclusions he sincerely believes to be best for society. For similar reasons, advocacy journalism or liberation theology are also anathema to those with the constrained vision, since both are seen as misuses of entrusted roles.

Sincerity is so central to the unconstrained vision that it is not readily conceded to adversaries, who are often depicted as apologists, if not venal. It is not uncommon in this tradition to find references to their adversaries' "real" reasons, which must be "unmasked." Even where sincerity is conceded to adversaries, it is often accompanied by references to those adversaries' "blindness," "prejudice," or narrow inability to transcend the status quo. Within the unconstrained vision, sincerity is a great concession to make, while those with the constrained vision can more readily make that concession, since it means so much less to them. Nor need adversaries be depicted as stupid by those with the constrained vision, for they conceive of the social process as so complex that it is easy, even for wise and moral individuals, to be mistaken—and dangerously so. They "may do the worst of things without being the worst of man," according to Burke.[87]

Related to the question of sincerity versus fidelity is the issue of roles or structured relationships. Fidelity to roles is central to the constrained vision, for in carrying out defined roles the individual is relying on the experiential capital of nations and of ages, in Burke's terms. Among contemporaries, he is leaving specific results to be determined by the values, knowledge, and capabilities of others, fulfilling his own role only to serve faithfully the processes which make this possible. But in the unconstrained vision, where the individual's own reason and sincerity are paramount, roles are seen as needlessly constricting. Those with the unconstrained vision tend to deplore "role stereotypes," to seek "less structured" situations, to "democratize" parent-child or student-teacher relationships, to de-emphasize titles and formalities.

All these patterns are consistent with their underlying vision of human capabilities in *ad hoc* decision-making. It is equally consistent for those with a more constrained vision of those individual capabilities to enlist roles and rules which tap the results of unarticulated historical experience, thereby restraining existing incumbents in these roles. Roles which involve enormous trust—parent-child or doctor-patient roles, for example—are also roles that preclude sex, for example, and those with the constrained vision are especially outraged if this taboo is broken. Others often are as well, but such opposition is not logically compelled by the unconstrained vision.

Both sincerity and fidelity can be seen as aspects of honesty—but as very different aspects, weighed differently in the opposing visions. The constrained vision in particular distinguishes sincerity from fidelity to truth: "The first thing a man will do for his ideals is lie," according to J. A. Schumpeter.[88] It is one reason why sincerity is given such light weight in the constrained vision. A modern defense of judicial activism by Alexander Bickel clearly put more weight on sincerity than on fidelity, when it urged that "dissimulation" was "unavoidable"[89] and referred to "statesmanlike deviousness" in the public interest.[90] When Bickel later turned against judicial activism, he also shifted moral grounds, now emphasizing fidelity over sincerity. It was now "a moral duty" of judges to "obey the manifest constitution," with improvements being left to the amending process.[91] In both positions, Bickel's conclusions were consistent with his respective visions.

The rationale for fidelity to the truth is very similar to the rationale for fidelity to roles. In both cases, one subordinates one's own *ad hoc* conception of what would be best for society in the particular case to adherence to a broader systemic process—accepted canons of morality, in this instance—in which one has greater confidence as to its long-run benefits to society.

Here again, it is necessary to note that none of the great historic visions has been either 100 percent unconstrained or 100 percent constrained. Differences of degree among unconstrained visions are often crucial as regards the significance of truth—and of force. In a very pure unconstrained vision, such as that of Godwin, reason is so powerful—"omnipotent" was his characterization[92] that neither deception nor force was justified in pursuing the public good.[93] Thus, even though the wisest and most beneficent might be on a far higher plane than most people as of a given time, their ultimate ability to gain public assent was virtually inevitable. But where the unconstrained vision of human potential postulates more resistant frictions en route to realizing the goal, falsehood and force become not merely rights but duties, for the enormous benefits of an irreversible breakthrough go on for centuries, over which time the initial costs are to be amortized.

If one believes, like Lenin, that the level of popular consciousness spontaneously achievable is inherently insufficient to the task,[94] then more far-seeing elites have an enormous historic role to play[95] and must employ whatever means are necessary. Although both Godwin and Lenin rejected the naturally evolved systemic processes which are central to the constrained vision, the differences in degree in their assumptions about human knowledge and reason produce profound differences in kind as to the role of truth and force. Relations between believers in Lenin's version of Marxism and believers in democratic socialism have historically been very bitter. A small shift of assumptions can have profound effects on the vision—and on the action that follows from it.

Youth and Age

With experience and articulated rationality having such vastly differing weights in the two visions, it is virtually inevitable that the young and the old should be seen in correspondingly different terms. In the constrained vision, which depends upon "the least fallible guide of human experience,"[96] the young cannot be compared to the old in wisdom. Adam Smith considered it unbecoming for the young to have the same confidence as the old.[97] "The wisest and most experienced are generally the least credulous," he said, and this depended crucially on time: "It is acquired wisdom and experience only that teach incredulity, and they very seldom teach it enough."[98]

By contrast, when knowledge and reason are conceived as articulated rationality, as in the unconstrained vision, the young have considerable advantages. Condorcet wrote, in the eighteenth century: "A young man now leaving school possesses more real knowledge than the greatest geniuses—not of antiquity, but even of the seventeenth century—could have acquired after long study."[99] In an unconstrained vision, where much of the malaise of the world is due to existing institutions and existing beliefs, those least habituated to those institutions and beliefs are readily seen as especially valuable for making needed social changes. According to Godwin:

> The next generation will not have so many prejudices to subdue. Suppose a despotic nation by some revolution in its affairs possessed of freedom. The children of the present race will be bred in more firm and independent habits of thinking; the suppleness, the timidity, and the vicious dexterity of their fathers, will give place to an erect mien, and a clear and decisive judgment.[100]

"Children are a sort of raw material put into our hands," according to Godwin.[101] Their minds "are like a sheet of white paper."[102] The young were viewed by

Godwin as a downtrodden group,[103] but from among them may be found "one of the long-looked-for saviors of the human race."[104] However, the constrained view, which seeks prudent trade-offs rather than dramatic solutions, cannot seek prudence in youth, for prudence was regarded as the fruit of experience.[105] Nor was moral fervor a substitute: "It is no excuse for presumptuous ignorance that it is directed by insolent passion," according to Burke.[106] Burke's American disciple, John Randolph, said: "I am not speaking to the groundlings, to the tyros and junior apprentices; but to the greyheaded men of this nation. . . ."[107] But to those with the unconstrained vision, old age merited no such special consideration. According to Condorcet, "prejudice and avarice" were characteristics "common to old age."[108]

SUMMARY AND IMPLICATIONS

The distribution of knowledge in society varies greatly according to the definition of knowledge. Where knowledge is defined, in the constrained vision, to include vast amounts of unarticulated but vitally important information and conclusions, summarized in habits, aversions, and attractions as well as in words and numbers, then it is far more broadly spread through a society than when its definition, as in the unconstrained vision, is restricted to the more sophisticatedly articulated facts and relationships. The constrained vision, which sees severe limits on man's conscious rationality, relies heavily on evolved systemic processes to convey and coordinate the broad array of knowledge necessary for human survival and progress. The unconstrained vision, which sees greater prospects for human mastery of knowledge, sees in those with special intellectual skills both the proof of its assumption and the vehicles of knowledge and reason for promoting social improvement.

Articulation plays an important role in the dissemination of knowledge, as knowledge is conceived in the unconstrained vision. "Discussion is the path that leads to discovery and demonstration," according to Godwin[109] who, as noted earlier, also considered accuracy of language to be "the indispensable prerequisite of sound knowledge."[110] But articulation plays no such crucial role in the constrained vision. "It has been the misfortune (not, as these gentlemen think it, the glory) of this age that everything is to be discussed," Burke declared.[111] He had no use for "pert loquacity,"[112] and argued that even reason, by frequent repetition, "loses its force."[113] Hamilton was suspicious of skilled articulation, which could be "mere painting and exaggeration"[114] or "artificial reasoning to vary the nature and obvious sense of words,"[115] and noted that "it is extremely easy, on either side, to say a great number of plausible things."[116] Hobbes declared that words are wise men's counters "but they are the mony of fooles."[117] Unarticulated social experience has remained a more effective guide to behavior than articulated rationality, in the tradition of the constrained vision. According to Hayek, it is enough that people *know how* to act in accordance with the rules without *knowing* that the rules are such and such in articulated terms."[118]

Articulate youth, idealistic and trained in the latest and most advanced forms of knowledge, as knowledge is conceived in the unconstrained vision, are a great

hope for the future to those with that vision. So are intellectuals. Neither is viewed in this way in the constrained vision. Where knowledge is more expansively
defined and consequently more widely distributed, as
in the constrained vision, intellectuals have no com-
manding advantage over the common man. According
to Hayek:

> Compared with the totality of knowledge which is con-
> tinually utilized in the evolution of a dynamic civiliza-
> tion, the difference between the knowledge that the
> wisest and that which the most ignorant individual can
> deliberately employ is comparatively insignificant.[119]

When Hayek referred to "that little extra knowledge" which intellectuals possessed,[120] he echoed a
skepticism about intellectuals that goes back for centuries among those with the constrained vision. Hobbes,
like Smith, found little natural difference among men,[121]
and such social differences as he found were by no
means always favorable to intellectuals. The common
man, according to Hobbes, seldom engaged in meaningless words, which he saw as the hallmark of intellectuals.[122] Moreover, the real differences among the quality
of people's decisions were due more to systemic incentives than to their individual knowledge or sophistication: "A plain husband-man is more Prudent in the affaires of his own house, than a Privy Counselor in the
affaires of other men."[123] In this view, the incentives fac-
ing intellectuals were to demonstrate their cleverness
rather than to be correct in terms of results affecting
other people. According to Hobbes, intellectuals "study

more the reputation of their own wit, than the successe of another's business."[124]

The arrogance and exhibitionism of intellectuals were likewise recurring themes in Burke[125] along with the dangers that such intellectuals posed to society. He spoke of their "grand theories" to which they "would have heaven and earth to bend."[126] Hobbes also saw those who "thinke themselves wiser, and abler to govern" as sources of distraction and civil war.[127] Hamilton likewise saw intellectuals as dangerous, because of their tendency to follow "the treacherous phantoms of an ever craving and never to be satisfied spirit of innovation."[128] Even where intellectuals were not conceived of as positively dangerous to the social order, their role as policy-makers was seen in the constrained vision as often inferior to that of ordinary people. John Randolph said that he knew men "who could not write a book, or even spell this famous word Congress" who nevertheless "had more practical sense" than any intellectual.[129]

But to believers in the unconstrained vision, intellectuals are "precursors to their fellows in the discovery of truth,"[130] in Godwin's words. Likewise, according to Condorcet, "the discovery of speculative truths" is "the sole means of advancing the human race."[131] However, those with a radically different conception of man, knowledge, and rationality see intellectuals as a danger—not simply to a particular society, but to any society.

Chapter 4

VISIONS OF SOCIAL PROCESSES

Differences in the vision of human nature are reflected in differences in the vision of social processes. It is not merely that social processes are seen as mitigating the shortcomings of human nature in one vision and as aggravating them in the other. The very ways that social processes function and malfunction are seen differently in the two visions, which differ not only in their view of morality but also in their view of causation.

Social processes cover an enormous range, from language to warfare, from love to economic systems. Each of these in turn comes in a great variety of forms. But there are also some things in common among social processes in general. Whether viewed within the framework of a constrained or an unconstrained vision, social processes have certain characteristics—an order, whether or not intentionally designed. Social processes also take time and have costs. Each of these—and other—aspects of social processes is seen differently in the constrained and the unconstrained visions.

ORDER AND DESIGN

A pattern of regularities may reflect either an intentional design or the evolution of circumstances not planned by any of the agents or forces involved in its emergence. Trees or vegetation of different kinds may grow wild at different heights on a mountainside, or a garden may be laid out with great care and forethought by a gardener. Both visions acknowledge the existence of both kinds of social processes, but they differ on the extent, efficiency, and desirability of evolved orders and planned designs.

The Constrained Vision

The constrained vision puts little faith in deliberately designed social processes, since it has little faith that any manageable set of decision-makers could effectively cope with the enormous complexities of designing a whole blueprint for an economic system, a legal system, or a system of morality or politics. The constrained vision relies instead on historically evolved social processes and evaluates them in terms of their systemic characteristics—their incentives and modes of interaction—rather than their goals or intentions.

Language is perhaps the purest example of an evolved social process—a systemic order without a deliberate overall design. Rules of language are indeed written down, but after the fact, codifying existing practices, and most people have begun obeying these rules in early childhood, before being explicitly taught them. Yet languages are extremely complex and subtle, and of course vital to the functioning of a society. Even for small children, language is not so much a matter of parroting what has been explicitly articulated, but rather of inferring complex rules never fully explained.[1]

Language is thus the epitome of an evolved complex order, with its own systemic characteristics, inner logic, and external social consequences—but without having been deliberately designed by any individual or council. Its rationality is systemic, not individual—an evolved pattern rather than an excogitated blueprint.

Language is, in effect, a model for social processes in legal, economic, political, and other systems, as viewed within the constrained vision.[2] It is not that languages *cannot* be created—Esperanto clearly was—but that they are more effective when evolved, because natural languages draw upon a more vast wealth of experiences over the centuries than will be at the command of any individual or council designing a language. Evolved language also serves a greater multiplicity of purposes than any given individual or council may be able to enumerate, much less weigh.

In much the same way, the complex characteristics of an economic system may be analyzed in skeletal outline, after the fact, but the flesh-and-blood reality has often evolved on its own—and it is considered more efficient when markets have evolved than when "planned" by central authorities. Deliberate action or planning at the individual level is by no means precluded by the constrained vision, just as individuals choose their own words and writing style, within the scope and rules of language. What is rejected in both cases by the constrained vision is individual or intentional planning of the whole system. Man, as conceived in the constrained vision, simply is not capable of such a feat, though he is capable of the hubris of attempting it. Systemic rationality is considered superior to individual or intentional rationality.

The constrained vision is not a static vision of the social process, nor a view that the status quo should not be altered. On the contrary, its central principle is evolution. Language does not remain unchanged, but neither is it replaced according to a new master plan. A given language may evolve over the centuries to something almost wholly different, but as a result of incremental changes, successively validated by the usage of the many rather than the planning of the few. In politics as well, evolution is the keynote of the constrained vision. Burke declared: "A state without the means of some change is without the means of its conservation."[3] Yet he would not subject whole political systems to "the mercy of untried speculations."[4] Individual brilliance was no substitute for pragmatic adjustments, even by people of less brilliance:

> I have never yet seen any plan which has not been mended by the observations of those who were much inferior in understanding to the person who took the lead in the business. By a slow but well-sustained progress, the effect of each step is watched; the good or ill success of the first gives light to us in the second; and so, from light to light, we are conducted safely through the whole series.[5]

The same basic view has been expressed in the twentieth century by F. A. Hayek:

Tradition is not something constant but the product of a process of selection guided not by reason but by success.[6]

The Hayekian view is even further removed from deliberate design than that of Burke, since Hayek incorporates a "survival of the fittest" culture-selection process which depends upon survival in competition with other social systems rather than simply on the basis of pragmatic individual judgments of success.[7] The intervening influence of Darwin between these two exponents of the constrained vision is apparent. It is not, however, a theory of the survival of the fittest *individuals* but of the fittest social processes.

The Unconstrained Vision

Without the underlying assumption that man's deliberate reason is too limited to undertake comprehensive social planning, an entirely different set of conclusions emerges in field after field. If, for example, effective rational planning and direct control of an entire economic system is possible, then it is clearly more efficient to reach desired results directly in this way, rather than as the end result of circuitous and uncontrolled processes. Where desirability can be specified by a small group of social decision-makers, rather than depending upon a multitude of mutually conflicting values among the populace at large, then social issues become very much analogous to engineering problems—an analogy often occurring among those with this approach, and equally often denounced from the opposing perspective of the constrained vision.[8]

One of the most striking visions which conceived of social issues as essentially engineering problems was that of Thorstein Veblen. This view, expressed in a number of Veblen's writings, was crystallized and elaborated in his *The Engineers and the Price System*. Here he explicitly rejected the systemic processes of the marketplace—the price system—in favor of direct control by the relevant experts, the engineers. Few others have carried this mode of thought to such a logical extreme, but elements of it appear in a number of later writers. John Kenneth Galbraith, for example, like Veblen, conceived of the pricing mechanism as inadequate and manipulated by powerful interests, if not wholly fraudulent.[9] Others with varying degrees of skepticism about economic and other systemic processes have likewise tended to seek more direct control by those with the requisite expertise and commitment to the public interest. Advocates of "industrial policy" are one of the latest in this tradition. Not all seek a special role for engineers, as such, but rely on an analogy between engineering problems and social issues.

In the engineering analogy, growing out of the unconstrained vision, one can begin with society's "needs" because it is possible to have an "objective analysis" of "what is really desirable."[10] The "public interest" can be specified, and therefore pursued rationally. It is then a question of assembling the relevant facts, and articulating them—"a full presentation of the items we can choose among,"—to determine how to achieve the resulting goals. Social issues thus reduce to a matter of "technical coordination" by experts.[11] Unlike the systemic vision, in which there are inherently conflicting uses because of multiplicities of conflicting values in the populace at large, in this rationalistic vision, select third parties can agree on what constitutes "needs," "waste," or the "spoiling" of the natural or man-made environment.

In this perspective, there are not only social solutions but often *obvious* solutions—though not necessarily easy solutions, given the opposition of those with a vested interest in the status quo. "Truth, and above all political truth, is not hard of acquisition," according to Godwin. What is required is "independent and impartial discussion" by "unambitious and candid" people.[12] "The nature of good and evil" was in Godwin's view "one of the plainest subjects" to understand.[13] What is needed is for "good sense, and clear and correct perceptions" to "gain ascendancy in the world."[14]

Very similar assessments are to be found in later writers with the unconstrained vision. Evil in the existing society is "neither incurable nor even very hard to cure when you have diagnosed it scientifically," according to George Bernard Shaw.[15] International conflicts are likewise neither inevitable nor inherently difficult to settle. The issues in military conflicts are usually things which warring nations "could have settled with the greatest ease, without the shedding of one drop of blood, if they had been on decent human terms with one another instead of on competitive capitalistic terms."[16] Existing society is "only an artificial system susceptible of almost infinite modification and readjustment—nay, of practical demolition and substitution at the will of Man," according to Shaw.[17] Every successful private business was an example of "the ease with which public ones could be performed as soon as there was the effective will to find out the way."[18]

In short, the *intrinsic* difficulties which dominate the constrained vision are not the real obstacle in the unconstrained vision, in which deliberate obstruction and obfuscation account for many evils, and in which what is crucially needed on the part of the public-spirited reformers is commitment.

In Edward Bellamy's famous social novel *Looking Backward*, a citizen of an advanced future society remarks to a man from the past on "the singular blindness" of the old society, in which "social troubles" and "dissatisfactions" necessarily portended changes,[19] that things had to be done "in the common interest."[20] To take control of the economy was not difficult, for "the larger the business the simpler the principles that can be applied to it. . . ."[21] Purely clerical devices provide "all the information we can possibly need."[22] A "simple system of book accounts" is all that is required.[23] Competition for resources was not intrinsic but due to "a system which made the interests of every individual antagonistic to those of every other. . . ."[24] Concepts of waste,[25] blindness,[26] and the public interest[27] abound—along with repeated assertions of the intrinsic simplicity of rationally managing a society.[28]

More sophisticated modern versions of the unconstrained or rationalistic vision are variations on the same themes. Even where societies are conceived to be more complex, modern expertise is able to master the complexities, making its central management still quite feasible. Thus, in more sophisticated versions of the unconstrained vision, whole societies remain readily manageable though by experts rather than by the mass of ordinary people. Third-party decision-making plays a key role: "Delegation to experts has become an indispensable aid to rational calculation in modern life."[29] What is "desirable" or "undesirable," "preferred," "satisfactory," or "unsatisfactory" are referred to in passing, without explanation, as apparently things too obvious to require explanation.[30] "Needs" are also treated in the same way.[31] There are analogies given to engineering or "scientific" social decision-making by third parties:

> Bureaucracy itself is a method for bringing scientific judgments to bear on policy decisions; the growth of bureaucracy in modern government is itself partly an index of the increased capacity of government to make use of expert knowledge.[32]

This modern promotion of the use of experts echoes a tradition which goes back at least as far as the eighteenth century, when Condorcet saw the physical sciences as providing a model which the social sciences should follow.[33] Indeed, he used the term "social science"[34] and urged that quantification and theories of probability be used in formulating social policies.[35]

Another recurring theme in the unconstrained vision is how profoundly different current issues are from those of the past, so that the historically evolved beliefs—"the conventional wisdom," in Galbraith's phrase[36] can no longer apply. Nor is this a new and recent conclusion. In the eighteenth century, Godwin declared that we cannot make today's decisions on the basis of "a timid reverence for the decisions of our ancestors."[37] Such terms as "outmoded" and "irrelevant" are common in dismissals of what, in the opposing vision, is called the wisdom of the ages.

The issue is not as to whether changes have occurred in human history, but whether these are, in effect, changes of costumes and scenery or changes of the play itself. In the constrained vision, it is mostly the costumes and scenery that have changed; in the unconstrained vision, the play itself has changed, the characters are fundamentally different, and equally sweeping changes are both likely and necessary in the future.

PROCESS COSTS

All social processes—whether economic, religious, political, or other—involve costs. These costs are seen very differently by those with the constrained and the unconstrained visions, just as they see differently the kinds of attitudes needed in these processes—sincerity versus fidelity, for example. These costs may be due to time or to violence, among other sources, their corresponding benefits may be apportioned justly or unjustly, and their recipients may be free or unfree. All these aspects are assessed differently in the constrained and the unconstrained visions.

Time

The passage of time, and its irreversibility, create special decision-making difficulties, social processes, and moral principles—all of which are seen quite differently by those with the constrained and the unconstrained visions. Both recognize that decisions made at one point in time have consequences at other points in time. But the ways of coping with this fact depend upon the capabilities of human beings, and especially of human knowledge and foresight.

Accretions of knowledge over time mean that individual and social decisions made under conditions of lesser knowledge have consequences under conditions of greater knowledge. To those with the unconstrained vision, this means that being bound by past decisions represents a loss of benefits made possible by later knowledge. Being bound by past decisions, whether in constitutional law cases or in marriage for life, is seen as costly and irrational. The unconstrained vision therefore tends toward seeking the greatest flexibility for changing decisions in the light of later information. In arguing against Locke's concept of a social contract, William Godwin took a position that was applicable to intertemporal commitments in general:

> Am I precluded from better information for the whole course of my life? And, if not for the whole life, why for a year, a week, or even an hour?[38]

To Godwin, "One of the principal means of information is time." Therefore, we needlessly restrict the effect of knowledge on our actions "if we bind ourselves today, to the conduct we will observe two months hence."[39] Future commitments require a man "to shut up his mind against further information, as to what his conduct in that future ought to be."[40] To live by "anticipating" future knowledge was to Godwin as "improvident" as living by anticipating future income.[41]

In the unconstrained vision, there are moral as well as practical consequences to intertemporal commitments. Gratitude, as well as loyalty and patriotism, for example, are all essentially commitments to behave differently in the future, toward individuals or societies, than one would behave on an impartial assessment of circumstances as they might exist at some future time, if those individuals and societies were encountered for the first time. Where two lives are jeopardized and only one can be saved, to save the one who is your father may be an act of loyalty but not an act of justice.[42] Thus, in behavioral terms, gratitude and loyalty are intertemporal commitments *not* to be impartial—not to use future knowledge and future moral assessments to produce that result which you would otherwise consider best, if confronting the same individuals and situations for the first time. From this perspective, loyalty, promises, patriotism, gratitude, precedents, oaths of fidelity, constitutions, marriage, social traditions, and international treaties are all constrictions imposed earlier, when knowledge is less, on options to be exercised later, when knowledge will be greater. They were all condemned by Godwin.[43] All were prior constraints on that "uncontroled exercise of private judgment"[44] which Godwin espoused.

The binding of judicial decisions by constitutions and legal precedents was seen by Godwin as another example of intertemporal commitments based on lesser knowledge impeding better decisions based on greater knowledge that emerges later. According to Godwin's principles:

An enlightened and reasonable judicature would have recourse, in order to decide the cause before them, to no code but the code of reason. They would feel the absurdity of other men's teaching them what they should think, and pretending to understand the case before them before it happened, better than they who had all the circumstances under their inspection.[45]

All those things condemned by Godwin—loyalty, constitutions, marriage, etc.—have been lauded and revered by those with a constrained vision. The process costs entailed by intertemporal commitments depend on (1) how much more knowledge, rationality, and impartiality human beings are capable of bringing to bear as a result of the passage of time and (2) on the cost of accepting the disadvantages of moment-to-moment decision-making. Where the capability of greater knowledge and understanding is considered to be large—as in the unconstrained vision—the case for avoiding commitment is strongest. Where this capability is considered to be inherently very limited—as in the constrained vision—the benefits are correspondingly smaller and more readily overbalanced by other considerations.

In social principles, especially, Burke saw no fundamental advance to be expected from the passage of time:

We know that *we* have made no discoveries, and we think that no discoveries are to be made, in morality; nor many in the great principles of government, nor in the ideas of liberty . . . [46]

More generally, the very concept of "social science," which largely originated among those with the unconstrained vision, beginning with Condorcet in the eighteenth century, is often viewed skeptically by those with the constrained vision, if not rejected outright as a pretentious delusion of being scientific where the prerequisites of science do not exist.[47] Changing historically evolved principles on the basis of "social science" theories or studies has become the hallmark of modern social thinkers with the unconstrained vision—and the *bête noir* of those with the constrained vision. Government, according to Burke, requires "more experience than any person can gain in his whole life."[48] Given this premise, the incremental gain in individual knowledge by avoiding commitments is trivial, compared to the gain to be made by fidelity to the accumulated experience of the society.

In a world where the individual is to be guided by the collective wisdom of his culture, in accordance with the constrained vision, culture must itself have some stability in order to serve as a guide. Without this stability, "no man could know what would be the test of honour in a nation continually varying the standard of its coin," according to Burke.[49] The judicial situation posed by Godwin may well lead to poorer decisions than if judges were completely free to decide each case *ad hoc*, but the constrained vision offsets such losses against the prospective guidance provided by known rules, leading to fewer criminal law violations or needs for civil litigation. To Burke, "the evils of inconstancy" were "ten thousand times worse than those of obstinacy and the blindest prejudice."[50] In short, process costs arising from unreliable social expectations outweighed the value of incremental individual knowledge, or its more finely tuned application.

Given the perspective of the constrained vision, a judge should not even *attempt* to reach the socially best decision in the case before him. According to Hayek: "The only public good with which he can be concerned is the observance of those rules that the individual could reasonably count on." The judge should "apply the rules even if in the particular instance the known consequences will appear to him wholly undesirable."[51] The cost is justified only because other (and larger) costs are entailed by alternative social processes, according to the constrained vision of human capabilities. Such a conclusion is, however, anathema to believers in the unconstrained vision. The courts "will never permit themselves to be used as instruments of inequity and injustice," according to a landmark court case.[52] To knowingly accept injustice is unconscionable in the unconstrained vision. But in the constrained vision, injustices are inevitable, with the only real question being whether there will be more with one process than another.

To Adam Smith as well, general stability was more important than particular benefits: "The peace and order of society is of more importance than even the relief of the miserable." Therefore, even though he believed that "the rich and the great are too often preferred to the wise and the virtuous," he noted that determining the former involved lower process costs, so that "the peace and order of society" would rest more securely "upon the plain and palpable difference of birth and fortune than upon the invisible and often uncertain difference of wisdom and virtue."[53]

Once again, where those with an unconstrained vision see a solution, those with a constrained vision see a trade-off. The unconstrained vision seeks the best individual decisions, arrived at seriatim and in *ad hoc* fashion. By contrast, the constrained vision trades off the benefits of both wisdom and virtue against the benefits of stability of expectations and standards. It may concede that one process offers abstractly better individual decisions, but deducts the *process costs* of those decisions to arrive at a net balance which may turn out to favor the less prepossessing alternative—palpable distinctions of rank versus less perceptible differences of wisdom and virtue, for example.

This calculation need not always come down on the side of the status quo; many of the leading exemplars of the constrained vision were advocates of unpopular and sometimes drastic changes, as noted in Chapter 3. But the fact that better decisions in themselves were not sufficient to justify change, because of process costs, provided a basis for those with the constrained vision to reject many proposed changes that would otherwise be compelling on the basis of the unconstrained vision. In short, human beings as conceived in the unconstrained vision should logically follow very different policies from those to be followed by human beings as conceived in the constrained vision.

Social rules are as central to the constrained vision as unfettered individual judgment and individual conscience are at the heart of the unconstrained vision. As F. A. Hayek has put it:

> We live in a society in which we can successfully orientate ourselves, and in which our actions have a good chance of achieving their aims, not only because our

fellows are governed by known aims or known connections between means and ends, but because they
are also confined by rules whose purpose or origin we
often do not know and of whose very existence we are
often unaware.[54]

Commonly shared implicit rules thus reduce process
costs. But process costs are less and less of a consideration, the greater is the individual's capacity to decide
each issue on its merits as it arises. Rules thus range
from a nuisance to an intolerable burden in the unconstrained vision. The difference between the two visions
is therefore especially sharp as regards rules and practices relating to intertemporal commitments—loyalty,
constitutions, and marriage, for example.

At the extremes, the constrained vision says, "My
country, right or wrong," while the unconstrained vision casts its exponent in the role of a citizen of the
world, ready to oppose his own country, in words or actions, whenever he sees fit. Patriotism and treason thus
become a meaningless distinction at the extremes of the
unconstrained vision, while this distinction is one of the
most central and most powerful distinctions in the constrained vision.

The constrained vision is premised on "necessary
and irremediable ignorance on everyone's part," in the
words of Hayek,[55] who also sees that individual, rationalistic decision-making of the unconstrained vision "demands complete knowledge of all the relevant facts." To
Hayek, the latter is utterly impossible, for the functioning of society depends upon social coordination of "millions of facts which in their entirety are not known to

anybody."[56] To Hayek, it is a delusion "that all the relevant facts are known to some one mind"[57] making a decision and considering its wider ramifications. In the constrained vision, the benefits of an advanced civilization derive from the better social coordination of widely dispersed fragments of knowledge—not from greater knowledge in the individual. According to Hayek:

> In civilized society it is indeed not so much the greater knowledge that the individual can acquire, as the greater benefit he receives from the knowledge possessed by others, which is the cause of his ability to pursue an infinitely wider range of ends than merely the satisfaction of his most pressing physical needs. Indeed, a "civilized" individual may be very ignorant, more ignorant than many a savage, and yet greatly benefit from the civilization in which he lives.[58]

In this vision, it is especially unwarranted for the individual to place himself outside or above the society which makes his life and his understanding possible. Even great achievements by an individual are deemed to be necessarily confined to a narrow slice of the sweeping spectrum of concerns which a society coordinates, and therefore provide no basis for him to imagine that he can disassemble and reassemble in a better way the complex society around him. "Their very excellence in their peculiar functions" may leave such outstanding individuals less than qualified in others, according to Burke.[59] In a similar vein, Hamilton argued that even the "greatest genius" would overlook decisive considerations which an ordinary man might see.[60]

While the comparison between the intellectually (or morally) superior individual and average people is the relevant one from the standpoint of the unconstrained vision, to those with the constrained vision even the most outstanding individuals—intellectually or morally—are inherently very limited in their grasp of the knowledge and of the innumerable interrelationships which make a society viable. Therefore, in the constrained vision, the historic and systemic wisdom expressed inarticulately in the culture of the many is more likely to be correct than the special insights of the few. Both processes mobilize human experience and understanding, but in very different ways. The very concept of "reason" is different in the two visions. In Hayek's words:

> "Reason," which has included the capacity of the mind to distinguish between good and evil, that is between what was and was not in accordance with established rules, came to mean a capacity to construct such rules by deduction from explicit premises.[61]

In the constrained vision, society is often analogized to a living organism, which cannot be comprehensively disassembled and reconstructed in a different way without fatal results. Burke, for example, wrote of hacking a body into pieces and then throwing the pieces "into the kettle of magicians," in hopes of regeneration.[62] In the constrained vision, the concept of "nation-building" is a fundamental misconception.[63] Nations may grow and evolve but cannot be built.

The intertemporal commitment of loyalty, seen as an abandonment of impartiality in future behavior by those with the unconstrained vision, was viewed very differently by those with the constrained vision. If one's view of human nature is very constrained, then the alternative to loyalty is not impartiality but pure selfishness. The kinds of emotional attachments which lead to loyalty are thus seen as beneficial social ties, essential to the functioning of the whole society. According to Burke:

> To be attached to the subdivision, to love the little platoon we belong to in society, is the first principle (the germ as it were) of public affections. It is the first link in the series by which we proceed towards a love of our country, and to mankind.[64]

In a similar vein, Hamilton said:

> We love our families, more than our neighbors: We love our neighbors more than our countrymen in general.[65]

By contrast, Godwin put his faith in the spread of reason, rather than "a brute and unintelligent sympathy."[66] He distinguished undisciplined feelings from feelings that have "ripened into virtue"—the latter embracing "the whole human race" in their concern. From Godwin's perspective, "the love of our country" is "a deceitful principle" which would establish "a preference built upon accidental relations, and not upon reason."[67]

Neither vision regards the smaller units as intrinsically more important than the larger units. The unconstrained vision simply regards man as ultimately capable of understanding that principle and acting upon it.

The constrained vision sees that as beyond human nature in practice, even if agreed to in theory, and that strong, naturally arising emotional attachments must therefore be socially utilized as a counter-weight to personal selfishness. Adam Smith, for example, rejected the rationalistic view which would attempt to establish directly the primacy of the species over the nation:

> We do not love our country merely as part of the great society of mankind—we love it for its own sake, and independently of any such consideration. That wisdom which contrived the system of human affections, as well as that of every other part of nature, seems to have judged that the interest of the great society of mankind would be best promoted by directing the principal attention of each individual to that particular portion of it which was most within the sphere both of his abilities and his understanding.[68]

As in his economic theories, so in his moral theories, Smith focused on individual behavior precisely as it conduces indirectly to *social* benefits—not simply because it benefits the individual. This indirection in both cases was due to Smith's conception of man as lacking either the knowledge or sufficient will to produce consistent social benefits directly. Hamilton likewise considered selfishness as an unchangeable part of human nature, so that wise social policy could, at best, "gently divert the channel, and direct it, if possible, to the public good."[69]

Those without this constrained vision of human nature equally logically proceed in the opposite way, by demanding an end of nationalism, and an assumption

of "social responsibility," by both individuals and institutions toward one's fellow human beings, whether at
home or overseas. The greater the capabilities of man,
the smaller the process costs, and the more directly the
social good can be pursued.

Freedom and Justice

The two visions judge social processes by fundamentally different criteria. In the unconstrained vision,
where individual intentions and individual justice are
central, it is enormously important whether individual
rewards are merited or merely reflect privilege and luck.
Both individual leaders and social policies ought to be
chosen with a view to their dedication to the goal of
ending privilege and promoting either equality or merit.
But in the constrained vision, social processes are to be
judged by their ability to extract the most social benefit
from man's limited potentialities at the lowest cost. This
means rewarding scarce and valuable abilities, which
include abilities which may be mere windfall gains to
the individuals possessing them, being in many cases either natural endowments or skills cultivated at prosper-
ous parents' expense, but too costly for most people's
means. Sometimes the scarce and valuable traits to be
rewarded may include skills and orientations picked up
almost by osmosis from being raised in families where
they exist.

In the unconstrained vision, the social benefits of individual skills can be elicited without individually unmerited rewards—if not immediately, then in some better society to develop over time. From this perspective,

continuing to pay vastly different rewards retards the development of such a society. But in the constrained vision of human nature, no such development is likely to become general, so that the injustice of paying unmerited rewards to individuals must be traded off against the injustice of depriving society of available benefits by not paying enough to provide incentives to their production and full utilization.

The two visions differ not merely in moral judgment but, more fundamentally, in their sense of social causation. In the constrained vision, the crucial characteristic of any social system is the set of incentives confronting the individuals in it. This includes not only the explicit rewards and penalties of the marketplace and the law, for example, but also the internal psychic rewards and punishments evolved by the culture and its values. Given an underlying human nature that is not fundamentally changing, these systemic characteristics largely determine individual endeavors.

These endeavors are not, however, directly realized. Systemic interactions are not simply—or even mainly—the fruition of individual plans. Adam Smith's businessman is not alone in producing results "which were no part of his intention." While social incentives are more important than individual intentions in the constrained vision, the specific characteristics of systemic interactions—the elaborate principles and channels of causation in a competitive economy, for example—are also essential to actual outcomes.

In short, the constrained vision takes human nature as given, and sees social outcomes as a function of (1) the incentives presented to individuals and (2) the conditions under which they interact in response to those incentives. These interactions—both conflicting and cooperative—are too complex to lead simply to an average of the intentions of agents. The results may in fact reflect no one's intentions, nor even an average of most people's intentions, even if it is the best result achievable with the disparate values and conflicting claims made on inherently insufficient resources. More thriftiness can lead to lower savings, for example, as a result of the circuitous effects of that thriftiness on aggregate demand, production, employment, investment, and income.[70] Similarly, in the legal system, more rights for particular groups can make those groups worse off.[71]

Such unexpected results are not "failures" of a given system, in the constrained vision. As limitations on man and nature are inherent, so disappointments are inherent. In this vision, the question is not whether "problems" are "solved"—they will not be—but whether the best trade-offs available have been made.

In the unconstrained vision, human nature itself is a variable, and in fact the central variable to be changed. The fact that particular individuals or groups have already exceeded the mass in intellect, morality, or dedication to the social good demonstrates what is possible. The great obstacles to its achievement are the opposition of those benefiting from the existing social order and the inertia and blindness of others. If these obstacles to progress are to be overcome, it must be by the commitment, intelligence, and imagination of those who have grasped the possibilities open to society.

In contrast to the constrained vision, which seeks to analyze, prescribe, or judge only processes, the unconstrained vision seeks to analyze, prescribe, or judge *results*—income distribution, social mobility, and equal or unequal treatment by a variety of institutions, for example. Processes are often condemned because their actual results are deemed unsatisfactory, whatever their abstract merits as processes. For example, the illusory nature of freedom or equality to the poor has been a recurrent theme of the unconstrained vision for centuries. The classic expression of this view was that of Anatole France:

> The law, in its majestic equality, forbids the rich as well as the poor to sleep under bridges, to beg in the streets, and to steal bread.[72]

Sometimes the inequality of results from apparently even-handed processes is deemed to be deliberate hypocrisy; at other times, merely a wrong result from an inadequate process. In a similar vein, one is not "really" free, in the unconstrained vision, merely because the political process does not legally confine one's actions. If the actual means of achieving one's goals are lacking, then there is no freedom in *result*, even if there is freedom in the *process*. In short, the very definition of freedom differs between the two visions. Regardless of the absence of legal restraints, one is not free by the definition of the unconstrained vision, "if one cannot achieve his goals. . . ."[73] For example, "Choosers are not free in the market if high costs prohibit a choice that could be made available to them by sharing the commodity through collective choice."[74] More generally:

> One's freedom finally depends on attaining important
> prime goals such as dignity, respect, love, affection,
> solidarity, friendship. To the extent that individuals
> lack these, they cannot be free.[75]

This results-definition of freedom in the unconstrained vision is anathema to those with the constrained vision, in which freedom is defined in terms of
process characteristics. Given the constrained vision of
man's wisdom and morality, he cannot successfully prescribe results but can only initiate processes, whose consequences are often the direct opposite of his intentions.
Moreover, even where certain results may be causally
attainable, they are not morally or intellectually justified
independently of the process which brought them
about. Equality of results for those who have contributed to production, abstained from production, and
hampered production is offensive to an equality of
process, in the constrained vision. Justice is likewise a
process characteristic in the constrained vision: If a
footrace is conducted under fair conditions, then the result is just, whether that result is the same person winning again and again or a different winner each time.
Results do not define justice in the constrained vision.

To those with the unconstrained vision, the best results should be sought directly. To those with the constrained vision, the best processes should be used and
protected, because the attempt to produce the best results directly is beyond human capacity. The two visions' original differences and assumptions about human nature dog their footsteps as they go from issue to
issue.

SUMMARY AND IMPLICATIONS

The two visions differ fundamentally as to the sources of human survival and progress. According to the unconstrained vision, the patterned behavior of society is successful, just, and progressive insofar as it reflects the articulated rationality of man in general and of the most intellectually and morally advanced people in particular. Order—and especially a just and progressive order—is the result of design, backed by the commitment of people dedicated to the general welfare. In broad outline, this is the vision of "the age of reason," which began in eighteenth-century France and has spread throughout the Western world and beyond.

In the constrained vision, where man—individually and collectively—lacks both the intellectual and moral prerequisites for such deliberate, comprehensive planning, order evolves historically without design, and more effectively then when it is designed. Language is one example of such order without design, and its complexity, subtlety, and effectiveness exemplify the power of systemic processes which tap the experience of all, instead of relying on the special wisdom or nobility of any individual or council. A prominent element within this tradition has applied the constrained vision to economics—beginning with the Physiocrats (also in eighteenth-century France), whose battle cry—*laissez-faire!*—was given its fullest expression by Adam Smith and is exemplified today in the writings of Milton Friedman and Friedrich Hayek.

Social processes in general are judged quite differently by the two visions. The unconstrained vision tends to judge processes by their results—"Is it *right*? Is it *good*?" in the words of Chief Justice Earl Warren. The constrained vision judges rightness and goodness as *process characteristics* rather than as results: A foot race is fair if it is run under the proper conditions—regardless of who wins or loses, or how often the same person wins. Justice, in the constrained vision, thus means adherence to agreed-upon rules, while in the unconstrained vision, something is just or unjust according to what end results occur.

According to Hobbes, "he that fulfilleth the Law, is Just."[76] But to Godwin justice is "a result, flowing from the contemplation of each individual case."[77] Results define justice for Godwin, because "whatever is not attended with any beneficial purpose, is not just."[78] Clearly, social processes ultimately exist for, or are justified by, beneficial results—in both visions. The two visions differ in their respective estimates of man's ability to directly produce those benefits. The following of rules instead— whether laws, contracts, customs, or constitutions—is an inferior substitute justifiable (if at all) only by the lower process costs involved. Even if it can be demonstrated in a given case that the result achieved by direct, *ad hoc* decision-making is more efficient, moral, or otherwise desirable, those with the constrained vision will assess its process costs in terms of how this violation of rules deranges the expectations of many others and adversely changes their future conduct, as they lose confidence in the general reliability of existing rules and agreements, and future rules and agreements. Whether the *ad hoc* benefits outweigh the systemic losses depends upon the capability of man—not only in law, but in economics, politics, and other areas.

Freedom, as well as justice, is defined differently by the two visions for this same reason. In the constrained vision, freedom is a process characteristic—the absence of externally imposed impediments. Hobbes applied this concept of freedom both to man and to inanimate things: A man was not free if chained or restricted by prison walls, and water was not free if hemmed in by river banks or by the walls of a container. But where the lack of movement was due to *internal* causes—a man "fastened to his bed by sicknesse" or a stone that "lyeth still"—that was not considered by Hobbes to be a lack of freedom.[79] The same concept of freedom continues to characterize the constrained vision today. Freedom to Hayek means "freedom from coercion, freedom from the arbitrary power of other men," but *not* release from the restrictions or compulsions of "circumstances."[80]

In the unconstrained vision, however, freedom is defined to include both the absence of direct, externally imposed impediments and of the circumstantial limitations which reduce the range of choice:

> Only when he can support himself and his family, choose his job and make a living wage can an individual and his family exercise real freedom. Otherwise he is a servant to survival without the means to do what he wants.[81]

As already noted, freedom may be so broadly defined in the unconstrained vision as to include not only economic prerequisites but also psychic benefits derivable only from emotional ties to others.[82] John Dewey perhaps best summarized this viewpoint when he defined liberty as "the effective power to do specific things."[83] With this definition, whether the limits on that effective power were internal or external, deliberate or circumstantial, did not matter.

These radically different conceptions of freedom reflect radically different conceptions of human capability. In the constrained vision, where man can at best initiate processes, the most that he can do for freedom through social processes is to establish widely known rules which limit how much power is granted to one individual over another, and limit the specific conditions under which the power-holder is authorized to exercise it. But in the unconstrained vision, where man is capable of both shaping and judging end results, there is a corresponding right and duty to ensure that those results maximize the scope of choice of individuals, that they remove impediments, whether deliberate or circumstantial. This may in some cases mean providing compensatory advantages to those whose social backgrounds would handicap them in competition with others, whether for deliberate or circumstantial reasons. But to those with the constrained vision, this is not only beyond the competence of any individual or council, but also an effort likely to derange the social processes to the general disadvantage and danger of society.

The complexity of social processes is a recurrent theme in both visions, but in very different senses. To those with the constrained vision, it is axiomatic that no individual or council can master this complexity, so that systemic processes—market economies, social traditions, constitutional law—are relied on instead. But to those with the unconstrained vision, individuals and councils can and must wrestle with social complexity. The summary descriptions of systemic processes by their adversaries are considered "simplistic," since they do not specify particulars, though specifying particulars would be self-contradictory under the assumption of the constrained vision, which is precisely that no one is capable of specifying the particular.

The preoccupation with process characteristics among those with the constrained vision extends to many specific kinds of social processes, just as in all the same processes those with the unconstrained vision seek directly to create particular results. Where there are, for example, people living below some economic level defined as poverty, those with the unconstrained vision tend to wish to subsidize them in some way to produce directly a more desirable *result* in the form of a higher standard of living. Those with the constrained vision focus on the process *incentives* created by such schemes and their consequences on future behavior, not only among these particular beneficiaries, but also on others who may become less assiduous in avoiding unemployment, teenage pregnancy, or other factors considered as contributing to the general incidence of poverty.

Now that the analysis of visions has proceeded from the two fundamentally different assumptions about man's moral and intellectual potentialities to the concepts of knowledge and reason appropriate to each assumption, and has now applied these concepts in social processes, the basic foundation for the conflict of visions has been established. What remains to be built on that foundation is (1) more awareness of the diversity of visions and their dynamics, and (2) special attention to visions of equality, visions of power, and visions of justice which are central to the ideological conflicts of the age. These are the subjects of the chapters that follow.

Chapter 5

VARIETIES AND
DYNAMICS OF VISIONS

Thus far the discussion has centered on what might be called pure visions or consistent visions, clearly either constrained or unconstrained. But, as noted at the outset, these are by no means the only possible kinds of visions. There are not only degrees in each vision but also inconsistent and hybrid visions. Moreover, beliefs in visions are not static. Both individuals and whole societies can change their visions over time. These changes may be sudden "road to Damascus" conversions, where a particular event reorients one's whole thinking, or the change may be more like water wearing away rock, so that one vision imperceptibly disappears, to be replaced by a changing set of implicit assumptions about man and the world. This second kind of change may leave no clear record of when or how it happened, nor perhaps even an awareness on the part of those concerned, except for knowing that things are no longer seen the same way they once were.

Some changes of visions tend to be associated with age. The cliché of radicals in their twenties becoming conservatives in their forties goes back many generations. Karl Marx predicted that the Russian radicals he met in Paris in the 1840s would be staunch supporters of the czarist regime in another twenty years—though he clearly did not expect any such conversion in his own case.

Although visions can and do change, the persistence and vitality of both constrained and unconstrained visions over a period of centuries suggest that such changes are not easy. The anguish of the apostate comes from within, as well as from the condemnation of his former comrades. Those who lose their faith but continue the outward observances, or who quietly withdraw if they can, are likewise testimony to the power of visions and the pain of change. The terms in which such changes of social vision are discussed—conversion, apostasy, heresy—are borrowed from religious history, though they apply equally to secular creeds which evoke similar emotional commitments.

No comprehensive survey of visions seems possible and none will be attempted here. However, it will be useful to consider a few kinds of visions and the dynamics of visions in general. But before surveying a variety of visions, it will be necessary to define more specifically constrained and unconstrained visions.

OPERATIONAL DEFINITIONS

No theory is literally 100 percent constrained or 100 percent unconstrained. To be totally unconstrained in the most literal sense would be to have omniscience and omnipotence. Religious visions may ascribe omniscience and omnipotence to God, but that in itself constrains man, and so precludes a completely unconstrained *social* vision. A 100 percent constrained vision would mean that man's every thought and action are predestined, and would be equally incompatible with advocating a particular social vision to be followed.

Although the classic social visions considered here do not go to such ultimate extremes, there are still very real differences in kind between them, as well as differences in degree within each kind. Once it is acknowledged that the dichotomy between constrained and unconstrained visions is simply a convenient way to separate some portions of a philosophical spectrum from others, the question becomes one of choosing operational criteria for placing a particular range of visions in one of these categories rather than the other—and of recognizing that still other ranges of visions cannot be fitted into either category, since constrained and unconstrained visions do not jointly exhaust all philosophies of man and society.

The simplest case is when someone such as William Godwin elaborates the scope of human reason and the individual and social decisions which fall within its domain. When the vast bulk of these decisions are deemed to be amenable to deliberately articulated rationality, then there is clearly an unconstrained vision—not in the sense that man is literally omniscient, but rather that whatever limitations there are in human knowledge and reason do not affect the analysis sufficiently to become an integral part of the theory. But few writers in either vision have systematically spelled out their assumptions, and the conclusions which follow from them, as explicitly as Godwin.

Adam Smith incorporated his vision of man's limitations into his social theory explicitly in *The Theory of Moral Sentiments* and largely implicitly in *The Wealth of Nations*. Others vary greatly in the extent to which they explicitly state their vision of man or connect that vision with their social conclusions. But where two thinkers have virtually identical social analyses and advocacy, to include one and exclude the other from the boundaries of a particular set of visions on the basis of their elaboration or non-elaboration of their premises would be arbitrary. Moreover it would be inconsistent with our initial definition of a vision as a "pre-analytic cognitive act"—a set of assumptions not necessarily spelled out even in the individual's own mind.

Seeking operational definitions of the two visions means going beyond suggestive contrasts to decisive distinctions. The difference between the trade-offs commonly found in constrained visions and the solutions found in unconstrained visions is suggestive but not decisive. So too is the distinction between seeking the social good through incentives rather than by changing the dispositions of human beings—this being a special case of trade-offs versus solutions. It is not simply the seeking of trade-offs but the systemic mode of trade-offs which is at the heart of the constrained vision. A central planning commission or an activist judge can make trade-offs, but this is clearly not what the constrained vision has in mind, however congenial that may be to the unconstrained vision.

The systemic versus the deliberate mode of social decision-making comes closer to the central issue of human capability. To allow social decisions to be made as collective decisions by given individuals acting as surrogates entrusted with the well-being of others is to claim a much larger capability for man than allowing those social decisions to be whatever systemic interaction produces from the innumerable individuals exercising their own individual discretion in their own individual interests.

In short, the two key criteria for distinguishing constrained and unconstrained visions are (1) the locus of discretion, and (2) the mode of discretion. Social decisions remain social decisions in either vision, but the discretion from which they derive is exercised quite differently. Social decisions are deliberately made by surrogates on explicitly rationalistic grounds, for the common good, in the unconstrained vision. Social decisions evolve systematically from the interactions of individual discretion, exercised for individual benefit, in the constrained vision—serving the common good only as an individually unintended consequence of the characteristics of systemic processes such as a competitive market economy.

Both visions acknowledge inherent limitations in man, but the nature and degree of those limitations are quite different. The need for food, the reality of death, or the ignorance of newborn babes are of course readily conceded by those with the unconstrained vision. What distinguishes those with the constrained vision is that the inherent constraints of human beings are seen as sufficiently severe to preclude the kind of dependence on individual articulated rationality that is at the heart of the unconstrained vision. The knowledge, the morality, and the fortitude required for successful implementation of the unconstrained vision are simply not there, according to the constrained vision—and are not going to be developed, either by the masses or by the elite. The best kind of world for man as conceived in one vision is disastrous for man as conceived in the other vision. Believers in the two visions are thus foredoomed to be adversaries on one specific issue after another. Issues new to both of them—such as compensatory preferences for disadvantaged groups—evoke the same opposition between them insofar as they depend on the implicit assumptions of different visions.

The Constrained Vision

A necessary but not sufficient condition for a constrained vision is that man's intellectual, moral, and other capabilities are so limited, relative to his desires (not only for material things but also for justice and love, for example), that his desires inherently cannot all be fully satisfied. However, insofar as man's reason is not only capable of grasping this in the abstract for mankind, but also of accepting it in the concrete for himself individually, and of voluntarily adjusting to it, there is no need for social institutions or systemic processes to impose trade-offs. Trade-offs freely accepted are essentially solutions. Such a world would be like that envisioned for the future by Godwin and Condorcet. It is the unconstrained vision.

For a constrained vision, it is necessary not only that (1) man's resources, both internal and external, are insufficient to satisfy his desires, but also that (2) individuals will not accept limits on the satisfaction of their own desires commensurate with what is socially available, except when inherent social constraints are forcibly imposed on them as individuals through various social mechanisms such as prices (which force each individual to limit his consumption of material goods) or moral traditions and social pressures which limit the amount of psychic pain people inflict on each other. The second criterion—the need for systemic processes to convey inherent social limitations to the individual—applies to all mankind, including the wisest thinker, the noblest leader, or the most compassionate humanitarian. Only when all are included within the human limitations it conceives is the constrained vision complete.

Man, as conceived in the constrained vision, could never have planned and achieved even the current level of material and psychic well-being, which is seen as the product of evolved systemic interactions drawing on the experiences and adjusting to the preferences (revealed in behavior rather than words) of vast numbers of people over vast regions of time. The constrained vision sees future progress as a continuation of such systemic interactions—and as threatened by attempts to substitute individually excogitated social schemes for these evolved patterns.

The enormous importance of evolved systemic interactions in the constrained vision does not make it a vision of collective choice, for the end results are not *chosen* at all—the prices, output, employment, and interest rates emerging from competition under *laissez-faire* economics being the classic example. Judges adhering

closely to the written law—*avoiding* the choosing of results per se—would be the analogue in law. *Laissez-faire*
economics and "black letter" law are essentially frame-
works, with the locus of substantive discretion being innumerable individuals.

The Unconstrained Vision

The operational definition of an unconstrained vision in
terms of locus of discretion and mode of discretion
avoids the ultimately impossible task of determining
just how unconstrained a vision must be to receive this
label. Even the classic unconstrained visions—such as
those of Godwin and Condorcet—acknowledged human mortality and the existence of erroneous ideas,
which they actively sought to banish. Success in this en-
deavor would lead ultimately to a society in which the
necessary social trade-offs would be voluntarily accepted individually, and so become for all practical purposes solutions. Both Godwin and Condorcet acknowledged that, even in such a world, man's biological
capacity to generate an ever-larger population would
contain the potentiality for producing catastrophic
poverty—but their crucial premise was that this potentiality would indeed be *contained* by rational foresight of
the consequences.[1] There would be an abstract trade-off
but a practical solution.

It is unnecessary for the unconstrained vision that
every single human being individually and spontaneously arrive at this ultimate level of intellectual and
moral solution, much less that he does so at the same
time or pace. On the contrary, those in the tradition of

the unconstrained vision almost invariably assume that some intellectual and moral pioneers advance far beyond their contemporaries, and in one way or another lead them toward ever-higher levels of understanding and practice. These intellectual and moral pioneers become the surrogate decision-makers, pending the eventual progress of mankind to the point where all can make social decisions. A special variant in Godwin is that each individual acts essentially as a social surrogate, making decisions individually but with social responsibility rather than personal benefit uppermost in his thinking. This tradition of "social responsibility" by businessmen, universities, and others implies a capacity to discern the actual social ramifications of one's acts—an assumption implicitly made in the unconstrained vision and explicitly rejected by those with the constrained vision.[2]

Central to the unconstrained vision is the belief that within human limits lies the potentiality for practical social solutions to be accepted rather than imposed. Those with the unconstrained vision may indeed advocate more draconian impositions, for a transitional period, than would be accepted by those with the constrained vision. But the very willingness of some of those with the unconstrained vision to countenance such transitional methods is predicated precisely on the belief that this is only necessary transitionally, on the road to far more freedom and general well-being than exist currently.

Moreover, not all believers in the unconstrained vision accept even a transitional necessity for forcible impositions. Godwin repudiated any use of force to bring about the kind of world he wished to see,[3] and Fabian socialists such as George Bernard Shaw considered it wholly unnecessary, at least in England.[4] In both cases, it was not merely that violence was deemed repugnant, but that alternative methods were deemed effective. The greater intellectual and moral capabilities of man in the unconstrained vision permit a greater reliance on the direct creation of social results by those with the requisite moral commitment and intellectual skills. It is this locus of discretion and mode of discretion, rather than the presence or absence of violence, which defines the vision.

Although modes of discretion are related to the locus of discretion, they are distinct considerations. Fascism, for example, heavily emphasizes surrogate decision-making but is not an unconstrained vision, because neither the mode of decision-making nor the mode of choosing the leader is articulated rationality. It is not merely that non-fascists find fascism non-rational, but that fascism's own creed justifies decisive emotional ties (nationalism, race) and the use of violence as political driving forces. It is only when both the locus of discretion and the mode of discretion consistently reflect the underlying assumptions of either the constrained vision or the unconstrained vision that a given social philosophy can be unambiguously placed under either rubric.

Operational definitions make it more feasible to place social theories—especially complex ones—under either constrained or unconstrained visions, or to leave them out of both categories, for these twin criteria provide a more definitive method than simply surveying an author's isolated remarks on human nature. It is, after all, not simply the presence of particular assumptions but the incorporation of those assumptions into the substantive analysis which determines the nature of a vision.

By the standards of locus of discretion and mode of discretion, John Rawls' *A Theory of Justice*, for example, is an unconstrained vision—even though its central theme is the trade-off between equality and the need to produce material well-being. In Rawls, the locus of discretion is the surrogate decision-maker "society" which can choose the trade-off collectively and arrange results in accordance with principles of justice—these principles being derived in explicitly rationalistic terms. While the principles of justice are logically derived from the presumed preferences of hypothetical individuals, "in the original position" of the yet unborn, deciding what kind of world they would like to inhabit,[5] the locus of discretion in applying these principles is "society" or a collective "we"—that is, surrogate decision-makers.

Rawls' unbiased unborn are similar in function to Adam Smith's "impartial spectator," from whom principles of morality are derived in *The Theory of Moral Sentiments*.[6] In both visions, these hypothetical beings are used to circumvent the bias of individual or class self-interest when deriving social principles. The difference is that Smith's "impartial spectator" is the conscience of each individual who remains the locus of moral (as well as economic) discretion, within a framework of laws and other social constraints, also reflecting the moral standards of the same "impartial spectator." In both visions, the hypothetical being defines social principles, but the locus of discretion remains real people—operating collectively through surrogates in Rawls, individually in Smith. A social framework is a collective product, in either constrained or unconstrained visions, but the ongoing exercise of discretion is what separates them into the self-interested individual decision-makers of the constrained vision and the collective surrogate decision-makers of the unconstrained vision.

The terms "collective decision-making" and "surrogate decision-making" are used here more or less interchangeably, though they are not precisely the same. "Town meeting democracy," for example, would mean collective decision-making without surrogates, even if officials then carried out the decisions made by the town meeting. Referendum government would likewise make possible collective decision-making, with official surrogates being in principle agents rather than major exercisers of discretion. However, neither the constrained nor the unconstrained vision devotes much attention to such special cases, which are not the situations of complex nation-states. Therefore, for present purposes, the collective, surrogate decision-making of the unconstrained vision can be contrasted with the individual, self-interested discretion of the constrained vision.

A given vision may fall anywhere on the continuum between the constrained and unconstrained visions. It may also combine elements of the two visions in ways which are either consistent or inconsistent. Marxism and utilitarianism are classic examples of hybrid visions, though in very different ways.

HYBRID VISIONS

Marxism

The Marxian theory of history is essentially a constrained vision, with the constraints lessening over the centuries, ending in the unconstrained world of communism.[7] However, at any given time prior to the advent of ultimate communism, people cannot escape—materially or morally—from the inherent constraints of their own era. It is the growth of new possibilities, created by knowledge, science, and technology which lessens these constraints and thus sets the stage for a clash between those oriented toward the new options for the future and those dedicated to the existing society. This was how Marx saw the epochal transitions of history—from feudalism to capitalism, for example—and how he foresaw a similar transformation from capitalism to communism.

This hybrid vision put Marxism at odds with the rest of the socialist tradition, whose unconstrained vision condemned capitalism by timeless moral standards, not as a once progressive system which had created new social opportunities that now rendered it obsolete.

Marx spoke of "the greatness and temporary necessity for the bourgeois regime,"[8] a notion foreign to socialists with the unconstrained vision, for whom capitalism was simply immoral. As in more conservative compromises with evil, Marx's temporary moral acceptance of past capitalism was based on the premise that nothing better was possible—for a certain span of past history, under the inherent constraints of those times. His efforts to overthrow capitalism in his own time were based on the premise that new options now made capitalism both unnecessary and counterproductive.

But just as Marx differed from other socialists because he believed in inherent constraints, he also differed from those like Smith and Burke who conceived of these constraints as being fixed by human nature. To Marx, the constraints were ultimately those of material production and the frontiers of those constraints would be pushed back by the march of science and technology. Eventually, the preconditions would exist for the realization of goals long part of the socialist tradition, including the production and distribution of output "from each according to his ability, to each according to his needs." But no such principle could be simply decreed, without regard to the stage of economic development and the human attitudes conditioned by it.

According to Marx, it was only "after the productive forces have also increased with the all-around development of the individual, and all the springs of co-operative wealth flow more abundantly—only then can the narrow horizon of bourgeois right be crossed in its entirety and society inscribe on its banner: 'from each according to his ability, to each according to his needs!'"[9] Marx's vision was therefore of a world constrained for centuries, though progressively less so, and eventually becoming unconstrained. Engels called this "the ascent of man from the kingdom of necessity to the kingdom of freedom."[10]

Marxian doctrine, as it applies respectively to the past and the future, reflects the reasoning respectively of the constrained and the unconstrained visions. Looking back at history, Marxism sees causation as the constrained vision sees it, as systemic rather than intentional. In Engels' words, "what each individual wills is obstructed by everyone else, and what emerges is something that no one willed."[11] When referring to the capitalist and pre-capitalist past, individual intention was as sweepingly rejected as a source of social causation in Marxism as in Adam Smith or any other exemplar of the constrained vision.[12] Unlike many others on the political left, Marx did not regard the capitalist economy as directly controlled by the individual intentions of capitalists, but rather as controlling them systemically—forcing them to cut prices, for example, as technology lowered production costs,[13] or even forcing them to sell below cost during economic crises.[14] Similarly, bourgeois democratic governments were seen as unable to control insurgent political tendencies threatening their rule.[15]

Marxian moral as well as causal conclusions about the past were consistently cast in terms of a constrained vision. For ancient economic and social systems, slavery and incest were considered by Marx to be historically justified, because of the narrower inherent constraints of those primitive times.[16] Nor would the immediate post-revolutionary regime envisioned by Marx sufficiently escape constraints to decide deliberately when to end the state; rather, systemic conditions would determine when and how the state would eventually "wither away."[17]

Only in some indefinite future was the unconstrained world, which Marxism sought, expected to be realized. In speaking of that world, and contrasting its desirable features with those of capitalism, Marx's language became that of the unconstrained vision. "Real" freedom of the individual, to be realized under Marxian communism, meant "the positive power to assert his true individuality," not merely the "bourgeois" freedom of the constrained vision—"the negative power to avoid this or that."

According to Marx and Engels:

> Only in community with others has each individual the means of cultivating his gifts in all directions; only in the community, therefore, is personal freedom possible.[18]

Looking backward, Marx and Engels saw the emergence of bourgeois freedom—political emancipation from deliberately imposed restrictions—as "a great step forward," though not "the final form of human emancipation." However, such freedom was "the final form *within* the prevailing order of things"[19] that is, within the constrained world before communism, as conceived by Marx. Under capitalism, Marx considered the worker to be only "nominally free"[20]; he was "compelled by social conditions" to work for the exploiting capitalist.[21] Real freedom was the freedom of the unconstrained vision to be realized in a future unconstrained world. This freedom was defined as a *result*, in the manner of the unconstrained vision, not as a *process* in the manner of the constrained vision.

Marx was not inconsistent in using the concepts of the constrained vision for his analysis of the past and the concepts of the unconstrained vision for criticizing the present in comparison with the future he envisioned. His overall theory of history was precisely that constraints lessened over time, with the advancement of science and technology, and that social changes followed in their wake.[22] As a system of contemporary political advocacy, it is an unconstrained vision—a theory that the ills of our time are due to a wrong set of institutions, and that surrogate decision-makers, making collective choices with specifically articulated rationality, are the proper locus and mode of discretion for the future.

Utilitarianism

Utilitarianism was a hybrid vision in a very different sense from Marxism, and to a different degree in its two chief proponents, Jeremy Bentham and John Stuart Mill. Bentham did not originate the basic concepts of utilitarianism,[23] but he systematized them, incorporated them into a body of political doctrine, and founded both an intellectually and politically active school in early nineteenth-century England. John Stuart Mill was the leader of the second generation of that school, but was also very consciously seeking to incorporate into his philosophy insights from very different schools of thought. Mill was in effect seeking a hybrid vision.

Man, as conceived by Jeremy Bentham, was thoroughly, relentlessly, and incurably selfish.[24] But, however severe this moral constraint, man's intellectual horizons were vast. In particular, it was within man's power to rationally structure the social universe, so as to produce the result of "the greatest good for the greatest number." The constrained aspect of the utilitarian vision consists of man's inherent moral limitations and the consequent need to rely on better *incentives* rather than better *dispositions*, in order to reconcile individual desires with social requirements. Bentham's own efforts were directed toward creating schemes of incentives, to be enforced by government, whose function was "to promote the happiness of the society, by punishing and rewarding."[25]

This reliance on surrogate decision-makers, however, seems to place Bentham's utilitarianism operationally in the category of the unconstrained vision, particularly since the mode of discretion was severely rationalistic.[26] However, Bentham's advocacy of government-structured incentives did not extend to wholesale government control of the economy. Indeed, Bentham repeatedly declared himself a believer in the *laissez-faire* economics of Adam Smith, whom he even chided for not carrying *laissez-faire* far enough when discussing usury laws.[27] Bentham rejected surrogate decision-making in the economy, where he argued that a free and rational adult should be unhindered in making any non-fraudulent financial bargain he chose.[28]

Bentham was not consistently in the tradition of either the constrained or the unconstrained vision. However, the work for which he is best known, in law and politics, reflects operationally the unconstrained vision, though not to the degree of Godwin or Condorcet. But Bentham's less known and less original work in economics essentially followed the constrained vision of Adam Smith—though not always with Smith's reasons. The reason for not allowing legislators to redistribute wealth, for example, was not that doing such things properly was beyond man's intellectual and moral capabilities, but rather that there were specifically articulated reasons against it—namely, that insecurity of property would reduce subsequent production.[29]

John Stuart Mill's respect for Bentham, and his carrying on—in modified form—the philosophy of utilitarianism (which name he popularized[30] did not prevent him from criticizing the scope and contents of Bentham's vision,[31] or from deliberately seeking in Samuel Taylor Coleridge an opposite, complementary, and corrective social vision.[32] Mill did not share "Bentham's contempt," as Mill saw it, "of all other schools of thinkers."[33] Indeed, Mill was remarkable among social thinkers in general for the range of other social theorists he not only studied but utilized in forming his own conclusions. Even when dealing with theories which he considered to be clearly erroneous, he was concerned with "seeing that no scattered particles of important truth are buried and lost in the ruins of exploded error."[34] This intellectual catholicity in Mill led to what might be characterized as either (1) a finely balanced consideration of issues or (2) an inconsistent eclecticism. In either case, it makes it difficult to put Mill unequivocally in the camp of either the constrained or unconstrained vision, though the general thrust of his philosophy was provided by the latter vision. Indeed, he gave one of the clearest statements of the unconstrained vision in its moral aspect:

> There are, there have been, many human beings, in whom the motives of patriotism or of benevolence have been permanent steady principles of action, superior to any ordinary, and in not a few instances, to any possible temptations of personal interest. There are, and have been, multitudes, in whom the motive of

conscience or moral obligation has been paramount. There is nothing in the constitution of human nature to forbid its being so in all mankind.[35]

On a number of issues Mill boldly asserted conclusions which derived from the unconstrained vision (that laws are made, not evolved, for example)—followed immediately by provisos from the constrained vision (that these changes in the law will be hopelessly ineffective unless they accord with the traditions and customs of the particular people). Similarly, with income distribution Mill combined both visions. He asserted that, unlike laws of production, constrained by diminishing returns, laws of income distribution are not constrained. While "opinions" and "wishes" do not affect production, they are paramount when it comes to distribution. The distribution of output "is a matter of human institutions solely." Mill declared:

> The things once there, mankind, individually or collectively, can do with them as they like. They can place them at the disposal of whomsoever they please, and on whatever terms ... The distribution of wealth, therefore, depends on the laws and customs of society. The rules by which it is determined, are what the opinions and feelings of the ruling portion of the community makes them, and are very different in different ages and countries; and might be still more different, if mankind so chose.[36]

This seems to be a clear statement of an unconstrained choice based on an unconstrained vision—but it only *seems* so. Mill's proviso in this case is that the "consequences" of particular rules of distribution are beyond man's control—"are as little arbitrary, and have as much the character of physical laws, as the laws of production."[37] Constraint has been explicitly repudiated only to be implicitly accepted. A similar pattern of bold assertion and devastating proviso appears even in Mill's more narrowly technical economic analysis, where there is a ringing defense of classical economics on the causes of depressions and the role of money in them—followed by provisos which repeat essential contentions of the critics.[38]

Much of Mill's rhetoric is the rhetoric of the unconstrained vision. His provisos from the constrained vision make the classification of his overall position ambiguous.

SUMMARY AND IMPLICATIONS

There are many striking features of constrained and unconstrained visions which, however, do not define them. The role of articulation, the relative importance of external incentives versus internal dispositions in determining human conduct, the meanings of knowledge and of reason, the role of fidelity versus sincerity—all these show characteristic differences between those with the constrained vision and those with the unconstrained vision. However, none of these specific features defines the two visions. What is at the heart of the difference between them is the question as to whether human capabilities or potential permit social decisions to be made collectively through the articulated rationality of surrogates, so as to produce the specific social results desired. The crucial issue is ultimately not what specifically is desired (a question of value premises) but what can in fact be achieved (a factual and cause-and-effect question), though in practical terms goals deemed unachievable are rejected even if conceded to be morally superior in the abstract. In the chapters that follow, even such apparently value-laden concerns as equality, power, and justice are analyzed as essentially questions about assumed facts and assumed chains of cause and effect.

Pending the ultimate achievement of an unconstrained society, the locus of discretion in the unconstrained vision is the surrogate decision-maker (individual or institutional), choosing a collective optimum, whether in economics, law, or politics, and whether for a limited range of decisions or for the structuring of the whole society. By contrast, in the constrained vision, the loci of discretion are virtually as numerous as the population. Authorities exist, but their role is essentially to preserve a social framework within which others exercise discretion.

The entire spectrum of social visions cannot be neatly dichotomized into the constrained and the unconstrained, though it is remarkable how many leading visions of the past two centuries fit into these two categories. Moreover, this dichotomy extends across moral, economic, legal, and other fields. This is highlighted by the fact that those economists, for example, who hold the constrained vision in their own field tend also to take a constrained vision of law and politics, while those with the unconstrained vision of law, for example, tend to favor economic and political policies which are also consistent with the unconstrained vision. This will become more apparent in the chapters that follow. Contemporary examples of this consistency across fields are no longer as numerous, simply because social thinkers who operate across disciplinary lines are not as numerous. The increasing specialization of modern times makes the kind of sweeping visions of the eighteenth century less common today. Contemporary visions are more likely to be confined to a particular field—"judicial activism" in law or *laissez-faire* in economics, for example—though there have been a small and dwindling number of twentieth-century thinkers, such as Gunnar Myrdal or Friedrich Hayek, whose writings on a wide range of issues have gone well beyond a single intellectual discipline. However, what makes a vision a vision is not its scope but its coherence—the consistency between its underlying premises and its specific conclusions, whether those conclusions cover a narrow or a broad range.

Nevertheless, despite the scope and consistency of both constrained and unconstrained visions, there are some other very important social visions—Marxism and utilitarianism, for example —which do not fit into either category completely. In addition, one of the hybrid visions which has had a spectacular rise and fall in the twentieth century is fascism. Here some of the key elements of the constrained vision—obedience to authority, loyalty to one's people, willingness to fight—were strongly invoked, but always under the overriding imperative to follow an unconstrained leader, under no obligation to respect laws, traditions, institutions, or even common decency. The systemic processes at the core of the constrained vision were negated by a totalitarianism directed against every independent social process, from religion to political or economic freedom. Fascism appropriated some of the symbolic aspects of the constrained vision, without the systemic processes which gave them meaning. It was an unconstrained vision of governance which attributed to its leaders a scope of knowledge and dedication to the common good wholly incompatible with the constrained vision whose symbols it invoked.

Adherents of both the constrained and the unconstrained visions each see fascism as the logical extension of the *adversary's* vision. To those on the political left, fascism is "the far right." Conversely, to Hayek, Hitler's "national socialism" (Nazism) was indeed socialist in concept and execution.

Inconsistent and hybrid visions make it impossible to equate constrained and unconstrained visions simply with the political left and right. Marxism epitomizes the political left, but not the unconstrained vision which is dominant among the non-Marxist left. Groups such as the libertarians also defy easy categorization, either on a left-right continuum or in terms of the constrained and unconstrained visions. While contemporary libertarians are identified with the tradition exemplified by F. A. Hayek and going back to Adam Smith, they are in another sense closer to William Godwin's atomistic vision of society and of decision-making dominated by rationalistic individual conscience than to the more organic conceptions of society found in Smith and Hayek. Godwin's views on war (see Chapter 7) also put him much closer to the pacifist tendency in libertarianism than to Smith or Hayek. These conflicting elements in libertarianism are very revealing as to the difference made by small shifts of assumptions.

Godwin's profound sense of a moral obligation to take care of one's fellow man[39] never led him to conclude that the *government* was the instrumentality for discharging this obligation. He therefore had no desire to destroy private property[40] or to have the government manage the economy or redistribute income. In supporting private property and a free market, Godwin was at one with Smith, with Hayek, and with modern libertarianism. But in his sense of a pervasive moral responsibility to one's fellow man, he was clearly at the opposite pole from those libertarians who follow Ayn Rand, for example. It was the power of reason which made it unnecessary for government to take on the task of redistribution, in Godwin's vision, for individuals were capable, eventually, of voluntarily sharing on their own. But were reason considered just a little less potent, or selfishness just a little more recalcitrant, the arguments and vision of Godwin could be used to support socialism or other radically redistributionist political philosophies. Historically, the general kind of vision found in Godwin has been common on the political left, among those skeptical of the free market and advocating more government intervention.

Logically, one can be a thorough libertarian, in the sense of rejecting government control, and yet believe that private decision-making should, as a matter of morality, be directed toward altruistic purposes. It is equally consistent to see this atomistic freedom as the means to pursue purely personal well-being. In these senses, both William Godwin and Ayn Rand could be included among the contributors to libertarianism.

The unconstrained vision is clearly at home on the political left, as among G. B. Shaw and the other Fabians, for example, or in Edward Bellamy's *Looking Backward* or in the contemporary writings of John Kenneth Galbraith in economics or of Ronald Dworkin and Laurence Tribe on the law. But the constrained vision, while opposed to such philosophies, is also incompatible with the atomism of thoroughgoing libertarians. In the constrained vision, the individual is allowed great freedom precisely in order to serve *social* ends—which may be no part of the individual's purposes. Property rights, for example, are justified within the constrained vision not by any morally superior claims of the individual over society, but precisely by claims for the efficiency or expediency of making social decisions through the systemic incentives of market processes rather than by central planning. Smith had no difficulty with the right of society to regulate individual behavior for the common good, as in fire regulations,[41] for example, and Oliver Wendell Holmes declared that "the public welfare may call upon the best citizens for their lives."[42]

Neither the left-right dichotomy nor the dichotomy between constrained and unconstrained visions turns on the relative importance of the individual's benefit and the common good. All make the common good paramount, though they differ completely as to how it is to be achieved. In short, it is not a moral "value premise" which divides them but their different empirical assumptions as to human nature and social cause and effect.

Another complication in making these dichotomies of social philosophy is that many twentieth-century institutions or legal precedents represent thinking that is "liberal" (in American terms) or social-democratic (in European terms), so that conservatives who oppose these institutions or precedents are often confronted with the argument that such things are "here to stay"— essentially a conservative principle. Those on the political right may thus end up arguing, on the ground of the political left, that certain policies are "irrational," while the left defends them as part of the accepted social fabric, the traditional position of the right. While these might be simply tactical debating positions in some cases, there is a very real philosophic difficulty as well. At the extreme, the long-standing institutions of the Soviet Union were part of the social fabric of that society, and communists who opposed reforming them were sometimes considered to be "conservative." Among fervent American supporters of the free-market principle, libertarians are often at odds with conservatives on welfare state institutions, including labor unions, which are now part of the American social fabric—an argument which carries little or no weight in libertarian thinking, though some conservatives find it important.

While it is useful to realize that such complications exist, it is also necessary to understand that a very fundamental conflict between two visions has persisted as a dominant ideological phenomenon for centuries, and shows no signs of disappearing. The inevitable compromises of practical day-to-day politics are more in the nature of truces than of peace treaties. Like other truces, they break down from time to time in various parts of the world amid bitter recriminations or even bloodshed.

The general patterns of social visions sketched in these chapters in Part I provide a framework for looking more deeply into the application of constrained and unconstrained visions to highly controversial issues involving equality, power, and justice in the chapters that follow in Part II. Finally, the role of visions will be assessed against related but very different concepts, such as "value premises" and paradigms.

PART II: APPLICATIONS

Chapter 6

VISIONS OF EQUALITY

Equality, like freedom and justice, is conceived in entirely different terms by those with the constrained vision and those with the unconstrained vision. Like freedom and justice, equality is a *process* characteristic in the constrained vision and a *result* characteristic in the unconstrained vision.

From Edmund Burke in the eighteenth century to Friedrich Hayek in the twentieth century, the constrained vision has seen equality in terms of processes. In Burke's words, "all men have equal rights; but not to equal things."[1] Alexander Hamilton likewise considered "all men" to be "entitled to a parity of privileges,"[2] though he expected that economic inequality "would exist as long as liberty existed."[3] A social process which assures equal treatment thus represents equality, as seen in the constrained vision, whether or not the actual results are equal. "Equal treatment," according to Hayek, "has nothing to do with the question whether the application of such general rules in a particular situation may lend to *results* which are more favorable to one group than to others."[4] There are, for Hayek, "irremediable inequalities,"[5] just as there is "irremediable ignorance on everyone's part."[6]

The constrained vision of man leads to a constrained concept of equality as a process within man's capabilities, in contrast to a results definition of equality, which would require vastly more intellectual and moral capacity than that assumed. The argument is not that it is literally impossible to reduce or eliminate specific instances of inequality, but that the very processes created to do so generate other inequalities, including dangerous inequalities of power caused by expanding the role of government. Milton Friedman exemplified this aspect of the constrained vision when he said:

> A society that puts equality—in the sense of equality of outcome—ahead of freedom will end up with neither equality nor freedom. The use of force to achieve equality will destroy freedom, and the force, introduced for good purposes, will end up in the hands of people who use it to promote their own interests.[7]

But to those with the unconstrained vision, such dangers are avoidable, if not illusory, and therefore to stop at purely formal process-equality is both needless and inexcusable. "What could be more desirable and just," Godwin asked, than that the output of society, to which all contribute, should "with some degree of equality, be shared among them?"[8] Both visions recognize degrees of equality, so the disagreement between them is not over absolute mathematical equality versus some degree of equalization, but rather over just what it is that is to be equalized. In the unconstrained vision, the results are to be equalized—to one degree or another—whereas the equality of a constrained vision is the equalization of processes. Godwin was prepared to concede some advantages to talents and wealth,[9] though other believers in the unconstrained vision varied in how far they would go in this direction. What they shared was a concept of equality—of whatever degree—as being equality of result. When Godwin lamented seeing "the wealth of a province spread upon the great man's table" while "his neighbors have not bread to satiate the cravings of hunger,"[10] he voiced a lament echoed many times throughout the history of the unconstrained vision.

Even when equality is phrased as "equality of opportunity" or "equality before the law," it still has different meanings in the two visions. Although these concepts are expressed in prospective rather than retrospective terms, they can be either (1) prospects of achieving a given result, or (2) prospects of being treated a given way by the rules of the process.

So long as the process itself treats everyone the same—judges them by the same criteria, whether in employment or in a courtroom—then there is equality of opportunity or equality before the law, as far as the constrained vision is concerned. But to those with the unconstrained vision, to apply the same criteria to those with radically different wealth, education, or past opportunities and cultural orientations is to negate the meaning of equality—as they conceive it. To them, equality of opportunity means *equalized probabilities of achieving given results*, whether in education, employment or the courtroom.

This may require the social process to provide compensatory advantages to some, whether in the form of special educational programs, employment preference policies, or publicly paid attorneys. Though the specific issues of "affirmative action" or "comparable worth" are quite recent in history, the thinking and the vision behind them go back at least as far as the eighteenth century. According to Condorcet, "a real equality" requires that "even the natural differences between men will be mitigated" by social policy.[11] Without equalized probabilities of achieving given results, formal equality was inadequate—if not hypocritical—according to the unconstrained vision. George Bernard Shaw, for example, ridiculed formal equality of opportunity:

> Give your son a fountain pen and a ream of paper, and tell him that he now has an equal opportunity with me of writing plays and see what he says to you.[12]

Those with the unconstrained vision see no need to neglect at least *trying* such efforts toward equalizing chances for particular results. But to those with the constrained vision, attempting to single out special individual or group beneficiaries is opening the floodgates to a dangerous principle whose ramifications go beyond the intentions or control of those initiating such a process. Again, it was not argued that it is literally impossible to reduce specified inequalities seriatim, but rather that the generation of new inequalities by this process defeats the overall purpose and creates additional difficulties and dangers. A landmark U.S. Supreme Court decision on preferential treatment rejected the idea that ethnic groups could be ranked by the levels of historic injustice suffered and the compensatory preferences to which they were correspondingly entitled:

> As these preferences began to have their desired effect, and the consequences of past discrimination were undone, new judicial rankings would be necessary. The kind of variable sociological and political analysis necessary to produce such rankings simply does not lie within the judicial competence. . . .[13]

The unconstrained vision was expressed by an opposing Justice in the same case, without regard to this argument. Instead, a lengthy elaboration of historic injustices and handicaps suffered was cited as arguments for compensatory preferences to achieve equalization of prospects.[14] The two visions argued past each other.

CAUSATION

For equality to become an issue between the two visions, there must first be inequality. The existence and persistence of inequality is causally explained very differently by those with the constrained vision and those with the unconstrained vision. Many leading exponents of a constrained vision do not explain inequality of result *at all*, while many leading exponents of an unconstrained vision find such inequality both intellectually and morally central.

It is not only the existence and persistence of unequal results which have long held the attention of those with the unconstrained vision, but the magnitude of these differences as well. For Godwin, the inequality of property ownership was at "an alarming height."[15] To Shaw, for one person to receive three thousand times the rate of pay of another "has no moral sense in it."[16] Moreover, it is not only the magnitude of unequal results but the source: According to Shaw, "landlords have become fabulously rich, some of them taking every day, for doing nothing, more than many a woman of sixty years drudgery."[17] Capitalists likewise were conceived to prosper in much the same way, profit being considered simply "overcharge."[18]

It was not merely that some have little and others have much. Cause and effect are involved: Some have little *because* others have much, according to this reasoning, which has been part of the unconstrained vision for centuries. In one way or another, the rich have *taken* from the poor. According to Godwin, the great wealth of some derives from "taking from others the means of a happy and respectable existence."[19] Such reasoning has been applied internationally as well as domestically. Imperial Britain was thus "a parasite on foreign labor," according to Shaw.[20] The correction of such exploitation has been a central concern in the unconstrained vision.

The theme of unjustified taking is not limited to direct employer-employee relationships, to business-consumer relationships, or to imperialist-and-colony relationships. When those incapacitated for work—"those less endowed with bodily strength or mental power"—do not share fully in the fruits of society, they are not merely denied compassion but robbed of rights, according to Edward Bellamy, for most of what makes modern prosperity possible comes from the efforts of past generations:

How did you come to be possessors of this knowledge
and this machinery, which represent nine parts to one
contributed by yourself in the value of your product?
You inherited it, did you not? And were not these others, these unfortunate and crippled brothers whom
you cast out, joint inheritors, co-heirs with you? Did
you not rob them when you put them off with crusts,
who were entitled to sit with the heirs, and did you
not add insult to robbery when you called the crusts
charity?[21]

The thesis that material deprivation has been aggra-
vated by the infliction of psychic pain has long been a
recurring theme in the unconstrained vision. In the
eighteenth century, Godwin declared:

Human beings are capable of enduring with chearful-
ness considerable hardships, when those hardships
are impartially shared with the rest of the society, and
they are not insulted with the spectacle of indolence
and ease in others, no way deserving of better advantages than themselves. But it is a bitter aggravation of
their own calamity, to have the privileges of others
forced on their observation, and, while they are per-
petually and vainly endeavouring to secure for themselves and their families the poorest conveniences, to
find others revelling in the fruits of their labors.[22]

Awareness of inequalities and revulsion toward
them have not been confined to those with the unconstrained vision. Similar reactions have been common to
Adam Smith in the eighteenth century and to Milton

Friedman in the twentieth century.[23] In Friedman's words:

> Everywhere in the world there are gross inequities in income and wealth. They offend most of us. Few can fail to be moved by the contrast between the luxury enjoyed by some and the grinding poverty suffered by others.[24]

While both Smith and Friedman (as well as others with the constrained vision) have proposed various ameliorative schemes to help the poor,[25] neither was prepared to make fundamental changes in the social processes in hopes of greater equalization. A vision of constrained options and greater dangers in alternative processes limits the scope of remedies. Moreover, these inequalities were not assumed to be products of the given social system, which Friedman saw as mitigating rather than aggravating them, but as a common misfortune far worse in other systems. According to Friedman: "Wherever the free market has been permitted to operate, wherever anything approaching equality of opportunity has existed, the ordinary man has been able to attain levels of living never dreamed of before."[26] While the material abundance of modern capitalist nations has created fortunes here and there, its main beneficiaries have been ordinary rather than wealthy people, according to Friedman. Modern technological wonders brought little improvement to what the rich already had, however much they revolutionized the lives of the masses:

> The rich in Ancient Greece would have benefitted little from modern plumbing: running servants replaced

running water. Television and radio—the patricians of Rome could enjoy the leading musicians and actors in their home, could have the leading artists as domestic retainers. Ready-to-wear clothing, supermarkets—all these and many other modern developments would have added little to their life. They would have welcomed the improvements in transportation and in medicine, but for the rest, the great achievements of Western capitalism have redounded primarily to the benefit of the ordinary person.[27]

In the constrained vision of Friedman and others, "exploitation" situations have been seen as more effectively eliminated by the systemic characteristics of a competitive economy than by the deliberate intervention of political leaders in complex economic processes that they cannot comprehend. The danger was not only in the adverse consequences of their intervention on the economy, but still more so in the dire consequences of such an increased concentration of political power. In short, attempts to equalize *economic* results lead to greater—and more dangerous—inequality in *political* power. This was the central theme of Hayek's *The Road to Serfdom*, where the goal of simultaneously combining freedom and equality of outcome in democratic socialism was declared "unachievable" as a result,[28] but dangerous as a process change pointing toward despotism.

Democratic socialists were not accused of plotting despotism, and were in fact regarded by Hayek as generally humane individuals lacking the "ruthlessness" required to achieve their social goals,[29] but were seen by him as paving the way for others—including both fascists and communists—who complete the destruction of freedom, after the principles of equality before the law and limitations on political power have been fatally undermined in pursuit of "the mirage of social justice."[30]

As in other issues, while followers of the unconstrained vision speak in terms of the *goals* being sought, followers of the constrained vision speak in terms of the *incentives* being created by the processes being changed.

Irremediable ignorance and irremediable inequality go hand in hand, according to Hayek. It is precisely our "inescapable ignorance" that makes general rules necessary[31] and general rules of social processes are incompatible with explicit determination of particular individual or group results. Those who "postulate a personified society"[32] assume an intention, purpose, and corresponding moral responsibility where there is in fact an evolved order—and "the particulars of a spontaneous order cannot be just or unjust."[33] *Government*, as a deliberately created entity, may act on intention and be morally judged by its acts, but not *society*.[34] Government, as a limited set of decision-makers, cannot possess all the knowledge in a society, or anything approaching it, and therefore lacks the omniscience in fact to prescribe just or equal results.

A "society of omniscient persons" would have no need for a process-conception of justice or equality. The "social justice" of the unconstrained vision could be imposed or agreed to in such a society, where—Hayek concedes—"every action would have to be judged as a means of bringing about known effects."[35] But the constrained vision of human knowledge precludes the existence of a society with any such capability, so that the moral criteria appropriate to such a society become moot. The moral principles insisted upon by those with the unconstrained vision are thus rejected, not as *wrong*, but as *irrelevant* to the social choices actually available, and dangerous in the concentration of governmental power implied by the pursuit of such ideals.

Because it is "absurd" to demand social justice from an uncontrolled process, according to Hayek,[36] such a demand implies the substitution of a very different kind of process. The moral issue thus becomes one of the relative merits of alternative processes. Hayek questioned "whether it is moral that men be subjected to the power of direction that would have to be exercised in order that the benefits derived by the individuals could be meaningfully described as just or unjust."[37]

In short, the constrained vision does not defend existing inequalities, or any given pattern of economic or social results, as just. According to Hayek, "the manner in which the benefits and burdens are apportioned by the market mechanism would in many instances have to be regarded as very unjust *if* it were the result of a deliberate allocation to particular people."[38] The moral justification of the market process rests on the general prosperity and freedom it produces.

The issue between the two visions is not simply one of the existence, magnitude, and persistence of inequalities but also of the extent to which those inequalities are merited. This issue, like the others, goes back for centuries. In the eighteenth century, Godwin wrote of "a numerous class of individuals, who, though rich have neither brilliant talents nor sublime virtues."[39] The privileged and powerful readily become "indifferent to mankind, and callous to their sufferings."[40] A king is "nothing but a common mortal, exceeded by many and equalled by more, in every requisite of strength, capability and virtue."[41] "Garlands and coronets," according to Godwin, "may be bestowed on the unworthy and prostituted to the intriguing."[42] His target was not simply inequality as such, but especially "unmerited advantage."[43] Variations on these themes have remained a prominent feature of the unconstrained vision. In the twentieth century, Shaw declared that "enormous fortunes are made without the least merit,"[44] and noted that not only the poor but many well-educated people "see successful men of business, inferior to themselves in knowledge, talent, character and public spirit, making much larger incomes."[45]

Because those with the unconstrained vision emphasize the *unmerited* nature of many rewards, it does not follow that those with the constrained vision assume rewards to be individually merited. Merit justifications have been very much the exception rather than the rule, and largely confined to secondary figures such as Samuel Smiles, Horatio Alger, and Social Darwinists like William Graham Sumner—all of whom have been explicitly repudiated by Hayek, for example.[46] Nor was Hayek unique. The leading figures in the tradition of the constrained vision have for centuries pointed out that many rewards are personally unmerited. The moral justification of the constrained vision is the justification of a social process, not of individuals or classes within that process. They readily concede that "inevitably some unworthy will succeed and some worthy fail," that rewards are "based only partly on achievements and partly on mere chance."[47] This is a trade-off they accept, on the conviction that no solution is possible. But those with the unconstrained vision do not share that conviction and therefore find acceptance of known inequities intolerable.

Although the two visions reach very different moral conclusions, they do so *not* on the basis of fundamentally different moral principles but rather because of their differences in analysis of causes and effects. The causal reasons for the inequalities in the first place, and the options available for dealing with them, are radically different in the two visions. Adam Smith and William Godwin were both offended by the privilege and arrogance of the wealthy and powerful in the eighteenth century, as Ronald Dworkin and Milton Friedman have both been offended by the economic inequalities of the twentieth century.[48] The constrained and the unconstrained visions differ, however, on the plane of *causation*, as to what can be done about it—at what cost and with what dangers.

Both visions agree that equality of process can mean vast inequalities of results, and that equal results may be attainable only by causing processes to operate very unequally toward different individuals or groups. The differences between the two visions are in the priority that they attach to each goal—and that in turn reflects the extent to which they conceive of man as capable of morally and causally determining the appropriate goal for society. One of the bitter contemporary clashes between the two visions, in various countries around the world, is over compensatory preferences for particular social groups, for purposes of enabling those groups to reach results more nearly like those of more fortunate groups in their respective societies. Although this specific issue has emerged very recently, as history is measured, it reflects a conflict of visions that goes back for centuries.

The relationship between equality and freedom is also seen in opposite terms in the two visions. In the unconstrained vision, equality and freedom are not in conflict, but are in fact twin applications of similar principles, sometimes summarized as "political democracy" and "economic democracy." As results, this is clearly so, since equalization is central to both concepts. As processes, it is by no means clear that it is so. The constrained vision, which focuses on processes, sees a major conflict between allowing freedom of individual action and prescribing equality of social results. Moreover, it is considered illusory in this vision to expect that prescription of economic results can be achieved while maintaining freedom in non-economic areas.[49]

KINDS OF EQUALITIES AND INEQUALITIES

If individuals were all equal in their developed capabilities and shared the same values and goals, then equal processes could produce equal results, satisfying both visions. But neither vision believes this to be the case. Some in both camps believe that innate potentialities do not differ greatly among individuals or groups, but this does little to reconcile the conflict of visions, since it is not potentialities but the actual application of developed capabilities which determines results.

No one believed in the innate equality of human beings more than Adam Smith. He thought that men differed less than dogs,[50] that the difference between a philosopher and a porter was purely a result of upbringing,[51] and he rejected with contempt the doctrine that whites in America were superior to the blacks they enslaved.[52] Yet the social inequalities of wealth and status that have been burning issues in the unconstrained vision were of little concern in Smith's constrained vision of man in society. He opposed slavery as a social *process*, on both moral and economic grounds.[53] But such general social *results* as differences in income and privilege were not deemed sufficiently important to override the process goals of freedom of civil and economic action.

Nor was this a matter of partisanship for the wealthy and powerful. Smith's low opinion of businessmen has already been noted in Chapter 2. He also repeatedly pointed out how the aristocracy, royalty, and the privileged or mighty in general were foolishly worshiped by the masses,[54] even to the point of imitating their vice,[55] and how this huge psychic windfall gain was taken for granted by its recipients, who did not even regard ordinary people as their fellow men.[56] A distinguished scholar once pointed out that several socialist orations could be put together out of quotations from Adam Smith.[57] But Smith's constrained vision of man and society led in the opposite direction—to *laissez-faire* capitalism.

Adam Smith's sweeping egalitarianism was by no means unique among those with the constrained vision. Alexander Hamilton, for example, had similar views regarding the moral level of different groups:

Experience has by no means justified us in the supposition, that there is more virtue in one class of men than in another. Look through the rich and poor of the community; the learned and the ignorant. Where does virtue predominate? The difference indeed consists, not in the quantity but kind of vices, which are incident to the various classes. . . .[58]

To those with the unconstrained vision, to say that people are innately equal, but that vast differences in economic and social results exist, and that privileges are both taken for granted and repaid only in arrogance, is to say that the existing society is intolerably unjust and must be drastically changed. Some would say that such a system must be changed "at all costs" or by "whatever means are necessary." At the very least, social mobility must be increased. Smith reached none of these conclusions. William Godwin once more serves as a perfect counter-example of the unconstrained vision, for he agreed completely with Smith on the innate equality of human beings,[59] on the inequalities of wealth and status,[60] and on the arrogance of privilege,[61] but reached opposite conclusions on the need for drastic change (though by entirely peaceful means in Godwin's case.[62] The difference between them was in their respective visions of man and of social causation.

Many of those with an unconstrained vision and a passionate opposition to inequality of results assume that those who oppose them must be in favor of inequality of results, either on philosophic grounds or as a matter of narrow self-interest. In reality, those with the constrained vision may be passionately devoted to certain processes (freedom to choose, the "rule of law," etc.) and only secondarily concerned with whether any particular result is equal or unequal. They may not be at all opposed to the advancement of untouchables in India or blacks in the United States, or similar groups in other countries—and may even have contributed efforts toward such advancement themselves—but nevertheless fight strongly against process changes intended (by those with an unconstrained vision) to aid such advancement.

While the belief that people's capabilities are equal can be found among exponents of both visions, so can the belief that these capabilities vary enormously between social groups. The view that races, classes, or sexes innately differ greatly in capabilities would be a conclusion for which a constrained vision would be necessary, but not sufficient, and is in fact rejected by many for whom intellectual or moral constraints apply to all human beings, without group distinction. As for developed capabilities, these are often conceived as being far more unequal by believers in the unconstrained vision than by believers in the constrained vision.

As noted in Chapter 3, the distribution of knowledge and reason is vastly more unequal in the unconstrained vision, because its definition of knowledge and reason as articulated information and syllogistic rationality puts them much more in the province of the intellectual elite. But the cultural conception of knowledge in the constrained vision makes it far more widely diffused, and the systemic logic of cultural evolution and survival in competition dwarfs to insignificance the special logical talents of the intellectual elite. Thus, while the common man was seen by Hobbes to be more capable in some respects than his more highly educated social superior,[63] and the latter's social claims were at least viewed very skeptically by Smith, Friedman, and Hayek, a vast chasm between the existing intellectual and moral capabilities of the common man and those of the intellectual elite has been an enduring characteristic of the tradition of the unconstrained vision.

In an eighteenth-century world where most people were peasants, Godwin declared that "the peasant slides through life, with something of the contemptible insensibility of an oyster."[64] Rousseau likened the masses of the people to "a stupid, pusillanimous invalid."[65] According to Condorcet, the "human race still revolts the philosopher who contemplates its history."[66] In the twentieth century, George Bernard Shaw included the working class among the "detestable" people who "have no right to live." He added: "I should despair if I did not know that they will all die presently, and that there is no need on earth why they should be replaced by people like themselves."[67]

While the unconstrained vision has featured egalitarianism as a conviction that people should share more equally in the material and other benefits of society, it tends to see the existing capabilities of people as far more unequal than does the constrained vision. Among contemporary economists proposing ways of advancing Third World nations out of poverty, those representing a constrained vision (P. T. Bauer and T. W. Schultz, for example) depict the peasant masses of the Third World as a repository of valuable skills and capable of substantial adaptations to changing economic conditions, if only the elite will leave them free to compete in the marketplace,[68] while those further to the left politically, such as

Gunnar Myrdal, depict the peasant masses as hopelessly backward and redeemable only by the committed efforts of the educated elite.[69]

It is only when estimating the potential intelligence of human beings that those with the unconstrained vision have a higher estimate than those with the constrained vision. When estimating the current intelligence of human beings, those with the unconstrained vision tend to estimate a lower mean and a greater variance. It is the greater variance which lends logical support to surrogate decision-making, whether in the form of more government planning in economics, judicial activism in the law, or international-agency efforts at population control or control of natural resources under the sea. Counter-examples can be found on both sides, of course, as for example among the leaders of the French Revolution or V. I. Lenin in modern times, both of whom praised the masses. But the public statements of those holding or aspiring to power are hardly decisive evidence. On the other side, Burke's famous outburst against the "swinish multitude" supporting the French Revolution was atypical even of Burke,[70] much less of the tradition of which he was part.

More important, it is the logic of each vision, rather than the isolated examples, which point in the direction each has tended to go. Except for that sub-set who are explicitly racist or Social Darwinists, followers of the constrained vision have no reason to expect the kind of vast differences in capabilities which are the logical consequence of conceiving knowledge and reason in ways which make them accessible to the few but not to the many. There is no need to question the sincerity of those with the unconstrained vision when they make the well-being of the masses their central concern, for it is not by choice but by the logic of their assumptions that this well-being of the masses is achievable only through the leadership and commitment of the elite.

Which vision is more of a vision of equality depends upon the particular aspect of equality considered salient. By and large, the elite and the mass are closer in capability and morality in the constrained vision, while they are more equally entitled to comparable shares of benefits in the unconstrained vision.

SUMMARY AND IMPLICATIONS

The crucial difference between the constrained and the unconstrained visions of man is not in their perceptions of people as they are. What fundamentally distinguishes the two visions is their respective perceptions of human potential. The average person as he exists today is not seen in optimistic terms by those with the unconstrained vision. On the contrary, some of the most sweeping dismissals of the current capabilities of ordinary people have come from those with the unconstrained vision, from Godwin in the eighteenth century to George Bernard Shaw in the twentieth—even as they urged sweeping economic equalization. Indeed, one of the arguments for sweeping equalization of material conditions is that it will enable the masses to improve themselves, in addition to enjoying life more fully. In short, the gap between the actual and the potential is greater in the unconstrained vision than in the constrained vision. So too is the gap between the existing masses of people and those who have advanced further toward the intellectual and moral potentialities of man.

The concept of "equality" thus has opposite implications in the two visions. To those with the unconstrained vision, a greater equalization of material conditions is imperative, even if the means of accomplishing this require the more morally and intellectually advanced to restrict the discretion of others in the marketplace, or through judicial activism in the law, or by other social or political devices. The concepts of compassion, leadership, commitment, and rationality are featured prominently in the unconstrained vision.

To those with the constrained vision, however, the gap between the actual and the potential is much smaller, and with it there is a correspondingly smaller difference between the intellectual and moral elite, on the one hand, and the ordinary person on the other. Vast differences may exist within given areas of specialization—hence Burke's reverence for authorities within their respective specialties[71]—but believers in this vision have long pointed out areas where ordinary people are greatly superior to intellectuals, so that there is no such general superiority as to justify one group's restricting the discretion of others and acting as surrogate decision-makers for them. To those with the constrained vision, equality of discretion is more important than equality of condition.

The two visions' respective estimates of existing human capability (intellectual and moral) differ not so much in their estimates of the mean as in their estimates of the variance. The extent to which the discretion of some should be substituted for the discretion of others—whether through influence or power—depends not on the average rationality of man in general but on the differential rationality of different sets of human beings. The greater this differential, the stronger the case for surrogate decision-makers to exercise discretion for others.

Where this differential is thought to exist only within given areas of specialization, individuals lacking particular expertise may remain "free to choose" to purchase such expertise as they see fit—from doctors, lawyers, photographers, etc.—but where the differential is thought to be general and pervasive, then the layman lacks the prerequisites even for choosing the amount and kind of surrogate decision-making needed, much less to reject their fundamental principles. Thus, "a more equal world is a better world, even if most people prefer inequality."[72]

It is not over the degree of equality that the two visions are in conflict, but over what it is that is to be equalized. In the constrained vision, it is discretion which is to be equally and individually exercised as much as possible, under the influence of traditions and values derived from the widely shared experience of the many, rather than the special articulation of the few. In the unconstrained vision, it is the material conditions of life which are to be equalized under the influence or power of those with the intellectual and moral standing to make the well-being of others their special concern.

Chapter 7

VISIONS OF POWER

The role of power in social decision-making has tended to be much greater in the tradition of the unconstrained vision than among those with the constrained vision. That is, much more of what happens in society is explained by the deliberate exertion of power—whether political, military, or economic—when the world is conceived in the terms of the unconstrained vision. As a result, unhappy social circumstances are more readily condemned morally—being the result of someone's exertion of power—and more readily seen as things which can be changed fundamentally by the exertion of power toward different goals. The constrained vision, in which systemic processes produce many results not planned or controlled by anyone, gives power a much smaller explanatory role, thus offering fewer opportunities for moral judgments and fewer prospects for sweeping reforms to be successful in achieving their goals.

Conflicting visions of the role of power are involved in a wide spectrum of issues. Power in the sense of direct force and violence is involved not only in issues of war and peace but also in issues of crime and punishment. Political power and its efficacy are also storm centers in the conflict of visions. The existence, magnitude, and effectiveness of various economic and social powers are also seen very differently by the two visions. Along with differences as to the magnitude, pervasiveness, or effectiveness of power, the two visions differ also as to the degree of inequality with which power is shared or concentrated, mitigated or amplified, by various social conditions. The role of legal rights as bulwarks against power is therefore seen in drastically different terms by those with the constrained and unconstrained visions. Moreover, power is defined to mean drastically different things in the two visions.

FORCE AND VIOLENCE

Force and violence take many forms, from crime to war, and including the implicit threat of force and violence behind government. The causal reasons and moral justifications for force differ completely as between the constrained and the unconstrained visions. Reason, as an alternative to force, likewise plays a different role in the two visions, in everything from child-rearing to international relations. It is not a difference in "value premises," however. Both visions prefer articulated reason to force, at a given level of efficacy. But they differ greatly in their assessment of the efficacy of articulated reason. The use of force is particularly repugnant to those with the unconstrained vision, given the effectiveness they attribute to articulated reason.

As in other areas of human life, the unconstrained vision seeks to discover the special reasons for evils involving force and violence—war and crime, for example—while the constrained vision takes these evils for granted as inherent in human nature and seeks instead to discover contrivances by which they can be contained—that is, to discover the causes of peace or of law and order.

War

Given the horrors of war, and the frequent outcome in which there are no real winners, those with the unconstrained vision tend to explain the existence and recurrence of this man-made catastrophe in terms of either misunderstandings, in an intellectual sense, or of hostile or paranoid emotions raised to such a pitch as to override rationality. In short, war results from a failure of understanding, whether caused by lack of forethought, lack of communication, or emotions overriding judgment. Steps for a peace-seeking nation to take to reduce the probability of war therefore include (1) more influence for the intellectually or morally more advanced portions of the population, (2) better communications between potential enemies, (3) a muting of militant rhetoric, (4) a restraint on armament production or military alliances, either of which might produce escalating counter-measures, (5) a de-emphasis of nationalism or patriotism, and (6) negotiating outstanding differences with potential adversaries as a means of reducing possible causes of war.

Those with the constrained vision see war in entirely different terms. According to this vision, wars are a perfectly rational activity from the standpoint of those who anticipate gain to themselves, their class, or their nation, whether or not these anticipations are often mistaken, as all human calculations may be. That their calculations disregard the agonies of others is no surprise to those with the constrained vision of human nature. From this perspective, the steps for a peace-seeking nation to take to reduce the probability of war would be the direct opposite of those proposed by people with the alternative vision: (1) raising the cost of war to potential aggressors by military preparedness and military alliances, (2) arousal of the public to awareness of dangers, in times of threat, (3) promotion of patriotism and willingness to fight, as the cost of deterring attack, (4) relying on your adversaries' awareness of your military power more so than on verbal communication, (5) negotiating only within the context of deterrent strength and avoiding concessions to blackmail that would encourage further blackmail, and (6) relying more on the good sense and fortitude of the public at large (reflecting culturally validated experience) than on moralists and intellectuals, more readily swayed by words and fashions.

Like other evils, war was seen by those with the constrained vision as originating in human nature and as being contained by institutions. To those with the unconstrained vision, war was seen as being at variance with human nature and caused by institutions. War was seen by Godwin as being a consequence of political institutions in general[1] and more specifically as a consequence of *undemocratic* institutions. "War and conquest," according to Godwin, "will never be undertaken, but where the many are the instruments of the few."

This *localization of evil* is one of the hallmarks of the unconstrained vision. There must clearly be some cause for evils, but insofar as these causes are not so widely diffused as to be part of human nature in general, then those in whom the evils are localized can be removed, opposed, or neutralized, so as to produce a solution. The specifics of this localization—whether in undemocratic institutions, as in Godwin, or in a capitalistic economy, as in some modern writers—are less crucial than the localization itself, which makes a solution possible. Evils diffused throughout the human race can only be dealt with by trade-offs, through artificial devices which themselves produce other unfortunate side effects.

War, as seen in the constrained vision of *The Federalist Papers*, seemed to require virtually no explanation. The Federalists considered it axiomatic that if the thirteen recently independent American colonies did not form one nation, they would inevitably and incessantly be at war with each other. To the Federalists, it was obvious that "nations in general will make war whenever they have a prospect of getting anything by it."[2] Far from seeing war as an evil with localized origins in despots, they argued that there were "almost as many popular as royal wars."[3] The idea of special causes of war was rejected out of hand:

> It is sometimes asked, with an air of seeming triumph, what inducements could the States have, if disunited, to make war upon each other? It would be a full answer to this question to say—precisely the same inducements which have, at different times, deluged in blood all the nations in the world.[4]

Within this constrained vision, war did not require a specific explanation. Peace required explanation—and specific provisions to produce it. One of these provisions was military power: "A nation, despicable by its weakness, forfeits even the privilege of being neutral."[5] This was the direct opposite of Godwin's unconstrained vision, in which a nation whose "inoffensiveness and neutrality" would present no military threat to cause a "misunderstanding" with other nations or to "provoke an attack."[6] To Godwin, the buildup of military power and the forging of military alliances, or balance-of-power policies, were likely to lead to war.[7] Godwin deplored the cost of maintaining military forces, which included not only economic costs but also such social costs as submission to military discipline[8] and the spread of patriotism, which he characterized as "high-sounding nonsense"[9] and "the unmeaning rant of romance."[10] Within this vision, the military man was a lesser man for his occupation.[11]

Within the constrained vision of Adam Smith, however, the demands on a soldier, and the weight of responsibility on him for defending his people, elevated his profession to a nobler plane than others,[12] even though Smith conceded that there is a "diminution of humanity" when one is repeatedly in a situation where one must either kill or be killed.[13] This was apparently an acceptable cost—or trade-off, a solution being impossible. Patriotism Smith saw as both natural and beneficial, as morally efficient, despite his acknowledgment of its perverse side effects.[14] Again, it was a trade-off that Smith accepted, with no sign of seeking a solution.

Crime

Crime is another phenomenon seen in entirely different terms by believers in the constrained and unconstrained visions. The underlying causes of crime have been a major preoccupation of those with an unconstrained vision of human nature. But those with the constrained vision generally do not look for any special causes of crime, any more than they look for special causes of war. For those with the constrained vision, people commit crimes because they are people—because they put their own interests or egos above the interests, feelings, or lives of others. Believers in the constrained vision emphasize social contrivances to prevent crime or punishment to deter it. But to the believer in the unconstrained vision, it is hard to understand how anyone would commit a terrible crime without some special cause at work, if only blindness. Condorcet asked:

> Is there any vicious habit, any practice contrary to good faith, any crime, whose origin and first cause cannot be traced back to the legislation, the institutions, the prejudices of the country wherein this habit, this practice, this crime can be observed?[15]

Godwin likewise said: "It is impossible that a man would perpetrate a crime, in the moment when he sees it in all its enormity."[16] In the twentieth century as well, it has been said in a highly acclaimed book that "healthy, rational people will not injure others."[17] Within this vision, people are forced to commit crimes by special reasons, whether social or psychiatric. Reducing those special reasons (poverty, discrimination, unemployment, mental illness, etc.) is therefore the way to reduce crime:

> The basic solution for most crime is economic—homes, health, education, employment, beauty. If the law is to be enforced—and rights fulfilled for the poor—we must end poverty. Until we do, there will be no equal protection of the laws. To permit conditions that breed antisocial conduct to continue is our greatest crime.[18]

In both visions, the conclusions follow logically from the initial assumptions. Both visions also recognize that most people are horrified at certain crimes and would be morally incapable of committing them. They differ as to why this is so. The constrained vision of human nature sees this revulsion at the thought of committing certain crimes as the product of social conditioning—a sense of general morality, personal honor, and humane feelings, all cultivated by the many traditions and institutions of society. The unconstrained vision sees human nature as itself averse to crime, and society as undermining this natural aversion through its own injustices, insensitivities, and brutality.

Society "drains compassion from the human spirit and breeds crime,"[19] according to a modern version of the unconstrained vision. Given human nature as seen in the unconstrained vision, such crimes as robbery, riots, rape, and mugging are "inherently irrational" and are explained only by irrational conditions imposed upon the unfortunate segment of society.[20] Such evils of society as poverty, unemployment, and overcrowding "are the fountainheads of crime."[21] From this perspective, criminals are not so much the individual causes of crime as the symptoms and transmitters of a deeper social malaise:

> Crime reflects more than the character of the pitiful few who commit it. It reflects the character of the entire society.[22]

In this vein, the assassinations of John F. Kennedy, Robert Kennedy, and Martin Luther King during the 1960s were regarded as reflections on American society in general, not just the particular assassins. Those who argued this way often reflected the unconstrained vision in a wide range of social, economic, and political issues.

But in the constrained vision of human nature, natural incentives to commit crimes are so commonplace that artificial counter-incentives must be created and maintained—notably moral training and punishment. Adam Smith acknowledged that the infliction of punishment is itself a negative experience to humane individuals, but again it was a cost he was willing to pay—a necessary trade-off in a situation with no solution:

> When the guilty is about to suffer that just retaliation, which the natural indignation of mankind tells them is due to his crimes; when the insolence of his injustice is broken and humbled by the terror of his approaching punishment; when he ceases to be an object of fear, with the generous and humane he begins to be an object of pity. The thought of what he is about to suffer extinguishes their resentment for the sufferings of oth-

ers to which he has given occasion. They are disposed to pardon and forgive him, and to save him from that punishment, which in all their cool hours they had considered as the retribution due such crimes. Here, therefore, they have occasion to call to their assistance the consideration of the general interest of society. They counterbalance the impulse of this weak and partial humanity, by the dictates of a humanity that is more generous and comprehensive. They reflect that mercy to the guilty is cruelty to the innocent, and oppose to the emotions of compassion which they feel for a particular person, a more enlarged compassion which they feel for mankind.[23]

But, whereas Smith saw the infliction of punishment as a painful duty, believers in the unconstrained vision have seen it as an unnecessary indulgence in vengeance, a "brutalizing throwback to the full horror of man's inhumanity in an earlier time."[24] With this vision, the criminal is seen as a victim—a "miserable victim" in Godwin's words[25] first, of the special circumstances which provoked the crime, and then of people with a lust for punishment. The criminal's "misfortunes," according to Godwin, "entitle him" to something better than the "supercilious and unfeeling neglect" he is likely to receive.[26] The death penalty, especially, imposed on "these forlorn and deserted members of the community" highlights the "iniquity of civil institutions."[27] True, the criminal inflicted harm on others, but this was due to "circumstances"—these circumstances being the only distinction between him and the highest members of the society.[28] Within the framework of this vision, executions are simply "cold-blooded massacres that are perpetrated in the name of criminal justice."[29]

Punishment as a trade-off is barbaric within the framework of the unconstrained vision, for there is a solution at hand: rehabilitation. This is in keeping with the unconstrained vision's general emphasis on internal disposition rather than external incentives. "Punishment," Godwin conceded, "may change a man's behavior," but "it cannot improve his sentiments." Punishment "leaves him a slave, devoted to an exclusive self-interest, and actuated by fear, the meanest of the selfish passions." Were he treated properly, "his reformation would be almost infallible."[30] That is, he would revert to a natural state of being unable to harm anyone, once he really understood what he was doing. This view likewise has a contemporary echo, that the rehabilitated criminal "will not have the capacity—cannot bring himself—to injure another or to take or destroy property."[31] This changed disposition represents a solution, whereas punishment represents only a trade-off. There would obviously be no point in accepting a trade-off, unless one's vision of human nature was constrained so as to preclude a solution.

Rehabilitation and its prospects of success are seen very differently by the two visions. In the unconstrained vision of human nature, rehabilitation is a process of returning a person to his more or less *natural* condition of decency—in principle, much like fixing a broken leg, which consists largely in putting the leg in condition to heal and restore itself, rather than attempting to create a new leg from scratch. In the constrained vision, however, decency is artificial rather than natural, and if it has not been created in the malleable years of childhood, it is unlikely to be created later on.

In the constrained vision, each new generation born is in effect an invasion of civilization by little barbarians, who must be civilized before it is too late. Their prospects of growing up as decent, productive people depends on the whole elaborate set of largely unarticulated practices which engender moral values, self-discipline, and consideration for others. Those individuals on whom this process does not "take"—whether because its application was insufficient in quantity or quality or because the individual was especially resistant—are the sources of antisocial behavior, of which crime is only one form.

THE LOCUS OF DISCRETION

Power lies at the end of a spectrum of causal factors which include influence, individual discretion, and systemic interactions whose actual outcomes were not planned or controlled by anyone. The question as to how much of what happens in the world is caused by the exercise of power is a question as to the locus of discretion—whether among millions of individuals, in groups such as the family, in structured political institutions, or in military forces that ultimately may make or unmake other people's decisions at gunpoint. The cause-and-effect question as to where current discretion lies is only one aspect of the role of power. The more fundamental conflict of visions is over where the locus of discretion should be.

In the unconstrained vision, where the crucial factors in promoting the general good are sincerity and articulated knowledge and reason, the dominant influence in society should be that of those who are best in these regards. Whether specific discretion is exercised at the individual level or in the national or international collectivity is largely a question then as to how effectively the sincerity, knowledge, and reason of those most advanced in those regards influence the exercise of discretionary decision-making. Godwin, who considered the power of reason—in the articulated syllogistic sense of the unconstrained vision—to be virtually irresistible in the long run, would diffuse discretion to the individual level, confident that the substance of what was to be decided by the many would ultimately reflect the wisdom and virtue of the few. However, those who have shared the unconstrained vision of man in general, but who lacked Godwin's conviction as to how effectively the wisdom and virtue of the few would spontaneously pervade the decisions of the many, wished to reserve decision-making powers in organizations more directly under the control or influence of those with the requisite wisdom and virtue. The unconstrained vision thus spans the political range from the anarchic individualism of Godwin to totalitarianism. Their common feature is the conviction that man as such is capable of deliberately planning and executing social decisions for the common good, whether or not all people or most people have developed this innate capability to the point of exercising it on their own.

The constrained vision sees no such human capability, in either the elite or the masses, and so approaches the issue entirely differently. It is not the sincerity, knowledge, or reason of individuals that is crucial but the *incentives* conveyed to them through systemic processes which forces prudent trade-offs, utilization of the experience of the many, rather than the articulation of the few. It is to the evolved systemic processes—traditions, values, families, markets, for example—that those with the constrained vision look for the preservation and advancement of human life. The locus of discretion may also range from the individual to the political collectivity among adherents of the constrained vision, but the nature of that discretion is quite different from what it is among those with the unconstrained vision.

Where adherents of the constrained vision emphasize the freedom of individuals to make their own choices—the theme of Milton Friedman's *Free to Choose*, for example—it is to be a choice within the constraints provided by the incentives (such as prices) conveyed to the individual and derived from the experiences and values of others. Where adherents of the unconstrained vision emphasize the freedom of the individual, it is either (1) the freedom of those individuals possessing the requisite wisdom and virtue—as in John Stuart Mill's *On Liberty*—or (2) the freedom of the masses insofar as they are deemed to be under the influence of the moral-intellectual exemplars.

Neither vision advocates that all individuals be utterly free to act without regard to others. It is the nature of what it is that is conveyed to them by others—and by which others—that differs. In the unconstrained vision, those with special wisdom and virtue convey this wisdom and virtue to others—through articulation, where that is deemed effective, and through coercive power where it is not. To those with the constrained vision, the special wisdom or virtue of moral-intellectual exemplars is far less important than the mass experience of the generations (embodied in traditional values) and the current experiences and economic preferences of the many (embodied in prices). In the unconstrained vision, the ordinary individual is to be responsive to the message of moral-intellectual pioneers; in the constrained vision, the ordinary individual is to be responsive to other ordinary individuals, whose rising and falling prices or rising and falling social disapproval convey their experience more effectively than words.

Individualism takes on entirely different meanings within the two visions. In the constrained vision, individualism means leaving the individual free to choose among the systemically generated opportunities, rewards, and penalties deriving from other similarly free individuals without being subjected to articulated conclusions imposed by the power of organized entities such as government, labor unions, or cartels. But in the unconstrained vision, individualism refers to (1) the right of ordinary individuals to *participate* in the articulated decisions of collective entities, and (2) of those with the requisite wisdom and virtue to have some *exemption* from either systemic or organized social constraints.

Mill's *On Liberty* was perhaps the classic statement of the second, the right of the moral-intellectual pioneers to be exempted from the social pressures of mass opinion. He did not believe the reverse—that the masses should be exempt from the influence of the moral-intellectual elite. On the contrary, many of his writings emphasized the leadership role of the intellectuals. While Mill opposed "social intolerance" on the part of the many,[32] he regarded democracy as most beneficial when "the sovereign Many have let themselves be guided (which in their best times they always have done) by the counsels and influence of a more highly gifted and instructed One or Few."[33]

Among contemporary followers of the unconstrained vision, individualism likewise centers on exemption of moral and intellectual pioneers from social pressures or even, in some cases, from laws. For example, conscientious objections to military service, or military advocacy of violence in the face of perceived social injustice, are among the exemptions Ronald Dworkin justifies, while denying that racial segregationists have any corresponding rights to violate civil rights laws.[34]

All these views on both sides are consistent with their initial premises. If man has moral-intellectual capabilities far in advance of those currently manifested in the mass of ordinary people, then the special wisdom and virtue of those who have already gone much further in that direction of those human potentialities must not only be made the basis for the decisions of others, whether by influence or power, but must itself be exempted to some extent from the social control of retrograde masses, and perhaps even from some laws reflecting retrograde views. But if the knowledge, virtue, and wisdom that matter most are those deriving from the experience of the masses, whether expressed in traditions, constitutions, or prices—as claimed in the opposing constrained vision—then the most that each individual can expect is to be left free to choose among the various rewards and penalties which emerge from systemic social processes, not exemption from any of them.

The Economy

The constrained vision sees market economies as responsive to systemic forces—the interaction of innumerable individual choices and performances—rather than to deliberate power shaping the ultimate outcome to suit particular individuals or organized decision-makers. A competitive market, as thus conceived, is a very efficient system for "the transmission of accurate information," in the form of prices.[35] These prices not only bring information as to changing scarcities, technological advances, and shifting consumer preferences, but also provide "an incentive to react to the information," according to Milton Friedman.[36] The unconstrained vision argues that this is *not* how the economy operates, that it is currently obeying the power of particular interests and should therefore be made in future to obey the power of the public interest. Deliberate price-setting "exists in the most basic American industries," according to this view. The answer is for "an angry public" to "appeal to its political government."[37] Thus "the market gods are increasingly brought within control of humanely exercised power."[38]

The point here is not to resolve this contradiction but rather to indicate how completely different are the worlds envisioned by those who see the role of power differently. The locus of discretion is in one case scattered among millions, in the other concentrated in a few large corporate hands, exercised by corporate managements in an "impregnable position," according to John Kenneth Galbraith.[39] Each dismisses the other's vision as a myth.[40]

It is hardly surprising that the reasons why government exercises power in the economy also differ between the two visions. In the unconstrained vision, it is a matter of intentions while in the constrained vision it is a matter of incentives. The government's intention to protect the public interest *forces* it to intervene in the economy to undo the harm done by private economic power, according to the unconstrained vision. But the government's inherent incentive to increase its own power leads it into intervention that is often both unneeded and harmful, according to the constrained vision. Incentives are central to the constrained vision— "the prime problem of politicians is not to serve the public good but to get elected to office and remain in power."[41]

These different conclusions apply not only to the industrialized nations in which such controversies have long been prominent but also to analyses of the poorer, less industrialized "Third World." Diametrically opposite views on the causes and cures of Third World poverty reflect the same underlying differences of opinion on the nature of man, the role of knowledge, the capabilities of the elites and masses which characterize the conflict of visions in many other areas. They of course disagree also on the role of power.

For convenience, the late Nobel Prize–winning economist Gunnar Myrdal can be considered as representative of the school of thought which has regarded political power and discretion as the key to the advancement of the poorer countries. The opposite view—the constrained vision—has long been exemplified by the distinguished economist from the London School of Economics Lord Peter Bauer. It is not merely in their conclusions but in a wide variety of underlying assumptions that they differ.

They differ at the most fundamental level, on the very question as to what it is that is to be explained. Myrdal has sought to discover those "conditions" in the Third World countries which are "responsible for their underdevelopment."[42] But rather than try to explain the lesser development of much of the world compared to the industrialized west, Bauer has instead sought to explain the causes of prosperity and development, refusing to designate "the position of the great majority of mankind as abnormal."[43] To Myrdal, it is poverty which needs explaining; to Bauer, it is prosperity.

To Myrdal, articulated rationality is crucial to development, which must be "rationally coordinated" in ways made "more explicit in an overall plan."[44] This planning "must continually reconcile competing interests and determine the order of precedence among them."[45] In short, the discretion of surrogates must determine the trade-offs. But to Bauer, economic performance and political articulation are completely different qualities:

> The market system delivers the goods people want, but those who make it work cannot readily explain why it is so. The socialist or communist system does

not deliver the goods, but those who operate it can readily explain away its failure.[46]

The relationship between the intellectual-moral leaders and the masses in the Third World is seen in the classically different terms which have marked the constrained and the unconstrained visions for centuries, though the specific economic problems of the Third World are a relatively recent issue. Myrdal has been very concerned (1) to promote greater material equality, within the Third World and between Third World and industrialized nations,[47] and (2) to enhance the influence and power of the westernized classes to cause the Third World masses to change their whole way of life and values, so as to increase material advancement.[48] In short, his immediate concern is for greater economic equality and, simultaneously, a shift in the locus of discretion to the intellectual-moral leaders, the westernized intellectuals.

To Myrdal, without more "social and economic equality" mere "political democracy would be an empty achievement."[49] His goal has been not simple equalization of processes but equalization of results. Moreover, "regulations backed by compulsion"[50] must be used to move the masses, for "economic development cannot be achieved without much more social discipline than the prevailing interpretation of democracy" would permit.[51] The "resistance to change" of the masses[52] must be overcome. Because of "hardened resistance" to change throughout Third World societies, "modernism will not come about by a process of 'natural' evolution" but only by "radical state policies" to "engender development by state intervention."[53] It is not the masses themselves but "those who think and act on their behalf"[54] who must direct economic development.

In short, this very modern controversy over Third World development elicits from Myrdal a centuries-old vision which combines economic equality and political inequality, giving power to intellectual-moral surrogate decision-makers—in short, the unconstrained vision. At the same time, it elicits from Bauer all the key features of another centuries-old viewpoint, the constrained vision.

To Bauer, the Third World masses have repeatedly demonstrated their responsiveness to systemic economic incentives.[55] He rejects "condescension toward the ordinary people" of the Third World,[56] "the classification of groups as helpless,"[57] and the notion that they "do not know what is good for them, nor even what they want"[58]—a view which "denies identity, character, personality, and responsibility" to them.[59] To Bauer, the evidence "refutes the suggestion that individual Africans and Asians cannot or do not take a long-term view."[60] He notes that proposed "sacrifices are not borne by those who so warmly advocate their imposition."[61] To Bauer, "the intellectuals so highly regarded by Professor Myrdal" were seen as a special danger rather than a special source of progress, for "their attempts to iron out differences in culture, language, status, wealth and income," and to "dissolve the bonding agents of society" could only lead to an "extreme concentration of power."[62] Their hostility to the market and "contempt for ordinary people" are to him "only two sides of the same coin."[63] Bauer rejects "Myrdal's conception of man and society" in general and in particular "Myrdal's practice of regarding poorer people as helpless victims of society."[64]

Whether Myrdal or Bauer is more in favor of equality depends entirely on whether equality is conceived as equality of economic results or equality of political process. Myrdal clearly believes more in equality of economic results—and Bauer equally clearly prefers equality of social processes. In this they are very representative of historic visions, even though contending over modern issues.

Their respective conceptions of power are likewise in the tradition of the two conflicting visions. According to Myrdal, power has shaped economic results in the Third World, for not only have Western nations "exploited the resources and peoples in the huge backward areas of the world and kept them politically and economically dependent,"[65] but also domestically "swarms of money lenders and middlemen" have "too many of South Asia's peasants in their grip today."[66] There is "economic power" by the Chinese minority in Malaysia,[67] for example. Economic planning is said to have failed when it did not lead to "a lessening of the concentration of economic power."[68] Bauer, by contrast, rejects the whole concept of economic power in a competitive market:

> The market order minimizes the power of individuals and groups forcibly to restrict the choices of other people. Forcible restriction of the choice of others is what coercion means. Possession of wealth does not by itself confer such power on the rich. Indeed, in modern market economies the rich, especially the very rich, usually owe their prosperity to activities which have

widened the choices of their fellow men, including those of the poor. Obvious examples are the fortunes made in mass production and mass retailing.[69]

Note that there is not simply a disagreement between Myrdal and Bauer on an empirical issue as to the magnitude or locus of power but also, and more fundamentally, a different *conception* of what power consists of. As with equality, freedom, and justice, power is defined as a result characteristic in the unconstrained vision (Myrdal) and as a process characteristic in the constrained vision (Bauer). Bauer's definition of coercion or power as "restrictions of the choices of others"—a *process* definition—is one that Myrdal's examples do not even attempt to meet. Such *results* as being "economically dependent" are sufficient for Myrdal's purposes as evidence of being subjected to economic power. Implicitly, this is a definition of power advanced long ago by Max Weber, endorsed more recently by John Kenneth Galbraith, and generally characteristic of the unconstrained vision—"the possibility of imposing one's will on the behavior of other persons."[70] The two definitions may seem at first to be very similar, but they are in fact quite different.

Whenever *A* can get *B* to do what *A* wishes, then *A* has "power" over *B*, according to the results-oriented definition of the unconstrained vision. For example, two modern theorists say: "A controls the responses of B if A's acts cause B to respond in a definite way." Even when a subordinate negotiates with another employer in order to induce his superior to grant him a raise," that is Control with a capital C in these authors' terminology, or power.[71] It is the result which defines power. But if B is in a process in which he has at least as many options as he had before A came along, then A has not "restricted" B's choices, and so has no "power over him, by the process definition used by Bauer and characteristic of the constrained vision. The "offer of some specific quid pro quo" by A to B would be an exercise of power according to Galbraith,[72] but not according to Bauer, for A has only enlarged B's options rather than restricted them. Even if the new option offered by A is so superior to B's existing options as to make B's choice virtually a foregone conclusion, a quid pro quo is still not power by this definition. Whether in a Third World context or otherwise, arguments about the magnitude and locus of economic power are not simply disputes about empirical facts, but go back to a basic conflict of visions and of definitions derived from those different visions.

Because the ability to affect particular results in one way or another is much more widespread than the ability to shape whole social processes, power is a more pervasive feature of the unconstrained vision than of the constrained vision. In modern times, the concept of "economic power" has been predominantly associated with those who, on other grounds as well, are in the tradition of the unconstrained vision, while those with the unconstrained vision remain skeptical, if not dismissive, of such a concept. The salient point here is that how much power exists, in whatever context, depends upon how power is defined. More important, the appropriate policy response to power depends upon what it is substantively that is being responded to, not the word used to describe it.[73]

To those with the constrained vision, to deal with the problems of an economic process, in which power is at most attenuated, by increasing and concentrating political power that is very real is to reduce rather than increase human freedom. But to those who with the unconstrained vision, with a different conception of power, the exercise of political power "is pale in contrast with that exercised by concentrated and organized property interests."[74] They use the same word, but they are talking about two different things, overlapping just enough to be confused with one another.

The Law

In many legal cases, the most fundamental decision is *who should decide*—the locus of discretion. The question of narrow versus expansive judicial interpretation of the Constitution is ultimately a question as to whether the courts should restrict themselves, as much as possible, to defining boundaries within which others may exercise relatively uninhibited choices, or whether instead the courts should reserve to themselves broad powers to review those choices with respect to their arbitrariness or reasonableness, bias or good faith, duress or freedom, or equality or inequality of bargaining power between the parties concerned. The locus of discretion under the law is one of the many questions seen in radically different terms by those with the constrained vision and those with the unconstrained vision.

To those with the constrained vision, the locus of discretion should be, as much as possible, with those individuals and organizations directly concerned and systemically responsible for the consequences, in the sense of personally gaining or losing. Once the law has drawn the boundaries of their discretion, courts should be very reluctant to second-guess their choices. Even if the decisions made were clearly for the purposes of avoiding taxes, for example, the real question—according to Oliver Wendell Holmes—was whether they were within the legal boundaries of individual discretion, for "the very meaning of a line in the law is that you intentionally may go as close to it as you can if you do not pass it."[75]

This principle was applied to many kinds of cases. Within limits, someone who makes a will may be "a despot" with his property, according to Holmes.[76] Within the bounds of their discretion, state legislatures may pass laws "so foolish as to kill a goose that lays golden eggs," Holmes declared. "Intelligent self-interest," he noted, "is not a constitutional duty."[77] He said, "it by no means is true that every law is void which may seem to the judges who pass upon it as excessive."[78] Nor was Holmes prepared to condemn legally someone who killed an assailant, even though his action "may seem to have been unnecessary when considered in cold blood" afterward. "Detached reflection cannot be demanded in the presence of an uplifted knife," he said.[79]

In all these very disparate cases, the underlying premise was that, once the law had drawn the boundaries of discretion, courts should avoid second-guessing the actual exercise of that discretion. Given the assumptions of the constrained vision, the principle could hardly be otherwise. It is the legal equivalent of *laissez-faire* in economics, based essentially on the same vision of man and society.

But to those with the unconstrained vision, such holding back by courts is simply allowing injustice to flourish unnecessarily. According to Ronald Dworkin, courts must supply "fresh moral insight" when judging "the acts of Congress, the states, and the President."[80] If someone has "a moral right to an equal education," then "it is wrong for the state not to provide that education," and courts should rule accordingly.[81] This view is skeptical of "the supposed natural right to the use of property"[82] and dismisses "the liberty of an employer to hire workers on such terms as he wishes" as not entitled to constitutional protection from statutory law.[83] To those with the unconstrained vision, it is not simply a question of the locus of discretion, but also of the morality, reasonableness, and equality or inequality with which that discretion was exercised. If third parties are able to make such judgments, as the unconstrained vision assumes, those with the power to change these decisions have little justification for their failure to do so.

To those with the unconstrained vision, such holding back by courts is simply allowing injustice to flourish unnecessarily. Laurence Tribe and Ronald Dworkin are among the most prominent contemporary advocates of this view. Tribe rejects the "substance-denying" idea of courts limiting themselves to drawing boundaries defining acceptable procedures, without judging the substance of what those procedures produce within those boundaries.[84] Judges should "question the trade-offs arrived at by the political branches" of government rather than be satisfied if "due process" is observed within the boundaries of legislative and executive discretion.[85] It is

not enough that explicit constitutional rules are followed; implicit constitutional "values" are to be dis-
cerned and applied by judges to the substance of decisions made by others. Ronald Dworkin likewise sees a
need for courts to go beyond demarcation of the boundaries within which other branches of government exercise their own discretion. According to Dworkin, there
must be a "fusion of constitutional law and moral theory"[86] again, based on values found in the Constitution,
rather than only on explicit rules of procedure prescribed by that document.

While discerning implicit values is inherently subjective, legal process cannot be "emptied of substance or
subjectivity," according to Tribe.[87] The fact that particular rulings have particular effects means, for Tribe, that
implicit choices have been made as to the substance. For
example, protection of property rights means, in effect,
"immunizing from majoritarian rearrangement extant
distributions of wealth and economic power."[88] Thus, the
U.S. Supreme Court, by overruling state laws infringing
property rights "reinforced the protection of existing
patterns of capital distribution."[89] There is a "deep bias
against economic redistribution" in constitutional requirements for "just compensation" by government
when private property is taken under eminent domain.[90]
The law's "built-in bias against redistribution of wealth"
is seen as a benefit to "entrenched wealth"[91]; that is, it is
seen in terms of its individual results rather than in
terms of the social processes facilitated by a property-
rights system of economic decision-making.

By contrast, legal theorists who support property
rights defend them on the entirely different ground that

they "have an effect on the efficiency with which the economic system operates."[92] It is not the retrospectively observed results for particular individuals or classes but rather the prospective incentives created throughout society—the effect of property rights on "the penalty-reward system"[93] that is central in the opposing vision. In short, Tribe does not simply reach a different conclusion, but argues on an entirely different ground, from those with the constrained vision.

According to Tribe, "seemingly neutral principles" of the law betray a "tilt decidedly in the direction of existing concentrations of wealth and influence."[94] What is needed is "a more substantive conception of equality," for "equality is essential to the Constitution's protection of free speech and association."[95] As in other versions of the unconstrained vision in other fields, so in the law, it is not the *process* but the *result* which defines equality. According to Tribe, "free speech has not been available at all."[96] Because "inexpensive methods of communication such as leafletting, picketing, and soapbox orating have given way to expensive media such as electronic broadcasting, newspaper advertising and direct mail,"[97] freedom of speech as a process does not mean freedom of speech as a result. While there is "equality of voting" there is not "equality of voice."[98]

Economic *power* and institutional *participation* are central to this reasoning. The importance of both is denied by those with the constrained vision, who see the "power" of a corporation as a "delusion," and "participation" in collective decision-making as often inefficient.[99] Once again, the points of disagreement are not purely empirical because "power" in the constrained vision means an ability to reduce someone else's options. It is the existence of power in this sense that is denied:

> What then is the content of the presumed power to manage and assign workers to various tasks? Exactly the same as one little consumer's power to manage and assign his grocer to various tasks. The single consumer can assign his grocer to the task of obtaining whatever the customer can induce the grocer to provide at a price acceptable to both parties. That is precisely all that an employer can to do an employee.[100]

Because the employer cannot reduce the employee's pre-existing set of options, he does not have "power" over him in this conception. But to those with the unconstrained vision, power or force is not defined in these process terms. In the unconstrained vision, where results rather than processes are central, if A's chosen behavior changes B's behavior, then A has forced B to behave in a particular way. For example, according to Tribe, if the government refuses to pay for abortions by indigent women, then it causes "coerced childbirth," acting in effect to conscript women (at least poor women) as "involuntary incubators," thereby "denying women power over both their bodies and their futures."[101] This is consistent with the general logic of defining power in terms of the ability to change someone else's behavior, though inconsistent with the definition of power as the reduction of pre-existing options. In the latter sense, the government would be exercising power over pregnant women if it forbade abortions but not when it simply declined to pay for them.

The clash of the two concepts of power is especially sharp in legal issues in which governmental power is put at the disposal of private parties to enforce contracts or property rights. Where the terms of contracts have been privately and voluntarily agreed to, the locus of discretion is in the private sector—both initially and when a breach of contract presents to the aggrieved party the option of resorting to the enforcement power of the state. Similarly, when property rights are trespassed, the locus of discretion is with the individual property-owner, who may choose to ignore the trespass or to invoke state power to eject and/or prosecute the trespasser.

In a landmark case involving "state action" at the behest of an aggrieved private party, a woman handing out leaflets in a privately owned residential development, in defiance of the development's rules against it, was arrested for trespass. In the constrained vision and the judicially restrained view of the law based upon it, the central question for the court to decide was whether the "state action" requested was within the boundaries of the owners' property rights. But in the more judicially activist view of the opposing vision, the court should inquire into whether the "state action" requested was consonant with the "values" emanating from the Constitution, not simply whether it was consonant with the explicit rules written there. Among these "constitutional values" would be freedom of speech under the First Amendment, which explicitly forbade government—but not private individuals—from restricting communications.

In this particular case—*Marsh v. Alabama* (1946)—the U.S. Supreme Court overruled the trespass conviction on grounds of freedom of speech. In subsequent cases involving similar trespass in shopping centers, the Supreme Court decision sometimes went one way and sometimes the opposite way.[102] What is relevant here are the rationales for each position and how they relate to the underlying conceptions of power and the locus of discretion in applying it. Where the state's enforcement of trespass laws is *procedurally* correct as an application of explicit property rights, those with the unconstrained vision have nevertheless argued that the courts should refuse to countenance "state action" when the net *result* will be to deny someone the exercise of free speech on that property or to exclude someone from that property because the owner does not like people of that race. Like so many issues between those with constrained and unconstrained visions, "state action" cases turn on whether it is process or result that is paramount.

While conceding that "the Constitution does not directly concern itself with private actors," Laurence Tribe nevertheless declares that "to put 'private' actors in a position to inflict injury" by resort to state power under trespass laws makes the state guilty of the substantive result.[103] Thus "state action" can be "a subterfuge for substantive choices."[104] But to those whose constrained vision limits what man should attempt to making *processes* operate according to agreed principles, the only question is whether the legal boundaries of property rights were rightly drawn, not what substantive result occurred within the bounds of the discretion permitted the owner. There are echoes of Oliver Wendell Holmes in a latter-day Supreme Court Justice's dissenting opinion that the right "to use and dispose of his property as he sees fit" means that within those boundaries the owner has the legal right to be "irrational, arbitrary, capricious, even unjust."[105]

SUMMARY AND IMPLICATIONS

The role of various forms of power is seen very differently by those with the constrained and the unconstrained visions. The amassing of military power by a peaceful nation is dangerously counterproductive, according to the unconstrained vision, and absolutely essential to preserve peace, according to the constrained vision. These opposing views are as common today as they were in the eighteenth century—and as highly correlated with their proponents' respective positions on unrelated domestic social issues involving income and wealth differences or crime and punishment. Even issues of more recent vintage, such as abortion or Third World development, divide controversialists along lines reflecting different underlying assumptions that go back for centuries.

The constrained vision of human intellectual and moral capabilities relies less on articulated rationality to convince and more on incentives to influence behavior. This vision sees unprovoked aggression—whether by criminals or nations—as something to be systemically deterred, rather than something that can be rooted out by better understanding conveyed to those lacking it, or by defusing emotions which might otherwise override judgment. Neither criminals, war-makers, or Third World peoples are seen as requiring, or likely to derive much benefit from, the articulated rationality of the intellectually or morally advanced segments of society. Nor is the law seen as benefiting from their fresh insights being substituted for the implicit wisdom of systemically evolved procedures.

By contrast, the unconstrained vision necessarily sees a larger gap between current human capabilities and the ultimate intellectual and moral potential of the species. It is consistent with, if not entailed by, this vision that the existing intellectual and moral variance between the ordinary person and those who have traveled further along the road toward larger human potentialities would be greater than in the constrained vision. This imposes on the elites a duty to seek more influence on the course of events, whether in law, international relations, or Third World development. In this context, deference to less advanced popular beliefs or ancient institutions and traditions would be an almost fetishistic abdication of responsibility. This is especially so where resort to force, or the threat of force, is involved. Proposals that they observe such deference often evoke amazement, scorn, or even a questioning of the honesty of those who make such proposals—which are indeed irrational, *given the assumptions* of the unconstrained vision. But those who make such proposals are often operating under entirely different assumptions.

Contemporary controversies revolving around differences in the very conception of power often go back to centuries-old differences in the visions of man and social causation. Whenever one individual or group can change the behavior of another, then the former has power over the latter, as power is conceived by J. K. Galbraith, Gunnar Myrdal, Laurence Tribe, or other modern thinkers in the tradition of the unconstrained vision. Those with the constrained vision reject this conception of power, when behavioral changes are made in response to a quid pro quo, and conceive of power as the ability to reduce someone's pre-existing options. The result may be the same in both cases, whether achieved by threat or reward, but the constrained vision is not a vision of results but of processes.

If one conceives it to be within the capabilities of man to control the exercise of power and to limit it to socially desirable results, as those with the unconstrained vision do, then it is arbitrary to do so only with power defined as the ability to reduce pre-existing options. But if monitoring the desirability of myriad individual results is in general beyond the capabilities of any individual or council, as those with the constrained vision assume it to be, then efforts to produce social benefits must focus on general processes and on power restrictions—meaning restricting the ability of some to reduce the options of others.

Both visions see the abuses of power, whether direct force or in other social forms. They disagree widely and fundamentally on the means of controlling it.

Chapter 8

VISIONS OF JUSTICE

A dam Smith and John Rawls each made justice the prime virtue of a society, but they said it in such different senses as to mean nearly opposite things. Moreover, the differences between them were not due simply to their very different conceptions of what constituted justice—a process in Smith, a result in Rawls—but more fundamentally were due to how they wanted the principle of justice applied. According to Rawls:

> Justice is the first virtue of social institutions, as truth is of systems of thought. A theory however elegant and economical must be rejected or revised if it is untrue; likewise laws and institutions no matter how efficient and well-arranged must be reformed or abolished if they are unjust. Each person possesses an inviolability founded on justice that even the welfare of society as a whole cannot override. For this reason justice . . . does not allow that the sacrifices imposed on a few are outweighed by the larger sum of advantages enjoyed by many. . . . The only thing that permits

us to acquiesce in an erroneous theory is the lack of a better one; analogously, an injustice is tolerable only when it is necessary to avoid an even greater injustice. Being first virtues of human activities, truth and justice are uncompromising.[1]

Rawlsian justice is not to be traded off, even for the existence of an otherwise well-run society. Others with a similar vision speak of rights based on justice as "trumps" which invariably prevail over other social considerations.[2] There are different values of trumps, so that one must give way to another, but all trumps prevail over all non-trumps. The "superior claims of justice" have been part of the unconstrained vision as far back as William Godwin.[3] Those with this vision may differ among themselves as to the specifics of justice, as there are differences within the tradition of the constrained vision as well, and they differ especially as to the extent to which government is the instrumentality of enforcing these moral principles.[4] But what is consistent in the unconstrained vision is that (1) justice is categorically paramount and that (2) rights derived from justice inhere in individuals and for individuals.

A very different view of justice is found in the constrained vision of Adam Smith, who said, "society cannot subsist unless the laws of justice are tolerably observed."[5] He said:

Society may subsist, though not in the most comfortable state, without beneficence; but the prevalence of injustice must utterly destroy it.[6]

Justice thus derived its importance from the need to preserve society—not society its *raison d'être* from the need to produce justice. Moreover, justice need only be "tolerably observed" to serve its social function of maintaining order, and that overriding need for social order was due to the limitations of man. According to Smith:

> Men, though naturally sympathetic, feel so little for another, with whom they have no particular connection, in comparison to what they feel for themselves; the misery of one, who is merely their fellow-creature, is of so little importance to them in comparison even of a small convenience of their own; they have it so much in their power to hurt him, and may have so many temptations to do so, that if this principle [justice] did not stand up within them and overawe them into a respect for his innocence, they would, like wild beasts, be at all times ready to fly upon him; and a man would enter an assembly of men as he enters a den of lions.[7]

Here the elements of Smith's constrained vision stand out in stark contrast to those of the unconstrained vision. While man, as conceived by Smith, had natural sympathy—that was the cornerstone of the moral code elaborated in his *Theory of Moral Sentiments*—this sympathy and man's reason serve to provide mankind with general principles for society, rather than with direct restraints on individual behavior. Where derived and refined principles of justice serve as an individual restraint, it is not because of sympathy and reason but because the social inculcation of justice serves to "overawe" the individual.

Because society "cannot subsist among those who are at all times ready to hurt and injure one another,"[8] justice is—instrumentally—society's prime virtue.

The instrumental nature of justice, and its consequent subordination at times to other social imperatives, is a recurring theme in the constrained vision—and is anathema to the unconstrained vision. Implicit in this subordination of justice to order in the constrained vision is the conclusion that man will suffer more by the breakdown of order—even an unjust order—than by some injustices. Those with the constrained vision accept this trade-off because the inherent limitations of man, as they conceive man, leave no solution to hope for. In this vision of incremental trade-offs, the categorical concept of "trumps" is completely inapplicable.

LEGAL JUSTICE

The Constrained Vision

Oliver Wendell Holmes illustrated the way in which the inherent limitations of human beings were central to the concept of legal justice, as seen in the constrained vision:

> The law takes no account of the infinite varieties of temperament, intellect, and education which make the internal character of a given act so different in different men. It does not attempt to see men as God sees them. . . . If, for instance, a man is born hasty and awkward, is always having accidents and hurting himself or his neighbors, no doubt his congenital defects will be allowed for in the courts of heaven but his slips are no less troublesome to his neighbors than if they

sprang from guilty neglect. His neighbors accordingly require him, at his proper peril, to come up to their standard, and the courts which they establish decline to take his personal equation into account.[9]

Holmes thus established two standards of justice—and deliberately chose the lower standard as the proper one for human beings to administer, given the inherent limitations of man. It was a conscious trade-off of justice for the interest of the society as a whole. Holmes said, "justice to the individual is rightly outweighed by the larger interests on the other side of the scales."[10] He opposed "confounding morality with law."[11] Law existed to preserve society. Criminal justice, for example, was primarily concerned with deterring crime, not with finely adjusting punishments to the individual:

Public policy sacrifices the individual to the general good. It is desirable that the burden of all should be equal, but it is still more desirable to put an end to robbery and murder.[12]

Once again, Holmes rejected the higher standard of justice—the "desirable" tailoring of punishment to the individual—in favor of the lower standard of justice. Implicit in putting aside the solution in favor of the trade-off was the assumption that the solution was beyond human capability—a point already made explicitly in his discussion of civil liability, where the courts of men were said to have to operate differently from the courts of heaven. Even when the civil law prescribed the forcible sterilization of the mentally incompetent, to prevent their breeding more incompetents, Holmes on the Supreme Court sustained the law in the name of "the public welfare," declaring: "Three generations of imbeciles are enough."[13]

Law, as Holmes conceived it, was not the deliberate logical creation of great minds, but rather represented the evolved and codified experience of vast numbers of people:

> The life of the law has not been logic: it has been experience. . . . The law embodies the story of a nation's development through many centuries, and it cannot be dealt with as if it contained only the axioms and corollaries of a book of mathematics.[14]

Holmes did not deny that there was logic in law or that great minds had in fact contributed to its development, nor did he fatalistically accept whatever law existed. He in fact became famous as "the great dissenter" on the Supreme Court. "I venerate the law," he said, but "one may criticise even what one reveres."[15] What Holmes denied was that law had historically evolved by the application of logic, though there was a general logic in its propositions, arising systemically. He recognized "the countless number of great intellects that have spent themselves in making some addition or improvement" in the law—"the greatest of which," he said, "is trifling when compared to the mighty whole."[16] Here, as in other areas of the constrained vision, it is the experience of the many rather than the brilliance of the few that is to be relied upon, and historical evolution rather than excogitated rationality that is paramount.

The social benefits of known law, as a framework within which the many could make their own decisions, were weighed in a similar fashion by the celebrated English legal theorist of the eighteenth century, William Blackstone. The trade-off between individual justice and the social benefits of certainty was particularly striking within the British legal tradition, where "courts of equity" were institutionally distinguished from "courts of law"—the former to make exceptional adjustments for the sake of individual justice. Blackstone said:

> Equity thus depending, essentially, upon the particular circumstances of each individual case, there can be no rules and fixed precepts of equity laid down, without destroying its very essence, and reducing it to positive law. And on the other hand, the liberty of considering all cases in an equitable light must not be indulged too far, lest thereby we destroy all law, and leave the decision of every question entirely in the breast of the judge. And law, without equity, tho' hard and disagreeable, is much more desirable for the public good, than equity without law; which would make every judge a legislator, and introduce most infinite confusion; as there would be almost as many rules of action laid down in our courts, as there are differences of capacity and sentiment in the human mind.[17]

The parallel of such reasoning with other conclusions in the tradition of the constrained vision was not merely coincidental. Blackstone's vision of man was that "his reason is corrupt, and his understanding full of ignorance and error." To Blackstone, "the frailty, the imperfection and the blindness of human reason"[18] made it an unreliable instrument for the direct creation of law. Reason was necessary but not sufficient. When Blackstone said, "what is not reason is not law," he added immediately:

> Not that the particular reason for every rule in law can at this distance of time be always precisely assigned; but it is sufficient that there be nothing in the rule flatly contradictory to reason, and then the law will presume it to be well founded. And it has been an antient observation in the laws of England, that whenever a standing rule of law, of which the reason perhaps could not be remembered or discerned, hath been wantonly broke in upon by statutes or new resolutions, the wisdom of the rule hath in the end appeared from the inconveniences that have followed the innovation.[19]

In short, like Holmes and like the constrained vision in general, Blackstone found evolved systemic rationality superior to explicitly excogitated individual rationality. Blackstone thus became the great expositor and advocate of the British common law—"doctrines that are not set down in any written statute or ordinance, but depend merely upon immemorial usage."[20] Moreover, in interpreting the written law, Blackstone urged following the original intentions of those who wrote the law, seeking to "interpret the will of the legislator" by "exploring his intentions at the time when the law was made," taking his words "in their usual and most known signification," establishing their meaning "from the context" if necessary, and only as a last resort "when the words are dubious" trying to carry out the intent or spirit of the law.[21]

Like Holmes later in the law, or like his contemporary Burke in politics, Blackstone did not advocate an unchanging law or society. What distinguished his position was the mode of change and the caution about change:

> The doctrine of the law then is this: that precedents and rules must be followed, unless flatly absurd or unjust: for though their reason be not obvious at first view, yet we owe such deference to former times as not to suppose they acted wholly without consideration.[22]

Though Blackstone and Holmes were the most famous exponents of the constrained vision in the laws of their respective countries, their views were not unique, nor confined to legal theorists. Other exponents of the constrained vision in other fields expressed similar views when they mentioned the law. To Burke, for example, jurisprudence "with all its defects, redundencies, and errors, is the collected reason of the ages."[23] To Hayek, the law "does not owe its structure to the design of either judges or legislators."[24] Adam Smith saw "the sacred and necessary law of retaliation" for murder as "antecedent to all reflections upon the utility of punishment,"[25] and natural resentment in general as "the safeguard of justice and the security of innocence."[26] With all, law evolved as an expression of the natural feelings and experiences of human beings in general, not the articulated rationality of intellectual or moral leaders. Moreover, human nature was not considered to vary fundamentally over time. Holmes assumed that "the earliest barbarian . . . had a good many of the same feelings and passions as ourselves."[27] Here too his assumptions were typical of the kind of equality conceived by the constrained vision.

The Unconstrained Vision

The unconstrained vision has likewise been consistent over the centuries in reaching opposite conclusions on justice and the law. Although the argument has been made that modern psychological and sociological thinking enables courts today to individualize punishments to the criminal rather than the crime, the argument for individualizing the application of law to the criminal goes back at least as far as the eighteenth century, and has been as much a part of the unconstrained vision as the opposite view has been part of the opposite vision.

William Godwin condemned both the "absurdity" and the "iniquity" of punishment according to the general category of crimes committed. "No crimes were ever alike" he said.[28] According to Godwin:

> There is no maxim more clear than this, "Every case is a rule to itself." No action of any man was ever the same as any other action, had ever the same degree of utility or injury. It should seem to be the business of justice, to distinguish the qualities of men, and not, which has hitherto been the practice, to confound them.[29]

It is not "real justice," according to Godwin, to proceed by "reducing all men to the same stature" according to the crime committed. Rather, justice requires "contemplation of all the circumstances of each individual case."[30] Note, however, that the opposite positions of Godwin and Holmes on individualized punishment do *not* reflect differences in "value premises." Holmes, like Godwin, regarded it as morally superior to individualize criminal punishments or civil liability judgments, but simply regarded this higher morality as beyond the capability of human courts. They differed in empirical assumptions rather than in value premises.

The emphasis on individualizing criminal justice has remained part of the unconstrained vision over the centuries. John Dewey, for example, said:

> The dawn of truly scientific criminal law will come when each individual case is approached with something corresponding to the complete clinical record which every competent physician attempts to procure as a matter of course in dealing with his subject.[31]

In the unconstrained vision, it is not only the justice of punishment but also its efficacy which is at issue. According to Godwin, punishment is "inimical to the improvement of the mind" because incentives of reward and punishment are distractions from the real reasons why one kind of behavior is socially preferable to another.[32] In Godwin's view, "moral improvement will be forwarded, in proportion as we are exposed to no other influence, than that of the tendency which belongs to an action by the necessary and unalterable laws of existence." Man needs to be "governed by the moral arithmetic of the case," realizing that the well-being of many others is more important than his own.[33]

While the constrained vision takes people's motives and predispositions as given, and emphasizes incentives to lead to socially desired behavior, the unconstrained vision attempts to change people's motives and predispositions, so that incentives in general are less important, whether in the economic marketplace or in the law.[34] The unconstrained vision seeks a *solution*—in Condorcet's words, "the reconciliation, the identification of the interests of each with the interests of all," so that "the path of virtue is no longer arduous."[35]

From the standpoint of the unconstrained vision, the issue is not how best to structure incentives currently but how to rely less and less on incentives over time—especially the incentive of punishment. Social institutions should aim at seeing "men influenced by other and better motives." The statesman should "be careful not to add rigor to the selfish passions," but instead to "gradually wean men from contemplating their own benefit," as incentives in general tend to cause them to do.[36] Godwin wished to see men more concerned with their duties and rights than with rewards and punishments.[37]

Just as the two visions see the nature and role of rewards and punishments very differently, so they see the development of law in quite different terms. For Condorcet, progress in the law was conceived as the deliberate work of outstanding individuals:

> Laws are better formulated and appear less often to be the vague product of circumstances and caprice; they are made by learned men if not yet by philosophers.[38]

Further advancement was conceived by Condorcet in similarly rationalistic terms:

> The creation of a system of criminal jurisprudence would be a huge enterprise demanding time, work, and a luminous intelligence in those undertaking it, and a profound mind in the man charged with responsibility for planning and executing it.[39]

The unconstrained vision has continued to emphasize the deliberate creation of law, by both legislators and judges, in order to produce desired social *results*. It rejects the emphasis of the constrained vision on the characteristics desirable in legal *processes*, as such, and especially the attempt to make the judge's role essentially that of a neutral transmitter of process principles created by constitutional or legislative enactments. Where process principles have disparate impact on different social groups, the neutrality of the principle and the judge are deemed illusory, if not hypocritical.

The emphasis on process has been called by Laurence Tribe "the dangerous allure of proceduralism." The attempt to evolve principles aimed at the general benefit of society without regard to their differential impact on subsets within society he characterized as "the paralyzing seduction of neutrality," and the vision of an incrementally evolving law he described as "the morally anesthetizing imagery of the natural." It was the social result that was crucial, "the hidden (and sometimes not-so-hidden) tilt of various constitutional doctrines toward the perpetuation of unjust hierarchies of race, gender, and class" which he found offensive, and the

attempt to "deflect judicial responsibility for crucial substantive choices" which he found questionable.[40]

Tribe's viewpoint "questions all formulas as devices
for concealing the constitutional choices that we must
make—and that we cannot responsibly pretend to 'derive' by any neutral technique."[41] In short, the issue is
not process principles but social results, not transmission of law derived from incremental evolution in the
past but deliberate *choices* made in the present. Tribe denies that this means "anything goes" in judicial interpretation,[42] but argues that interpretation of texts is "in-
escapably subjective," so that the interpreter has "no
escape from the need to make commitments of signifi-
cant premises" of social morality.[43]

> We must make choices but renounce the equally illu-
> sory freedom to choose however we might *wish* to
> choose. For it is a Constitution—a specific, necessarily
> imperfect Constitution—in whose terms we are, after
> all, choosing.[44]

Judges thus must get into "the kind of controversial
substantive choices that the process proponents are so
anxious to leave to the electorate and its representatives."[45]
To Tribe, "the Constitution is inevitably substantive"[46] so
that those who interpret it must decide issues taking substantive results into account. In short, to Tribe the written
law is neither irrelevant nor all-determining. The Constitution "is not simply a mirror, nor is it an empty vessel
whose users may pour into it whatever they will."[47]

As an example of the difference between process-
based judicial decisions and a more substantively based

decision, Tribe criticized court rulings which upheld the legality of applying certain physical standards to particular job applicants, regardless of sex, "blithely ignoring sex-specific physical differences that make the 'similar' treatment of men and woman invidious discrimination."[48] A number of sex-difference cases demonstrate to Tribe that "pervasive inequalities in the distribution of power and status are overlooked," that "the evils to be extirpated" are instead allowed to flourish as part of "the omnipresent realities that the legal order simultaneously reflects and re-creates with relentless rationality."[49]

In a similar vein, Ronald Dworkin called for "a fusion of constitutional law and moral theory." The Constitution itself "rests on a particular moral theory" and must be understood as appealing to moral concepts rather than laying down particular conceptions"—that is, it is to be interpreted broadly as moral values to be applied rather than as explicit rules to follow. Any court that undertakes the burden of applying constitutional clauses "must be an activist court, in the sense that it must be prepared to frame and answer questions of political morality."[50]

INDIVIDUAL RIGHTS

Both visions believe in rights. But rights as conceived in the unconstrained vision are virtually a negation of rights as conceived in the constrained vision. Social theorists in both traditions recognize that rights are not absolute, and there are variations within both visions as to the weights given one right over another when they conflict, as well as differences in the scope accorded a particular right. But the fundamental difference between the two visions is in what the very concept of rights means.

The Constrained Vision

As already noted in Chapter 7, the constrained vision thinks of legal boundaries within which private individuals and groups may make their own decisions, without being second-guessed by political or legal authorities as to whether those decisions are wise or foolish, noble or mean. From the standpoint of the constrained vision, the scope of those boundaries of immunity from public authority are the scope of people's rights. This is a *process* conception of rights—the legal ability of people to carry on certain processes without regard to the desirability of the particular *results*, as judged by others.

Although these rights, as zones of immunity from public authority, belong to individuals, their whole purpose is social, in the constrained vision. In that vision, the sacrifice of the individual for the social good has a long tradition going back at least as far as Adam Smith in philosophy and economics, and Holmes and Blackstone in American and British law, respectively. Yet it is precisely this tradition which has consistently emphasized the importance of individual property rights, for example. The crucial benefits of property rights have been conceived as *social*—as permitting an economic process with greater efficiency,[51] a social process with less strife,[52] and a political process with more diffused power and influence than that possible under centralized political control of the economy.[53] The beneficiaries of such processes are conceived to be the population at large, and the justification or lack of justification of property rights is made to rest on that basis.

In the same way, rights of free speech are zones of immunity from public authority, without regard to whether what is said is wise or foolish, noble or mean. In two of Holmes' best-known free-speech opinions on the Supreme Court, he rested his conclusion in favor of free speech on *social* expediency, not the superior rights of the individual. In *Abrams v. United States*, Holmes pointed out that this social expediency derived from the inherent limitations of man's knowledge and the crucial trade-off this implied. "Persecution for the expression of opinion" would be "perfectly logical," he said, provided "you have no doubt of your opinion." Holmes continued:

> But when men have realized that time has upset many fighting faiths, they may come to realize even more than they believe the very foundation of their own conduct that the ultimate good desired is better reached by free trade in ideas—that the best test of truth is the power of the thought to get itself accepted in the competition of the market, and that truth is the only ground upon which their wishes safely can be carried out. That at any rate is the theory of our Constitution. It is an experiment, as all life is an experiment. Every year if not every day we have to wager our salvation upon some prophecy based upon imperfect knowledge.[54]

This opinion encapsulated key features of the constrained vision: (1) the test of truth by social process rather than articulated rationality, (2) inherent human limitations—man's "imperfect knowledge"—as the reason for relying on social processes, and (3) reliance on experience as the overall rationale ("time has upset many fighting faiths").

The primacy of social interests over those of the individual appeared both in this opinion and later in *Schenck v. United States*. In *Abrams*, while Holmes urged eternal vigilance against the suppression of opinions considered loathsome and dangerous, his proviso was "unless they so imminently threaten immediate interference with the lawful and pressing purposes of the law that an immediate check is necessary to save the country."[55] This was a clear forerunner of his more famous proviso of a "clear and present danger" standard in *Schenck*. In both cases, the public interest was considered paramount, with free speech being a derivative right of the individual, precisely in order to serve that public interest—and therefore subject always to annulment when it directly and unmistakably threatened the public interest itself. Finally, the right of free speech, whatever its scope or limitations, meant purely and simply an exemption from public authority. It did not imply any facilitating activity by the authorities.

The Unconstrained Vision

Unlike the constrained vision, which sees individual rights as instrumentalities of the social process—their scope and limits justified by the social processes from which they are derived—the unconstrained vision sees rights as inhering in individuals for their own individual benefit and as fundamental recognitions of their human-

ity. Free-speech rights or property rights are therefore justified or not by their relative importance to the individuals who exercise them. Given the uneven distribution of
property and the universality of speech, freedom of
speech logically becomes a far more important right than
property rights in this vision. Free-speech rights are thus
entitled to sweeping exemptions from interventions of
public authority, but not so property rights. Dworkin dismissed "the silly proposition that true liberals must respect economic as well as intellectual liberty. . . ."[56]

Issues involving property rights are seen in a *results*
context in the unconstrained vision of Dworkin and
Tribe, rather than a process context. While those with a
constrained vision focus on the incentive effects of a
property-rights system on the economic process, those
with the unconstrained vision focus on such social results as the existing distribution of property. Laws safe-
guarding property rights are thus viewed in the unconstrained vision of Laurence Tribe as "immunizing from
majoritarian rearrangement extant distributions of
wealth and economic power, almost as though such patterns and distributions of capital reflected something
decreed and indeed sanctified by nature rather than
something chosen by the polity."[57] Property-rights issues
are to Tribe issues concerning "the existing distribution
of capital."[58] Doctrines espousing property rights represent a "tilt against redistribution."[59] The "rights of property and contract" supported by the framers of the U.S.
Constitution represent "substantive values." Therefore,
Tribe finds is "puzzling that anyone can say, in the face
of this reality, that the Constitution is or should be predominantly concerned with *process* and *not* substance."[60]

According to Tribe, "seemingly neutral principles" in theory turn out in practice to "tilt decidedly in the direction of existing concentrations of wealth and influence."[61]

Free-speech rights have likewise been viewed by Tribe in a substantive results context:

> The decline of traditional public forums such as parks and streets has been accompanied by the rise of privately owned shopping centers as key locations for reaching the public; inexpensive methods of communication such as leafletting, picketing, and soapbox orating have given way to expensive media such as electronic broadcasting, newspaper advertising, and direct mail.[62]

In short, "speech, as it now comes to us, is usually anything *but* 'free,'"[63] according to Tribe, and "free expression has *not*, in truth, been available to all."[64] This conception of free speech, like the conception of freedom in general in the unconstrained vision, is clearly a results conception, unlike Holmes' process conception in which all that was at issue was exemption from limitation by governmental authority. This cost conception of free speech has not been limited to Laurence Tribe or other legal theorists. The U.S. Supreme Court, in a series of cases involving the handing out of leaflets on private property (housing developments, shopping malls) in violation of the owners' prohibitions, ruled in favor of those handing out the leaflets, citing the expensiveness of alternative modes of exercising free-speech rights as a reason for overriding property rights.[65] Had the court not sided with those arrested under trespass laws, according to Tribe, it would have meant that local property laws would have "denied the protection of the First Amendment to the residents of company towns and those who wished to communicate with them."[66] There would have been a denial of free speech, by this conception, even though the content of what was said—at some other location—would have remained exempt from government authority.

SOCIAL JUSTICE

William Godwin's *Enquiry Concerning Political Justice* in 1793 may have been the first treatise on social justice. The term "political" in its title was used in the sense common at the time, referring to organized society—much as the contemporary expression "political economy" referred to the economics of society, as distinguished from the economics of the household. In short, Godwin wrote on social justice, as that term is used today. Social justice, as depicted by Godwin, was a pervasive and demanding duty. He said "our debt to our fellow men" includes "all the efforts we could make for their welfare, and all the relief we could supply to their necessities." According to Godwin: "Not a talent do we possess, not a moment of time, not a shilling of property, for which we are not responsible at the tribunal of the public, which we are not obliged to pay into the general bank of common advantage."[67] He rejected "the supposition that we have a right, as it has been phrased, to do what we will with our own." He denied its premise: "We have in reality nothing that is strictly speaking our own."[68]

However, these were all *moral* duties, not political duties, such as might be imposed by a welfare state or a socialist government. It was the imperative moral force of such heavy social duties which made it unnecessary for Godwin (or Condorcet) to invoke governmental power to effect the kind of social changes today identified with the state—and for both to support property rights and *laissez-faire*,[69] as far as government's role was concerned. It is not difficult, however, to see how the kind of social analysis pursued by Godwin and Condorcet has led others to oppose *laissez-faire* economics and to have reservations about property rights, if not outright opposition to the concept. It was their faith in the power of reason to eventually make moral duties effective guides to individual conduct which made it unnecessary for Godwin or Condorcet to resort to government as the instrument of the sweeping social changes they sought. (This also illustrates the pitfalls of mechanically translating unconstrained and constrained visions into the political left and right, since Godwin and Condorcet were more "radical" than many on the left who would not share their reluctance to touch property rights or invoke government planning.)

Whatever its mechanisms or details, social justice has been the dominant theme of the unconstrained vision, from Godwin to Rawls. Like other forms of justice, it is conceived as a result rather than a process. But while the imperative of social justice pervades the unconstrained vision, it is virtually non-existent in the constrained vision. Social thinkers in the tradition of the constrained vision deal with issues of income distribution as a process, and consider its humane aspects as well as efficiency issues, but there is no implication that one income distribution result is more *just* than another.

F. A. Hayek is one of the few writers with a constrained vision who discusses social justice at all—and he characterizes it as "absurd,"[70] a "mirage,"[71] "a hollow incantation,"[72] "a quasi-religious superstition,"[73] and a concept that "does not belong to the category of error but to that of nonsense."[74] Other contemporaries of his in the tradition of the constrained vision—Milton Friedman and Richard Posner, for example—do not bother to discuss it, even as something to be rebutted.

The concept of social justice thus represents the extremes of the conflict of vision—an idea of the highest importance in one vision and beneath contempt in the other.

The Unconstrained Vision

Humane efforts to help the less fortunate have been part of both visions over the centuries. Adam Smith took part in such efforts, both in theory and in practice.[75] So did John Stuart Mill.[76] The campaign against slavery was also supported by leading figures in both traditions—by Burke and Smith, as well as by Godwin and Condorcet.[77] In the twentieth century, schemes of income transfer to the poor have been proposed by Milton Friedman and by George Bernard Shaw.[78]

What distinguishes the unconstrained vision is not that it prescribes humane concern for the poor, but that it sees transfers of material benefits to the less fortunate not simply as a matter of humanity but as a matter of justice. Edward Bellamy's novel, *Looking Backward*, protested not only that the poor were relegated to receiving crusts, but that insult was added to injury by calling the crusts charity. As co-inheritors of a prosperity created largely through the efforts of preceding generations, they were entitled to more—in the name of justice.

Central to the concept of social justice is the notion that individuals are entitled to some share of the wealth produced by a society, simply by virtue of being members of that society, and irrespective of any individual contributions made or not made to the production of that wealth. Whether they are entitled to a full share or a smaller share—perhaps only some minimum of "decency"—is a question answered variously by different social thinkers in this tradition, but the crucial point is that everyone is seen as entitled to some share as a matter of justice, not simply as a matter of charity. According to Godwin:

> The doctrine of the injustice of accumulated property has been the foundation of all religious morality. Its most energetic teachers have been irresistibly led to assert the precise truth in this respect. They have taught the rich, that they hold their wealth only as a trust, that they are strictly accountable for every atom of their expenditure, that they are merely administrators, and by no means proprietors in chief. But, while religion thus inculcated on mankind the pure principles of justice, the majority of its professors have been but too apt to treat the practice of justice, not as a debt, which it ought to be considered, but as an affair of spontaneous generosity and bounty.
>
> The effect which is produced by this accommodating doctrine, is, to place the supply of our wants in the disposal of a few enabling them to make a show of gen-

erosity with what is not truly their own, and to purchase the submission of the poor by the payment of a debt. Theirs is a system of clemency and charity, instead of a system of justice. It fills the rich with unreasonable pride, by the spurious denominations with which it decorates their acts; and the poor with servility, by leading them to regard the slender comforts they obtain, not as their incontrovertible due, but as the good pleasure and grace of their opulent neighbors.[79]

Similar themes have remained part of the tradition of the unconstrained vision. George Bernard Shaw, disdained people who "plunge into almsgiving to relieve their sickly consciences," partly because "it fills the paupers with humiliation, the patrons with evil pride, and both with hatred," but more fundamentally because "in a country justly and providently managed there could be neither excuse for it on the pauper's part nor occasion for it on the patron's."[80]

While the concept of social justice in the unconstrained vision revolves around issues of income distribution—conceived as a statistical result—there is also a subsidiary concern for social mobility, also conceived as a result. All of these concerns are viewed in radically different terms in the constrained vision.

The Constrained Vision

Although F. A. Hayek is exceptional among leading figures in the constrained vision in discussing social justice at all, the nature of his discussion may provide clues as to why so many others in this tradition do not bother to discuss it. While those with the unconstrained vision define social justice as a *result*, which they warmly embrace, Hayek treats social justice as a *process*, which he bitterly rejects—"the atrocious principle implied that all rewards should be determined by political power."[81] Hayek neither challenges, accepts, nor denies the results characterized by others as social justice. His objection is not that some alternative pattern of income results is preferable, but rather that the attempt to create such preconceived results means creating processes which "can destroy a civilization."[82]

Hayek's whole method of thinking is directly the opposite to that of Rawls. When Rawls repeatedly speaks of reasons of justice why society should "arrange"—somehow—one result rather than another, he abstracts from social processes to concentrate on social goals. But Hayek abstracts from these social justice goals to concentrate on the characteristics of the processes created in pursuit of these goals—and the dangers that such processes are deemed to represent to freedom and general well-being. In short, each has assumed away the primary concern of the other—primary not simply as to whether freedom or justice is more important, but as to whether process characteristics or goal characteristics are more important.

Hayek treats much of the rhetoric of social justice as a confused evasion of harsh realities inherent in the processes required to move toward such goals. To Hayek, those things commonly modified by the adjective "social"—justice, conscience, democracy—are by their very nature inherently social, so that this adjective is meaningless by reason of redundancy, if the word is used in an honest and straightforward way. It is "incredibly empty of meaning," according to Hayek,[83] so that "to employ it was either thoughtless or fraudulent."[84]

Although Hayek found the concept of "social justice" to be devoid of specific meaning, he found it fraught with insinuations which he considered both erroneous and dangerous. Many "who habitually employ the phrase do not know themselves what they mean by it,"[85] he said, but others who have used it were not simply engaging in "sloppy thinking" but "intellectual dishonesty."[86] According to Hayek, "the phrase 'social justice' is not, as most people probably feel, an innocent expression of good will towards the less fortunate," but has become in practice "a dishonest insinuation that one ought to agree to a demand of some special interest which can give no real reason for it."[87] The dangerous aspect, in Hayek's view, is that "the concept of 'social justice' . . . has been the Trojan Horse through which totalitarianism has entered"[88] Nazi Germany being just one example.[89]

At the social policy level, Hayek objected to the very notion of "the 'actions' of society, or the 'treatment' of individuals and groups by society" as "anthropomorphism or personification" incompatible with the concept of systemic social processes.[90] "To demand justice from such a process is clearly absurd," according to Hayek, for "the particulars of a spontaneous order cannot be just or unjust,"[91] because "the results are not intended or foreseen, and depend on a multitude of circumstances not known in their totality to anybody."[92] The hidden—and dangerous—significance of the demand for social justice, in Hayek's view, was that it implied a drastic change in whole processes under the bland guise of a mere preference for better distribution. According to Hayek, "society, in the strict sense in which it must be distinguished from the apparatus of government, is incapable of acting for a specific purpose," so that "the demand for 'social justice' becomes a demand that the members of society should organize themselves in a manner which makes it possible to assign particular shares of the product of society to the different individuals or groups."[93]

In short, those who argue for social justice argue for a particular set of *results* while Hayek's objections are to the *process* implied by seeking these or any other specific social results for particular individuals or groups. What he objected to was "a desire for a comprehensive blueprint of the social scene as a whole."[94] For him, "personification" of society as "a thinking, collective entity" capable of producing specifically desired social results presupposed a mastery of social details inherently "beyond our ken."[95]

It was not merely the futility of the attempt but the dangerousness of the attempt that was central to Hayek's objections. In his view, human freedom was crucially dependent on rules in general, and especially on rules which carved out domains of exemption from government power. These *rights*—as conceived in the constrained vision—"protect ascertainable domains within which each individual is free to act as he chooses"[96] and are thus the very opposite of rights to social justice, which imply expansion of the governmental domain to produce social results to which particular individuals and groups are morally entitled. Whether they are or are not morally entitled—a subject dealt with at great length by various writers in the tradition of the unconstrained vision—is a subject totally ignored in Hayek's various writings on social justice. This is logically consistent with his view of the futility of the attempt and its dangerousness. It may also explain why other writers with a constrained vision do not discuss the general concept of social justice at all, though they deal with such specifics as income distribution or the "social responsibility" of business,[97] or—in the case of Richard Posner—write a whole treatise on justice.[98] Given the assumptions of the unconstrained vision, social justice is at the heart of all discussions of policy or societies. Given the assumptions of the constrained vision, it is hardly worth talking about, just as square circles are not worth talking about, however great the desirability of such things might be if they were possible.

The greatest danger of the concept of social justice, according to Hayek, is that it undermines and ultimately destroys the concept of a rule of law, in order to supersede merely "formal" justice, as a process governed by rules, with "real" or "social" justice as a set of results to be produced by expanding the power of government to make discretionary determinations in domains once exempt from its power. While Hayek regarded some advocates of social justice as cynically aware that they were really engaged in a concentration of power, the greater danger he saw in those sincerely promoting the concept with a zeal which unconsciously prepares the way for others—totalitarians—to step in after the undermining of ideological, political, and legal barriers to government power makes their task easier. Thus he regarded Nazism as "the culmination of a long evolution of thought"[99] in Germany by socialists and others whose goals were vastly different from those of the Nazis, but who promoted the erosion of respect for legal rules in favor of the imperatives of specific social results.[100]

Communism has likewise been seen by Hayek as a residual beneficiary of the way of thinking promoted by people who may have no desire to see communism triumph. According to Hayek, "distributive justice" is inherently "irreconcilable with the rule of law,"[101] and the ideal of a government of laws and not of men is all that stands between a free society and totalitarianism. He quotes a Soviet writer who declared that "communism means not the victory of socialist law, but the victory of socialism over any law."[102] To Hayek, that is what social justice as an overriding goal ultimately means, as an alternative to merely "formal" justice as impersonal rules of a process.

SUMMARY AND IMPLICATIONS

The Unconstrained Vision

In the unconstrained vision, where man is capable of foreseeing and controlling the social consequences of his decisions, both the individual and society are causally and morally responsible for having made choices whose social results are what they are. The nature of socially just results is therefore a central concern of this vision, which has produced a number of treatises on the principles of social justice, from William Godwin's *Enquiry Concerning Political Justice* in the eighteenth century to John Rawls' *Theory of Justice* in the twentieth. This vision demands for the less fortunate not merely charity but justice. It demands of its laws not merely procedural rules but just results—with the former yielding to the latter in case of conflict.

Judges are not to limit themselves to the application of procedural rules, in disregard of the resulting justice or injustice, according to the unconstrained vision, but are to apply moral standards implicit in the law, which rules are essentially attempts to suggest. Judges cannot pretend, to themselves or others, that they are only applying prescribed procedural rules when in fact particular legal rules produce particular social results, so that social choices have been made implicitly by judges, whether they acknowledge them or not. Those with the unconstrained vision want these choices made explicitly, based on constitutional values and norms, rather than on narrow readings of constitutional rules on the one hand, or purely *ad hoc* judicial preferences on the other.

In this vision, the rights of individuals are to be "taken seriously" as essential recognitions of their humanity, and social expediency is to yield when basic human rights such as free speech or the right of the accused to constitutional protection are at issue.[103] In conflicts between rights, those which define the human being as a subject rather than an object are to have categorical preference over other rights, such as rights to property, and all rights are to trump all interests, such as a general interest in social peace, or economic efficiency. Inconveniences caused by pickets or those handing out leaflets are deemed a small price to pay for the basic right to free speech, and the fact that some criminals escape the law due to constitutional protections essential to the recognition of the basic humanity of all is likewise a price worth paying, to those with the unconstrained vision.

Given the greater ability of individuals and social decision-makers to foresee the consequences of their actions in the unconstrained vision, there is a correspondingly greater moral burden on them to exhibit "social responsibility," rather than simply to pursue their own individual interests within procedural rules. In William Godwin's vision especially, each individual thus becomes in effect a surrogate decision-maker for society, even when making purely individual and unofficial decisions—a surrogate not in the sense of controlling others' decisions but in the sense of making his own available choices in such a way as to promote the general well-being, rather than his own. Thus the radical individualism of Godwin, which is procedurally the same as that of modern libertarianism in its sweeping rejection of a government role in the economy, is substantively much closer to modern socialism in wanting specific social results to be the direct object of the decision-making process.

Equality has been at the heart of the tradition of the unconstrained vision, in its conception of justice, as elsewhere. Degrees and modifications of equality have varied among those in this tradition but, in whatever degree or modification, equality has meant equality of results. Given man's ability to shape social results, this has included compensatory rather than equal treatment of some. While the modern form of this approach in "affirmative action" policies is quite recent, the idea of compensatory social treatment goes back at least as far as Condorcet in the eighteenth century.[104]

In addition to being logically consistent with the unconstrained vision, "affirmative action" also illustrates the role of rights and interests in that vision. Members of the general population are deemed to have an *interest* in particular jobs, college admission, and other benefits to which compensatory preferences for selected groups may apply. But the members of those selected groups have a *right* to be where they would have been except for historical patterns of discrimination. Interests therefore give way to rights, which are "trumps." Individuals from either the majority population or selected minorities have equal interests and suffer equal losses of those interests when denied a job, college admission, or other benefits. But members of the selected minority groups are also deemed to have suffered past stigmatizing implications of inferiority through discrimination, which current rejected applicants from the majority population do not suffer in "reverse discrimination." Since stigmas of inferiority are seen as denials of basic humanity, they violate rights, as rights are conceived in the unconstrained vision, while "reverse discrimination" can violate only interests. Once again, in this vision, rights take precedence over interests.

Moral rights in the unconstrained vision are rights to results. Their political and judicial enforcement justify the extension of government power to domains of interest, such as those protected by property rights. Those other interests are not annihilated but are abridged to the extent made necessary to vindicate more fundamental rights and constitutionally protected values. This process involves judges weighing competing values—making complex "constitutional choices" in Laurence Tribe's phrase—rather than simply applying procedural rules.

The Constrained Vision

Much of what the unconstrained vision sees as morally imperative to do, the constrained vision sees man as incapable of doing. Because of the crucial premise that man cannot effectively monitor the social ramifications and reverberations of his individual choices—whether he acts for himself or in the name of society—the constrained vision treats as moot vast ranges of moral principles encompassed under the heading of social justice. There are no "constitutional choices" to make, if man cannot choose social results anyway. Even when the individual's decision has major social impact, it will seldom be the result he intended, given the assumption of the constrained vision that deliberately determining social results rationalistically is beyond the capabilities of man. A central concern of those with the constrained vision is precisely that there will be major social impacts of a kind completely different from the intentions, including the destruction of the rule of law in the quest for an illusory social justice.

In the constrained vision, the principles of justice are subordinated to the *possibilities* of justice. Oliver Wendell Holmes acknowledged that taking account of the inborn clumsiness of an individual who innocently inflicted damage on others would be a higher form of justice, but dismissed it as a principle of civil litigation beyond human capability. The whole literature on social justice issuing from those with an unconstrained vision is almost totally ignored by these with the constrained vision. Particular issues are covered in both visions, but the general principles of modern social justice theory are neither contested nor evaluated by the leading contemporaries in the constrained vision. Even Hayek, who has paid more attention to this literature than others of his persuasion, spends virtually no time on its general principles, being concerned instead with determining the likely social consequences of attempting to pursue such goals—their actual realization being implicitly deemed impossible.

Social processes are central to the constrained vision. Individual rights originate, take their meaning, and find their limits in the needs of social processes. However, that does not mean that incumbent judges or political leaders are authorized to expand or contract these rights in *ad hoc* fashion, according to their changing assessments of social needs. On the contrary, these rights are domains of exemption from the judgments of political or legal authorities. The assessment of *long-run* social expediency is already implicit in that exemption. This is symptomatic of a more general difference between the constrained and the unconstrained visions. They differ not only in the locus of discretion and the mode of discretion, but also in the locus of assessment and the mode of assessment.

In the constrained vision, man is capable of making long-run and general assessments of social processes, comparing constitutional government with alternative governments or competitive economies with politically directed economies, for example. The mode of assessment is experiential, and the revealed preference of the many—especially when they "vote with their feet"—is from this perspective more persuasive than the articulation of the few. By contrast, the unconstrained vision implicitly sees man as capable of judging more immediately, and more minutely, when it offers discrete solutions to numerous social problems seriatim.

While those with the unconstrained vision often stress the complexity of the social choices to be weighed by judges and other surrogate decision-makers, those with the constrained vision see such complexity as too great even to attempt to prescribe specific social results, leaving surrogate decision-makers with the more manageable task of applying rules which allow the substantive trade-offs to be made at the discretion of innumerable other individuals.

With ordinary social results so difficult to control, in the world as conceived in the constrained vision, compensatory justice is beyond consideration. The moral rationales of such policies as "affirmative action" receive little or no attention, given the remoteness of any possibility of their being realized. What is examined instead are the incentives created by such policies and their effect on social processes, especially the rule of the law as contrasted with the issuance of edicts prescribing results. The argument concerning "stigma" was rejected in the *Bakke* case, not on grounds that it was not true, but on grounds that it was not part of the constitutional rules which the Supreme Court was authorized to apply.[105]

In the constrained vision, with justice as with everything else, "the best is the enemy of the good."

Chapter 9

VISIONS, VALUES, AND PARADIGMS

Visions differ both morally and intellectually. Moreover, social visions differ in some respects—though not all—from visions which play an important role in science. A central question from a moral perspective is the extent to which different social visions reflect differences in value premises. A central concern from an intellectual perspective is the very different history of visions of society and visions underlying scientific theories of natural phenomena. It is also useful to understand whether social issues represent conflicts of values, of visions, or of interests.

PARADIGMS AND EVIDENCE

While visions involve assumed facts and assumed causes, a vision is not a "paradigm" in Thomas Kuhn's sense of a theoretical model of causation.[1] A vision is an almost instinctive *sense* of what things are and how they work. Kuhn's "paradigm" is a much more intellectually developed entity, including scientific "law, theory, application, instrumentation together."[2] Visions may lead to paradigms, whether in science or in politics, economics, law, or other fields, but visions and paradigms are different stages in the intellectual process. Whether in science or in social thought, visions or inspirations come first, and are subsequently systematized into paradigms, which embrace specific theories, and their narrowly focused hypotheses, which can be tested against evidence.

In these general intellectual terms, visions of scientific phenomena and visions of society proceed in parallel ways. However, opposing paradigms in science do not persist for centuries, as paradigms derived from the constrained and unconstrained visions have in politics, economics, law and social thought in general. The phlogiston theory and the oxidation theory did not coexist and endure together in chemistry. Scientific paradigms tend to succeed each other in history, not coexist through centuries. While still in the *early states* of the development of science, "men confronting the same particular phenomena" might "describe and interpret them in different ways." But these divergences, according to Kuhn, "disappear to a very considerable extent and then apparently once and for all."[3] No such process has yet become general in social thought.

The fundamental difference between science and social theory is not at the level of visions, or even paradigms, but at the point where theories produce empirically testable hypotheses. The uncontrollable variations which prevent laboratory experiments with societies prevent the decisive confrontations which shatter particular hypotheses, reverberating backward to shake theories and perhaps even topple paradigms and the visions they embody. Moreover, the biological continuity of the human race means that experiments which fail cannot be begun over again from scratch, as a chemist throws out a batch of chemicals from a failed experiment and tries again with a fresh batch of chemicals. We can never know what Germany would be like today if there had been no Hitler, or how Western civilization would have developed, had there been no decline and fall of the Roman Empire. In short, evidence is not as decisive in social visions. This is due not only to the nature of the evidence but also to the strength of commitments to social values.

Although opposing views begin with visions, they do not end there. Visions are only the raw material from which theories are constructed and specific hypotheses deduced. In principle, the opposing conclusions reached can be checked against evidence and the conflict of visions resolved. There are a number of reasons why this does not happen on such a scale as to produce a decisive victory for one social vision over others, though individuals may find particular evidence sufficient to change their thinking.

Definitive evidence cannot be expected on the grand general sweep of a vision. A great deal of partial evidence may be accumulated on each side, but the evidence for and against one's own vision can be weighed differently, and being convinced is ultimately a subjective process. Even in those cases where a clear confrontation in empirical terms can be arranged and evidence produced, every lost battle on one front does not signal the end of the war, much less unconditional surrender. When hypotheses deriving from a particular vision are contradicted by evidence in the form in which they were first asserted, they may nevertheless be salvageable in a less extreme or more complex form.

Evidence is not irrelevant, however. "Road to Damascus" conversions do occur. Even if this conversion is only on a single issue, the repercussions on one's general vision may lead to a domino effect on other assumptions and beliefs. Responses to evidence—including denial, evasion, and obfuscation—likewise testify to the threat that it represents. At one extreme in the relationship of evidence to visions is the total subordination of evidence to conclusions based on a vision or the theories deriving from it. Those Western intellectuals who for years ignored, evaded, denied, or explained away the growing evidence of Stalin's mass murders and slave labor camps are a classic example of this phenomenon.

Similar cases can be found for both constrained and unconstrained visions. While evidence on particular issues may be falsified, this phenomenon is itself true and weighty evidence for the power of visions. In many cases, there are no personal economic, political, or career gains to be made by the individual that would explain the falsification. It is done simply for the sake of the vision.

Evidence need not be falsified in order to be evaded. The very formulation of a theory may be such as to insulate it from direct confrontation with contrary evidence. In other words, the theory may be so stated that nothing could possibly happen that would prove it wrong. In this case, the theory is reduced to empirical meaninglessness; since all possible outcomes are consistent with it, it predicts nothing. Yet, though it specifically predicts no single concrete outcome, it may *insinuate* much and be enormously effective in its insinuation. Malthus' theory of population is a classic example of a theory of this sort, based ultimately on a constrained vision, but in later years adapted by others for use as part of an agenda deriving from an unconstrained vision.

The population principle expounded by T. R. Malthus in 1798 projected a grim picture of a highly unconstrained world inhabited by highly constrained man. It was explicitly set forth in opposition to the ideas of William Godwin and of Condorcet,[4] whose constrained visions of man were anathema to Malthus.

Malthus' theory began with two postulates—that (1) "food is necessary to the existence of man" and that (2) "the passion between the sexes is necessary and will remain nearly in its present state." These he called "laws of our nature"[5] in short, constraints unlikely to disappear. Implicit also was the law of diminishing returns, so that an increase of population would not lead to a proportionate increase in the food supply as more people grew food.[6] Thus there were differential constraints on the increase of population and on the increase of food. It was logically sufficient for his purposes that population could grow faster than food, though by calling the former rate of increase "geometrical" and the latter "arithmetical" he dramatized the difference in a way that made the idea indelible and historic.

Because population is ultimately constrained by the food supply, the empirical implication of the original Malthusian theory is that the observed rates of growth of the two must be similar. According to Malthus, "the population constantly bears a regular proportion to the food that the earth is made to produce."[7] This is the crucial conclusion from Malthus' two postulates, and it constitutes the empirical test of the truth or falsity of Malthusian theory. If, in the long run, the food supply grows faster than the population, then the average nourishment per person rises and the Malthusian theory is false. Given two possible outcomes which would, respectively, confirm or deny the Malthusian theory, there would seem to be little room for controversy after sufficient time had passed and sufficient data had been collected.

Yet no such clear confrontation of evidence and theory has occurred, because of Malthus' shifting formulations under stress of critical attack. In later years, Malthus declared that higher incomes among the masses could lead to either of "two very different results"—an increase of population or "improvements in the modes of subsistence."[8] With both possibilities now being considered consistent with the Malthusian principle, there was no possible evidence that could conceivably prove it wrong—whether it was in fact right or wrong. In reality, as census and other data accumulated over the years, the food supply—and other elements of the general standard of living—tended to increase faster than population. Yet the Malthusian population theory has survived and flourished.

Malthus clearly had a constrained vision. "To prevent the recurrence of misery, is alas! beyond the power of man,"[9] he said, and he even doubted whether there had ever been a permanent increase in the span of life.[10]

He spoke of "laws inherent in the nature of man, and absolutely independent of all human regulations,"[11] and declared: "The vices and moral weakness of mankind, taken in the mass, are invincible."[12] However, though Malthus' theory of population was within the tradition of the constrained vision, it was not the only population theory consistent with that vision. Adam Smith's theory of population was quite different in analysis and conclusion.[13] Moreover, the Malthusian population principle has re-emerged, with modifications, on the political left, among people with an unconstrained vision.

In the modified version, overpopulation is neither inherent nor invincible, but simply cannot be effectively prevented by relying on the discretion of individuals. However, with political leadership, which may range from hortatory to draconian, there is a "solution" through birth control and abortions. In short, ideas originating in one vision may be adapted to another. But, for the Malthusian population theory to last long enough for this to happen, it first had to survive more than a century of contradictory evidence. Its success in doing so suggests that evasions and tautological formulations may protect a theory against evidence as effectively as outright falsification.

While falsification is clearly a conscious decision, evasion is not necessarily conscious, and misperceptions of what constitutes evidence still less so. Theories may persist because the difficult task of bringing them to confrontation with evidence has simply not been performed with sufficient skill and care. This may be especially so when the person testing the theory has a different vision of his own, and reads the opposing vision in his terms, rather than in its own terms. This happened in a celebrated controversy in economics which erupted right after World War II, between distinguished economists of radically different schools of thought—and voluminous evidence failed completely to resolve the issue.

The traditional economic theory was that artificial imposition of wage rates (by government or labor unions) higher than those emerging in a competitive labor market would tend to cause employment to be less than it would be otherwise. This was a direct corollary of the more general economic principle that more of anything tends to be bought at a lower price than at a higher price. In order to test this theory, a critic of this view sent questionnaires to hundreds of employers, asking how they had acted or would act, under various possible conditions involving wage rates. Most employers did not indicate in their replies that they would react to wage increases by firing workers. The critic regarded this as disproof of the prevailing economic theory.[14]

However, the prevailing economic theory was not set forth in terms of what individual employers would say, but in terms of what the economy as a whole would do. While this survey asked employers for their own chosen mode of adjustment, the economic theory being tested dealt with the opposite phenomenon—how a competitive economy *imposed* modes of adjustments on individuals. For example, an employer might well react to a wage increase by maintaining employment and trying to pass the cost increase along to consumers in higher prices, but if this price increase results in a decline in the sales of his product, forcing him then to reduce production and employment, the net result is the same as if he had deliberately chosen to fire workers because of the imposed wage increase.

The real issue was whether externally imposed wage increases reduce employment, not whether this takes the particular form of (1) individual employer decisions to lay off workers; (2) the bankruptcy of marginal firms; (3) a reduction in the number of new firms entering the industry; or (4) a decline in sales and employment as cost increases are passed on to the consumer. In short, the theory being tested was a systemic theory of market adjustments, while the questionnaire asked about individual intentions among surviving businesses. The voluminous evidence collected was irrelevant to the issue.

These examples are not meant to prove the already obvious point that mistakes or shortcomings mar the use of evidence. Instead, they are illustrations of particular ways in which disparate and conflicting visions survive together, despite an abundance of factual evidence which might otherwise be expected to shift the balance decisively to one side or another over a long span of time—such as the centuries during which the constrained and the unconstrained visions have survived and flourished together.

In the extreme case, evidence may simply be falsified, or it may be evaded by verbal expedients which empty the theory of empirical meaning while leaving it full of powerful insinuations. Conversely, evidence may be made to appear to conflict with a theory merely because the specific terms of the theory are misunderstood by those collecting the evidence. But perhaps the most striking demonstration of the power of a vision occurs when *no evidence at all* is either asked or offered for assertions which are consonant with a prevailing vision.

A recent example of this phenomenon has been the oft-repeated assertion that higher rates of broken homes and teenage pregnancy among black Americans are a "legacy of slavery." Only after decades of widespread repetition of this assertion was a comprehensive factual study done—revealing that broken homes and teenage pregnancy were far less common among blacks under slavery and in the generations following emancipation than they are today.[15] Again, the point is not that a particular conclusion was mistaken but that a sweeping and unsupported assertion went *unchallenged* for many years because it fit a particular vision. The ability to sustain assertions without any evidence is another sign of the strength and persistence of visions.

The process of moving from a vision, as an inchoate sense of causation, to a specific set of theories and corollaries—a paradigm or intellectual model representing what is believed to happen—is both intellectually and psychically difficult. The precise definition of terms, the careful construction of causal links, and the derivation of specific hypotheses unambiguously differentiated from the hypotheses derived from alternative theories—all this requires not only skill but discipline and dedicated efforts. To the extent that one has become emotionally committed to, or publicly identified with, a particular theory, its failure in the face of evidence imposes psychic costs that can be painful. In an attempt to reconcile the paradigm with the incoming discordant evidence, an initially simple principle may be modified and complicated until it resembles a Rube Goldberg contraption.

Ridicule of these *ad hoc* complications is not refutation. Moreover, any paradigm—being a model rather than reality—will necessarily not fit the evidence perfectly. The scientific formula for the speed of a falling object ignores the effect of atmospheric resistance, but no one considers the law of gravity refuted because actual scientific observations show deviations between the acceleration predicted by the theory and that observed as things fall through the air. Nor are people who believe in the law of gravity accused of denying the existence of the atmosphere. Rather, they do not consider the atmosphere essential to the theory of gravity and omit it as a needless complication, except in special cases (such as helium-filled balloons, which rise instead of fall).

In much the same way, believers in an unconstrained vision do not deny that man has any limitations. They simply do not treat these limitations as decisive in theories of social phenomena, whose causal elements are explained in entirely different terms, with the limitations of man playing a peripheral role, much like that of the atmosphere in the theory of gravity. What distinguishes those with the constrained vision is that the limitations of man are at the heart of their theories—it plays the role of gravity rather than that of atmospheric resistance—and many of the elements emphasized by those with the unconstrained vision are omitted as incidental (atmospheric). But both visions must omit things which exist in reality, and which most proponents of these visions would admit exist in reality, however much they would disagree as to the prevalence or effect of the omitted factors.

Given, then, that no vision and no paradigm derived from it can fit the facts perfectly, efforts to adjust and modify visions to accommodate discordant evidence are not inherently mere self-deception, much less dishonesty toward others. But the gray area this provides can shelter rationalizations that do fit these descriptions. Moreover, resistance to the abandonment of paradigms has marked the history of science, as well as the history of social theories. There are simply fewer places to hide from scientific evidence. Nevertheless, a scientific paradigm which encounters discordant evidence is not usually abandoned in favor of nihilistic agnosticism, but is instead patched up and complicated until there is another paradigm to replace it.

Visions and paradigms exist at many levels. Karl Marx and a street-corner radical on a soapbox may have shared the same vision but at widely varying levels of sophistication. The more sophisticated versions of any vision are in part a tacit concession to discordant evidence which might otherwise be fatal. This general need for complexity can itself become, obliquely, a further protection against clear-cut evidence refuting a social theory. When no other reply to such evidence is possible, because it so clearly contradicts what is asserted, it is always possible to dismiss the evidence as "simplistic," because the issue *must* be more complex than that. In science, however, a simple explanation is preferred to a more complex explanation with no greater empirical accuracy.

While visions can survive and thrive on their own inner logic, in defiance of empirical evidence, the social dangers of such insulated dogmatism are obvious. It is no less arbitrary and dogmatic to declare *a priori* that "the truth lies somewhere in between." It may. It may not. On some highly specific issue, it may lie entirely on one side—and on another issue, with the other side. On still other issues, it may in fact lie in between. The point here is simply that there is no *a priori* way to say, or to avoid the difficult task of formulating hypotheses and testing them against evidence. Nor is this an exercise in futility. Even zealots may be forced to abandon some extreme outposts of a given vision as indefensible under empirical attack, while the contracted perimeter of the vision continues to be defended fiercely. Intellectual struggles can be wars of attrition as well as wars won or lost in a single battle. The visions of science, rather than those of social thought, seem to lend themselves to single decisive confrontations.

The growing complexity of social theories in general reflect in part the growing difficulties of defending them in their purer forms. Burgeoning empirical data, and even more sophisticated ways of analyzing them, may fail to deliver a single fatal blow to either of the great opposing visions which have dominated the past two centuries. But some important strategic retreats have been made on both sides. Neither vision can confidently maintain the air of incontrovertible truth which some of its eighteenth-century exponents exhibited. It is an advancement even to admit that we are dealing with a conflict of visions.

VISIONS AND VALUES

Both constrained and unconstrained visions are fundamentally and essentially visions of *causation*. Only derivatively do they involve clashes of moral principles or different hierarchies of social values. The much-vaunted need to make our "value premises" explicit is irrelevant in this context. Thinkers with identical moral values and social preferences must nevertheless reach opposing conclusions if their initial senses of reality and causation—their visions—are different.

Identical twins, bred to revere the same moral qualities in the same order, must differ in their conclusions if somewhere along the way one conceives of human attributes and social causation as described in the constrained vision and the other conceives them as described in the unconstrained vision. Just as travelers seeking the same destination must head in opposite directions if one believes it to be to the east and the other believes it to be to the west, so those seeking "the greatest good for the greatest number" (or any other similarly general moral precept) must favor opposite kinds of societies if opposite kinds of human beings are assumed to inhabit those societies, leading to opposite kinds of social causation. Things must *work* first before they can work to any given end, and what will work depends on the nature of the entities involved and their causal connections.

In this sense, physical science and the analysis of social phenomena both begin with visions. It is the ability of the physical sciences to winnow out conflicting visions by systematic experiment which marks a major difference between the intellectual patterns in the two areas. However, the ability of science to resolve its conflicts of visions does not mean that scientists share the same "value premises," but rather that "value premises" are neither necessary nor sufficient to explain conflicts of visions or their resolution.

People with the same moral values readily reach differing political conclusions. Convinced religious believers can split into opposite camps on social and political issues if they see worldly or divine causation in different terms. So too do philosophic materialists, such as Hobbes, and Holbach, or believers in a variety of other creeds. Where a particular creed implies a particular set of social, economic, and political conclusions—as in Marxism, for example—it is because that creed contains a particular vision of *causation*, not simply a particular moral premise.

Labeling beliefs "value premises" can readily become one more means by which conclusions insulate themselves from confrontation with evidence or logic. To say that a preference for "free speech" rights over "property rights" is simply a "value premise" is to deny that it rests on particular beliefs as to facts or causation, and to make it simply an opaque preference, like that for plums over tangerines. But if in fact the preference for free speech over property rights results from assumptions as to the magnitude of their respective benefits to society at large, and the extent to which the less fortunate members of society are helped or made more vulnerable by the two kinds of rights, then it is not simply an opaque "value premise."

With exactly the same preferences for helping the many rather than the few, and for protecting the vulnerable more so than those able to protect themselves, one would annihilate the preference for free speech over property rights if one's vision of social causation made property rights extremely beneficial to people who own *no* property (as in Hayek's vision, for example).[16] It is precisely the correctness or incorrectness of particular beliefs about social causation that requires scrutiny—a scrutiny arbitrarily barred by the phrase "value premises." ("Value premises" are, ironically, a sort of property right in conclusions, not to be trespassed on by evidence or logic.)

The persistence of opposing visions in the same society contrasts with major changes of visions that occur in individuals. The large numbers of people, including leading intellectuals, who have both embraced Marxism and then repudiated Marxism are a striking example. So too are those who embrace or relinquish various religious or secular creeds. These suggest that, while the psychic costs of changing visions may be high, they are not prohibitive—especially if the changes are gradual, rather than "road to Damascus" conversions.

If conversions to and from Marxism turned on differing moral valuations given to the same factual perceptions of the consequences of capitalism and communism, it would be difficult to explain why so many conversions occurred in one direction during the Great Depression of the 1930s and in the opposite direction after the Nazi-Soviet pact in 1939 or the Hungarian uprisings of 1956. The reordering of fundamental moral values so suddenly and simultaneously among a large number of people throughout the Western world hardly seems credible.

Such conversions are far more readily reconciled with changes in visions than in values. What these cases in capitalist and communist countries brought was new, massive, and intrusively insistent factual information about each social system—not necessarily conclusive evidence but certainly painful facts sufficient to cause many to reconsider. The heavy impact of startling new information may shake or shatter an individual's vision, but does not in itself realign moral values. Mass unemployment, hunger, the killing of innocents, the deliberate degradation of the human spirit, or the cynical unleashing of war, all inspire the same horror as before. What changes is the perception of who or what is doing it and why.

The thrust of organized, systematic propaganda, especially in totalitarian states, centers precisely on facts and causation as the pivots of belief. Similarly, in places and times where religious authorities have wielded oppressive control of ideas, people such as Copernicus and Galileo have become targets *not* because they offered alternative value systems but because they presented alternative visions of facts and causation. Existing values seemed threatened only because the vision on which they had been based seemed threatened—not because Copernicus or Galileo were propagandizing for alternative values.

Values are vitally important. But the question addressed here is whether they precede or follow from visions. The conclusion that they are more likely to derive from visions than visions from them is not merely the conclusion of this particular analysis, but is further demonstrated by the actual behavior of those with the power to control ideas throughout a society, whether those authorities be secular or religious.

If individuals in substantial numbers find it possible to change their visions, whether suddenly or gradually, how do sharply opposed visions persist over the centuries in society at large? Insofar as visions are (1) simplified projections of reality and (2) subject to contradiction by facts, all visions must encounter facts contrary to their simplified premises. This implies that all visions must also develop both intellectual and psychic means of coping with contradiction, and that any prospect of conversion must contend with the contradictions of whatever alternative vision beckons. Therefore, the instantaneous conversion of a whole society seems very unlikely—and once the conversion process becomes drawn out, individual mortality alone is enough to guarantee that many conversions will never be completed, and that new individuals must begin the process of vision allegiance and doubt all over again from the beginning.

In the physical sciences, however, the preservation of decisive evidence and the logically demonstrative methods of scientific analysis under controlled experimental conditions means that conversion from one vision to another can be sudden and irreversible, not only for given individuals but for future individuals as well, and therefore for society as a whole. No one needs to re-enact in his own mind the time-consuming process by which the Ptolemaic vision of astronomy gave way to the visions of Copernicus, Galileo, or Einstein.

While books likewise preserve records of social, political, and economic events and theories, the absence of controlled experiments, decisive evidence, and decisive techniques for analyzing it mean that these records themselves become battlegrounds in the conflict of visions. Disputes still rage over the reasons for the rise of Hitler or the decline and fall of the Roman Empire.

VISIONS AND INTERESTS

Believers in both the constrained and the unconstrained visions have long recognized that special interests and special pleading are major factors in day-to-day politics, and that what is said in these political struggles has no necessary connection with the truth, or even with what anyone believes to be the truth.

Businessmen, according to Adam Smith, are a class whose interests are often "to deceive and even to oppress the public," so that any statements coming from them should be "long and carefully examined, not only with the most scrupulous, but with the most suspicious attention."[17] He warned against "the clamorous importunity of partial interests" in general[18] and "the clamour and sophistry of merchants and manufacturers" in particular.[19] Of political propaganda, Smith observed that "those who taught it were by no means such fools as they who believed it."[20] Much the same views have characterized modern thinkers with the constrained vision, such as Friedman or Hayek.[21] It has equally been part of the tradition of the unconstrained vision, going back to Godwin and coming forward to Shaw, Galbraith, or other twentieth-century thinkers.[22]

The relationship between special interests and any vision—constrained or unconstrained—may be conceived of as a question whether there is (1) a direct corruption, (2) a class bias, or (3) a case of particular visions proving attractive to particular interests. Direct corruption may be due to bribes, economic self-interest, or careerism determining what is said, independently of what is actually believed about the facts or causation.

Although such explanations are sometimes attributed to Karl Marx, they are much closer to the theories of Charles A. Beard, who depicted the Constitution of the United States as shaped by special interests. Marx's theory was one of class bias distorting the thinker's perception of reality, with sincerely held beliefs being opposite and antagonistic in content when the thinkers drew upon different class experiences. The weakest of the three assertions above is that visions—however they originate—will be pressed into service by whatever special interests find them useful.

Examining first the strongest of the special-interest explanations of visions produces virtually no evidence that the leading figures in either the constrained or unconstrained tradition stood to gain personally from the views advocated, and much evidence to the contrary.

The entire tradition of the unconstrained vision, with its equalization emphasis, has been led by individuals who stood to lose both financially and in status terms by the equalization they advocated. Some were of modest means but still almost invariably above the average of their respective societies, and some like Condorcet or Holbach were quite rich. The policies advocated by the leading exponents of the constrained vision have likewise seldom advanced their personal interests. Adam Smith, who promoted both domestic and international free trade, was the son of a customs official and engaged in no trade at all, being primarily an academic—a profession whose practices he severely criticized.[23] Virtually none of the leading advocates of *laissez-faire* have been businessmen, from the time of Adam Smith to Milton Friedman or F. A. Hayek two centuries later.[24]

Burke's *Reflections on the Revolution in France* represented views that cost him the political alliances and friendships of a lifetime, and though it eventually brought him royal favor, this was hardly something he could have counted on, after years of having opposed royal interests in Parliament.

While political thinkers who were also political practitioners may create ambiguities as to their motivations, which may be either ideological or careerist, increasing specialization over the centuries has made the theorist-practitioner in politics almost as rare as the theorist-businessman. Leading social theorists who were at the same time leading political figures were more common in the eighteenth century, when Burke and the Federalists flourished, than in later times. But John Stuart Mill's brief career in Parliament in the nineteenth century or Joseph A. Schumpeter's brief career in business in the twentieth century were oddities having little significance for their own intellectual history, much less for visions in general.

The less extreme claim that visions represent the bias of class position is no more readily supported by evidence. The class positions of those with the constrained vision have not been consistently higher or lower than the class positions of those with the unconstrained vision, and differences in class position have been considerable among those with similar views on either side.

Milton Friedman was far more similar in social origins to Tom Paine than to Friedrich Hayek or James Madison. While Condorcet and Holbach were aristocrats, their philosophic compatriots Paine and Godwin knew what it was to struggle to make ends meet. At the individual level, the class explanation of ideas breaks down completely, while the tracing of assumptions about human nature to conclusions about social policy show a remarkable and enduring consistency.

The numerous other sociological explanations of ideological orientation need not all be rejected *a priori*, nor is it necessary to enter into their specifics here. To "explain" the social composition of those holding particular visions—whether the explanations be correct or incorrect—is only to assert that people are not randomly distributed in their visions, any more than they are randomly distributed in sports, religion, or a thousand other human activities. None of this denies that class bias exists or plays a potent role in political struggles. The question is whether its influence operates by controlling those who shape social visions or in other ways. That class bias, where it exists, will seize upon a vision which can serve as a rationalization is scarcely denied by anyone. But that has nothing to do with either the origins or validity of the vision.

The very reason visions are useful to those with a special interest to promote is that it helps recruit political allies who do *not* share that special interest, but who may be won over by the principles or rhetoric generated by a social vision. In short, the resort to visions as a means of recruiting political allies is evidence of the limited appeal of special interests, as such, and the independent power of visions. The relative weights of the two forces in the short run are not the issue here. However much the special interests may predominate as of a given time, the special interests of one generation need not be the same as the special interests of the next generation, while the constrained and unconstrained visions have both been viable for centuries.

SUMMARY AND CONCLUSIONS

This final set of summaries and conclusions must summarize not only this chapter but the whole work, and derive some of its implications. Behind the episodic eruptions of specific political and social controversies is a pattern of beliefs about the world, about man, and about causation. These implicit assumptions or visions repeatedly divide controversialists at all intellectual levels, on a wide spectrum of issues, and across the boundaries of the law, the economy, the polity, and the society, as well as across international boundaries. Though these controversies often become emotional, the opposing views tend to cluster, not around an emotion, but around the logic of a vision. Each vision tends to generate conclusions which are the logical consequences of its assumptions. That is why there are such repeated conflicts of visions in such a range of otherwise unrelated issues. The analysis here is not intended to reconcile visions or determine their validity, but to understand what they are about, and what role they play in political, economic, and social struggles. The question is not what particular policy or social system is best but rather what is *implicitly assumed* in advocating one policy or social system over another.

Whatever one's vision, other visions are easily misunderstood —not only because of caricatures produced by polemics but also because the very words used ("equality," "freedom," "justice," "power") mean entirely different things in the context of different presuppositions. It is not merely misunderstanding but the inherent logic of each vision which leads to these semantic differences, as well as to substantively different conclusions across a wide spectrum of issues. Visions are inherently in conflict, quite aside from the misunderstandings, hostility, or intransigence generated in the course of polemics.

Both constrained and unconstrained visions are ultimately concerned with social results. The unconstrained vision seeks directly to achieve those results socially—that is, through collective decisions prescribing the desired outcomes. The constrained vision considers it beyond the capability of any manageable set of decision-makers to marshal the requisite knowledge, and dangerous to concentrate sufficient power, to carry out their decisions, even if it were possible.

Given the unconstrained vision, which permits results to be directly prescribed, its basic concepts are expressed in terms of results. The degree of freedom is thus the degree to which one's desires can be realized, without regard to whether the obstacles to full realization be the deliberately imposed restrictions of government or the lack of circumstantial prerequisites. Justice is likewise a question of outcomes, and the justice or injustice of a society can therefore be determined directly by those outcomes, whether they be the result of conscious decisions, social attitudes, or circumstances inherited from the past. Power is likewise defined by results: If A can cause B to do what A wants done, then A has power over B, regardless of whether A's inducements to B are positive (rewards) or negative (penalties).

Equality too is a result, the degree of equality or inequality being a directly observable fact.

All these basic terms are defined in profoundly different ways under the assumptions of the constrained vision. One consequence of this is that those with different visions often argue past each other, even when they accept the same rules of logic and utilize the same data, for the same terms of discourse signify very different things. In the constrained vision, where man cannot directly create social results but only social processes, it is as characteristics of those processes that freedom, justice, power, and equality have significance. A social process has freedom to the extent that it refrains from interfering with the choices of individuals—whether or not the circumstances of those individuals provide them with many options or few. A social process has justice to the extent that its rules are just, regardless of the variety of outcomes resulting from the application of those rules. Power is exerted in social processes, by individuals or by institutions, to the extent that someone's existing set of options is reduced—but it is not an exertion of power to offer a quid pro quo that adds to his existing options. Equality as a process characteristic means application of the same rules to all, without regard to individual antecedent conditions or subsequent results. Results matter—they are the ultimate justification of processes—but it is only the *general* effectiveness of particular processes (competitive markets, constitutional government) that can be gauged by man, not each individual result in isolation.

The clash between the two visions is not over the actual or desirable *degree* of freedom, justice, power, or equality—or over the fact that there can only be degrees and not absolutes—but rather over what these things consist of, in whatever degree they occur. Moreover, the relationship between the two visions reflects not only logical differences, but also the historical ascendancy of one or the other vision at a given time. Because some of the key concepts used by both sides were first defined primarily in the terms of the constrained vision, those with the unconstrained vision have had to distinguish their concepts as "real" freedom, or "real" equality, for example, as contrasted with merely "formal" freedom or equality. However, the later ascendancy of the unconstrained vision forced those with the constrained vision into a defensive posture in which they tried to re-establish the former, more limited definitions of such terms as process characteristics.

In addition to these changing asymmetric relationships between the two visions, there is an enduring asymmetric relationship based on how they see each other as adversaries. Each must regard the other as mistaken, but the reasons for the "mistake" are different. In the unconstrained vision, in which man can master social complexities sufficiently to apply directly the logic and morality of the common good, the presence of highly educated and intelligent people diametrically opposed to policies aimed at that common good is either an intellectual puzzle or a moral outrage, or both. Implications of bad faith, venality, or other moral or intellectual deficiencies have been much more common in the unconstrained vision's criticisms of the constrained vision than vice versa.

In the constrained vision, where the individual's capacity for direct social decision-making is quite limited, it is far less surprising that those who attempt it should fail—and therefore far less necessary to regard the "mistaken" adversary as having less morality or intelligence than others. Those with the constrained vision tend to refer to their adversaries as well-meaning but mistaken, or unrealistic in their assumptions, with seldom a suggestion that they are deliberately opposing the common good or are too stupid to recognize it. Personality variations cut across these patterns on both sides—Burke was less generous to adversaries than Hayek, Shaw less accusatory than Condorcet—but the patterns themselves have persisted for centuries.

Malthus said: "I cannot doubt the talents of such men as Godwin and Condorcet. I am unwilling to doubt their candor."[25] But when Godwin wrote of Malthus, he called him "malignant,"[26] questioned "the humanity of the man,"[27] said "I profess myself at a loss to conceive of what earth the man was made,"[28] and hinted that Malthus' appointment as Professor at East India College was a reward for apologetics for the privileged.[29] In the twentieth century, Friedrich Hayek's landmark book, *The Road to Serfdom*, made him a moral leper to many,[30] though in that book he was very generous to his adversaries, whom he characterized as "single-minded idealists"[31] and as "authors whose sincerity and disinterestedness are above suspicion."[32] Further examples could be multiplied almost without limit. The point here is that these differences reflect more than personality differences, and are themselves part of an enduring pattern growing out of the fundamental assumptions of the two visions.

The two visions differ not only in how they see differences between themselves but also in how they see differences between ordinary individuals and those more intellectually or morally advanced. In the unconstrained vision, where the intellectual and moral potential of man vastly exceeds the levels currently observable in the general population, there is more room for individual variation in intellectual and moral performance than in the constrained vision, where the elite and the masses are both penned within relatively narrow limits. Striking moral and intellectual differences are recognized by those with the constrained vision, but are regarded as either too exceptional to form the basis of social policy or as confined to a small area out of a vast spectrum of human concerns. Given the inherent limitations of human beings, the extraordinary person (morally or intellectually) is extraordinary only within some very limited area, perhaps at the cost of grave deficiencies elsewhere, and may well have blind spots which prevent him from seeing some things which are clearly visible to ordinary people.

Differences between the moral-intellectual elite and the masses are crucial, especially to modern conflicts of visions over the degree of surrogate decision-making, whether by politicians, judges, or various agencies and commissions. Both visions try to make the locus of discretion coincide with the locus of knowledge, but they conceive of knowledge in such radically different terms as to lead to opposite conclusions as to where discretion should be vested.

To those with the unconstrained vision, who see knowledge and reason as concentrated in those who have advanced furthest toward the ultimate potential of man, surrogate decision-making—economic "planning," judicial activism, etc.—is essential. These surrogate decision-makers must attempt both to influence beforehand and to revise afterward the decisions made by those less accomplished in intellectual or moral terms. But to those with the constrained vision, each individual's knowledge is so grossly inadequate, compared to the knowledge mobilized systemically through economic markets, traditional values, and other social processes, that surrogate decision-makers in general—and non-elected judges in particular—should severely limit themselves to drawing up rules defining the boundaries of others' discretion, not second-guess the decisions actually made within those boundaries. In the constrained vision, the loci of discretion should be as widely scattered as possible, the inevitable errors resulting being accepted as a trade-off, no solution being possible.

Conflicts of visions affect not only such large and enduring issues as economic planning versus *laissez-faire*, or judicial activism versus judicial restraint, but also such new issues as the most effective modes of Third World development, "affirmative action," or "comparable worth." In each of these controversies, the assumptions of one vision lead logically to opposite conclusions from those of the other. All these issues turn ultimately on whether, or to what extent, surrogate decision-makers can make better decisions than those directly transacting. Even with perfect agreement on "value premises" as to what outcome would be ideal, differences in beliefs as to the efficacy of particular policies would put those with different visions in sharp conflict.

Visions help explain ideological differences, which are of course only one source of political differences. Yet, in the long run, these ideological conflicts seem to shape the general course of political trends as much as "practical" political considerations dominate day-to-day events. To a considerable extent, the ideological presuppositions of the times set the limits and the agenda which determine what is feasible, realistic, or imperative to practical politicians.

Powerful as ideology may be, it is not omnipotent. Inescapable and brutal facts—the Great Depression of the 1930s, the Nazi-Soviet pact of 1939—have caused many to simultaneously embrace or abandon an ideology. Even short of such cataclysmic events, the rules of logic and evidence have historically led many to change ideological positions, suddenly or gradually. Moveover, even when an ideological bias persists, the empirical or logical work of those with such a bias may not necessarily suffer—by empirical or logical standards—however much the semantics used to characterize the findings may betray the ideological leanings of the analyst.[33] For still others, however, ideology may totally overwhelm evidence.

Emotions and value judgments are important—but derivative. It is as *logical* for those with the unconstrained vision to put freedom of speech above property rights as it is for those with the constrained vision to bitterly oppose them on this, as in so many other issues.

While not all social theories can be neatly divided into constrained and unconstrained visions, what is remarkable is how many of the leading theories of the past two centuries or more fall into one or the other of these two categories. Personal and stylistic differences, as well as differences of subject, emphasis, and degree are all superimposed on this dichotomy, but the dichotomy itself still shows through nevertheless.

Logic is of course not the only test of a theory. Empirical evidence is crucial intellectually, and yet historically social visions have shown a remarkable ability to evade, suppress, or explain away discordant evidence, to a degree that scientific theories cannot match. Yet, for individuals, changes of visions have not been uncommon, and catastrophic historic events have created many "road to Damascus" conversions. The hybrid vision of fascism, once touted as "the wave of the future," has been devastated by the experience of World War II.

In short, evidence is not wholly irrelevant even to visions, even historically—and it is of course crucial logically. Historic evasions of evidence are a warning, not a model. Too often the mere fact that someone is known to disagree widely on other issues is considered sufficient reason not to take him seriously on the issue at hand ("How can you believe someone who has said . . . ?") In short, the fact that an opposing vision has as much consistency across a range of issues as one's own is used as a reason to reject it out of hand. This is especially so when the reasons for the differences are thought to be "value premises," so that opponents are conceived to be working toward morally incompatible goals.

Emphasis on the logic of a vision in no way denies that emotional or psychological factors, or narrow self-interest, may account for the attraction of some people to particular visions. The point is that neither the validity nor the consequences of a vision can be determined by examining such factors—that the vision has a logic and a momentum of its own, going beyond the emotions or intentions of its constituency at a given moment. Moreover, those subsequently attracted to a particular vision may be quite different from those initially attracted, and attracted for quite different reasons, as the consequences of the vision unfold.[34]

While visions conflict, and arouse strong emotions in the process, merely "winning" cannot be the ultimate goal of either the constrained or the unconstrained vision, however much that goal may preoccupy practical politicians. The moral impulse driving each vision cannot be jettisoned for the sake of winning, without making the victory meaningless. While defections from one vision to another may be occasioned by empirical evidence, it is usually the relevance of that evidence for the prospects of achieving some morally desirable goal that is decisive.

An analysis of the implications and dynamics of visions can clarify issues without reducing dedication to one's own vision, even when it is understood to be a vision, rather than an incontrovertible fact, an iron law, or an opaque moral imperative. Dedication to a cause may legitimately entail sacrifices of personal interests but not sacrifices of mind or conscience.

NOTES

PREFACE

1. The epigraph is from Bertrand Russell, *Skeptical Essays* (New York: W. W. Norton and Company, Inc., 1938), p. 28.

Chapter 1: THE ROLE OF VISIONS

1. Joseph A. Schumpeter, *History of Economic Analysis* (New York: Oxford University Press, 1954), p. 41.

2. *Vilfred Pareto, Manual of Political Economy (New York: Augustus M. Kelley, 1971), p. 22.*

Chapter 2: CONSTRAINED AND
UNCONSTRAINED VISIONS

1. Walter Lippmann, *Public Opinion* (New York: The Free Press, 1965), p. 80.

2. Adam Smith, *The Theory of Moral Sentiments* (Indianapolis: Liberty Classics, 1976), pp. 233–234.

3. *Ibid.*, p. 238.

4. *Ibid.*, p. 108.

5. Edmund Burke, *The Correspondence of Edmund Burke* (Chicago: University of Chicago Press, 1967), Vol. VI, p. 48.

6. Alexander Hamilton, *Selected Writings and Speeches of Alexander Hamilton*, ed. Morton J. Frisch (Washington, D.C.: American Enterprise Institute, 1985), p. 390.

7. Adam Smith, *The Theory of Moral Sentiments*, p. 235.

8. *Ibid.*, p. 234.

9. *Ibid.*, p. 235.

10. Adam Smith, *An Inquiry into the Nature and Causes of the Wealth of Nations* (New York: Modern Library, 1937), p. 423.

11. William Godwin, *Enquiry Concerning Political Justice* (Toronto: University of Toronto Press, 1969), Vol I, p. 156.

12. *Ibid.*, pp. 433, 435.

13. *Ibid.*, pp. 421–438.

14. *Ibid.*, pp. 434–435.

15. *Ibid.*, Vol. II, p. 122.

16. Edmund Burke, *The Correspondence of Edmund Burke*, Vol. VI, 392.

17. *Ibid.*, Vol II, p. 308.

18. *Ibid.*, Vol I, p. 172.

19. *Ibid.*, p. 171.

20. Antoine-Nicolas de Condorcet, *Sketch for a Historical Picture of the Progress of the Human Mind* (Westport, Conn.: Hyperion Press, Inc., 1979), pp. 52–53.

21. Edmund Burke, *Reflections on the Revolution in France* (London: J. M. Dent & Sons, Ltd., 1967), p. 60.

22. Edmund Burke, *The Correspondence of Edmund Burke*, Vol. VI, p. 47. "Prudence . . . in all things a Virtue, in Politicks the first of Virtues . . . ," *ibid.*, p. 48. Prudence was indeed the "presiding" virtue, giving "orders" to all other virtues, according to Burke, *ibid.*, Vol. VII, p. 220.

23. William Godwin, *Enquiry Concerning Political Justice*, Vol. VI, p. 438.

24. Quoted in Keith Michael Baker, *Condorcet: From Natural Philosophy to Social Mathematics* (Chicago: University of Chicago Press, 1975), p. 217.

25. William Godwin, *Enquiry Concerning Political Justice*, Vol. I, p. 448.

26. *Ibid.*, p. 451.

27. *Ibid.*, Vol. II, p. 193.

28. *Ibid.*, p. 211.

29. *Ibid.*, p. 313.

30. Antoine-Nicolas de Condorcet, *Sketch for a Historical Picture of the Progress of the Human Mind*, p. 4.

31. *Ibid.*, pp. 49, 65, 99, 117, 150, 169, 175, 193.

32. *Ibid.*, p. 185.

33. *Ibid.*, p. 184.

34. *Ibid.*, p. 133.

35. *Ibid.*, p. 200.

36. Robert A. Dahl and Charles E. Lindblom, *Politics, Economics and Welfare* (Chicago: University of Chicago Press, 1967), p. 522.

37. Antoine-Nicolas de Condorcet, *Sketch for a Historical Picture of the Progress of the Human Mind*, p. 192.

38. William Godwin, *Enquiry Concerning Political Justice*, Vol. I, pp. 156, 433.

39. *Ibid.*, p. 152.

40. *Ibid.*

41. Adam Smith, *The Wealth of Nations*, p. 423.

42. *Ibid.*, p. 460.

43. *Ibid.*, p. 128.

44. *Ibid.*, pp. 98, 128, 249–250, 429, 460, 537.

45. William Godwin, *Enquiry Concerning Political Justice*, Vol. II, p. 129n.

46. John Stuart Mill, "Utilitarianism," *Collected Works* (Toronto: University of Toronto Press, 1969), Vol. X, p. 215. This will be illustrated in later discussions of Mill in Chapters 3 and 5.

47. However, Mill's pattern of making ringing assertions based on one set of premises and attaching devastating provisos from another system of thought extended to economic doctrines as well. See, for example, Thomas Sowell *Classical Economics Reconsidered* (Princeton: Princeton University Press, 1974), pp. 95–97; *idem, Say's Law* (Princeton: Princeton University Press, 1972), pp. 143–154.

48. Harold J. Laski, "Political Thought in England: Locke to Bentham," *The Burke-Paine Controversy: Texts and Criticisms* (New York: Harcourt, Brace and World, Inc., 1963), p. 144.

49. Thomas Robert Malthus, *Population: The First Essay* (Ann Arbor: University of Michigan Press, 1959), p. 67.

50. William Godwin, *Of Population* (New York: Augustus M. Kelley, 1964), p. 554.

51. Edmund Burke, "Thoughts on the Cause of the Present Discontent," *Burke's Politics: Selected Writings and Speeches of Edmund Burke on Reform, Revolution, and War*, eds. R. J. S. Hoffman and P. Levack (New York: Alfred A. Knopf, 1949), p. 5.

52. Thomas Hobbes, *Leviathan* (London: J. M. Dent & Sons, Ltd., 1970), p. 89.

53. William Godwin, *Of Population*, p. 480.

54. Thomas Robert Malthus, *Population: The First Essay*, p. 54.

55. Quoted in Lewis Coser, *Men of Ideas* (New York: The Free Press, 1970), p. 151.

56. Alexander Hamilton et al., *The Federalist Papers* (New York: New American Library, 1961), p. 33. Elsewhere, Hamilton said: "We may preach till we are tired of the theme, the necessity of disinterestedness in republics, without making a single proselyte," Alexander Hamilton, *Selected Writings and Speeches of Alexander Hamilton*, p. 63.

57. Alexander Hamilton, et al., *The Federalist Papers*, p. 322.

58. Adam Smith, *The Theory of Moral Sentiments*, p. 308.

59. Alexander Hamilton et al., *The Federalist Papers*, p. 110.

60. Keith Michael Baker, ed., *Condorcet: Selected Writings* (Indianapolis: The Bobbs-Merrill Company, Inc., 1976), p. 80.

61. *Ibid.*, p. 87.

62. *Ibid.*, p. 157.

63. Adam Smith, *The Theory of Moral Sentiments*, p. 380. Very similar views are expressed in *The Correspondence of Edmund Burke*, Vol. VII, p. 510.

64. Keith Michael Baker, ed., *Condorcet: Selected Writings*, p. 80.

65. Antoine-Nicholas de Condorcet, *Sketch for a Historical Picture of the Progress of the Human Mind*, p. 147.

66. Alexander Hamilton, *Selected Writings and Speeches of Alexander Hamilton*, p. 455.

67. Thomas Jefferson, Letter of January 3, 1793, *The Portable Thomas Jefferson*, ed. Merrill D. Peterson (New York: Penguin Books, 1975), p. 465.

68. Adam Smith, *The Theory of Moral Sentiments*, p. 369.

69. Jean-Jacques Rousseau, *The Social Contract* (New York: Penguin Books, 1968), p. 49.

70. *Ibid.*, p. 55.

71. Thomas Hobbes, *Leviathan*, pp. 64, 70, 87.

72. *Ibid.*, p. 65.

73. Keith Michael Baker, ed., *Condorcet: Selected Writings*, p. 8.

74. F. A. Hayek, *Law, Legislation and Liberty* (Chicago: University of Chicago Press, 1979), p. 168.

75. Edmund Burke, *The Correspondence of Edmund Burke*, Vol. IX, p. 449.

Chapter 3: Visions of Knowledge and Reason

1. F. A. Hayek, *The Constitution of Liberty* (Chicago: University of Chicago Press, 1960), p. 26.

2. F. A. Hayek, *Law, Legislation and Liberty* (Chicago: University of Chicago Press, 1979), Vol. III, p. 157.

3. Alexander Hamilton, *Selected Writings and Speeches of Alexander Hamilton*, ed. Morton J. Frisch (Washington, D.C.: The American Enterprise Institute, 1985), p. 222.

4. Edmund Burke, *Reflections on the Revolution in France* (New York: Everyman's Library, 1967), p. 84.

5. *Ibid.*, p. 93.

6. Edmund Burke, *Speeches and Letters on American Affairs* (New York: E. P. Dutton and Company, Inc., 1961), p. 198.

7. Edmund Burke, *Reflections on the Revolution in France*, p. 140.

8. Gerald W. Chapman, *Edmund Burke: The Practical Imagination* (Cambridge, Mass.: Harvard University Press, 1967), Chapters II, VI; Isaac Kramnick, *The Rage of Edmund Burke: Portrait of An Ambivalent Conservative* (New York: Basic Books, Inc., 1977), Chapter 7; Edmund Burke, *The Correspondence of Edmund Burke* (Chicago: University of Chicago Press, 1968), Vol VII, pp. 122–125; Vol. VIII, p. 451n.

9. Adam Smith *An Inquiry into the Nature and Causes of the Wealth of Nations* (New York: Modern Library, 1937), pp. 553–555, 559–560, 684, 736–737, 740, 777, 794, 899–900; Adam Smith, *The Theory of Moral Sentiments* (Indianapolis: Liberty Classics, 1976), p. 337.

10. William Godwin, *Enquiry Concerning Political Justice* (Toronto: University of Toronto Press, 1969), Vol. II, p. 172.

11. *Ibid.*, Vol. I, p. 85.

12. Keith Michael Baker, ed., *Condorcet: Selected Writings* (Indianapolis: The Bobbs-Merrill Company, Inc., 1976), p. 86.

13. Antoine-Nicholas de Condorcet, *Sketch for a Historical Picture of the Progress of the Human Mind* (Westport, Conn.: Hyperion Press, Inc., 1955), p. 11.

14. William Godwin, *Enquiry Concerning Political Justice*, Vol. II, p. 206.

15. *Ibid.*, Vol. I, p. 34.

16. *Ibid.*, Vol. II, p. 299.

17. Edmund Burke, *Reflections on the Revolution in France*, pp. 95–96.

18. *Ibid.*, p. 31.

19. William Godwin, *Enquiry Concerning Political Justice*, Vol. I, p. 70.

20. *Ibid.*, p. 82.

21. *Ibid.*, p. 104.

22. Quoted in Lewis Coser, *Men of Ideas* (New York: The Free Press, 1970), p. 232.

23. Antoine-Nicolas de Condorcet, *Sketch for a Historical Picture of the Progress of the Human Mind*, p. 109.

24. Jean-Jacques Rousseau, *The Social Contract* (New York: Penguin Books, 1968), p. 115.

25. Quoted in Lewis Coser, *Men of Ideas*, p. 231.

26. John Stuart Mill, *Collected Works* (Toronto: University of Toronto Press, 1977), Vol. XVIII, p. 86.

27. *Ibid.*, p. 121.

28. *Ibid.*, p. 139.

29. *Ibid.*, Vol. XV, p. 631.

30. *Ibid.*, Vol. XVIII, p. 86.

31. *Ibid.*, p. 129.

32. Edmund Burke, *Reflections on the Revolution in France*, p. 76.

33. Russell Kirk, *John Randolph of Roanoke* (Indianapolis: Liberty Press, 1978), p. 57.

34. Thomas Hobbes, *Leviathan* (London: J. M. Dent & Sons, Ltd., 1970), p. 4.

35. *Ibid.*, p. 20.

36. Edmund Burke, *Reflections on the Revolution in France*, p. 108.

37. Adam Smith, *The Theory of Moral Sentiments* (Indianapolis: Liberty Classics, 1976), pp. 380–381.

38. *Ibid.*, p. 381.

39. F. A. Hayek, *Individualism and Economic Order* (Chicago: University of Chicago Press, 1948), p. 80.

40. [Pierre Joachim Henri Le Mercier de la Riviere], *L'Ordre Naturel et essentiel des sociétés politiques* (Paris: Jean Nourse, libraire, 1767).

41. Adam Smith, *The Wealth of Nations*, p. 423.

42. William Godwin, *Enquiry Concerning Political Justice*, Vol. I, p. 66.

43. *Ibid.*, p. 315.

44. *Ibid.*, p. 385.

45. *Ibid.*, Vol. II, p. 320.

46. *Ibid.*, p. 211.

47. Antoine-Nicolas de Condorcet, *Sketch for a Historical Picture of the Progress of the Human Mind*, p. 192.

48. See, for example, Thomas Sowell, "Economics and Economic Man," *The Americans: 1976*, eds. Irving Kristol and Paul Weaver (Lexington, Mass.: Lexington Books, 1976), pp. 191–209.

49. See Jacob Viner, *The Role of Providence in the Social Order* (Philadelphia: American Philosophical Society, 1972).

50. Oliver Wendell Holmes, Jr., *The Common Law* (Boston: Little, Brown and Company, 1923), p. 1.

51. *Chicago, Burlington & Quincy Railway Co. v. Babcock*, 204 U.S. 585, at 598.

52. Oliver Wendell Holmes, *Collected Legal Papers* (New York: Peter Smith, 1952), p. 26.

53. *Ibid.*, p. 180.

54. *Ibid.*, p. 185.

55. John Stuart Mill, *Collected Works* (Toronto: University of Toronto Press, 1977), Vol. XVIII, p. 41.

56. *Ibid.*, pp. 41–42.

57. *Ibid.*, p. 43n.

58. *Ibid.*, pp. 42–43.

59. F. A. Hayek, *Law, Legislation and Liberty*, Vol. I, p. 81.

60. *Ibid.*, p. 85.

61. Ronald Dworkin, *Taking Rights Seriously* (Cambridge, Mass.: Harvard University Press, 1980), p. 147.

62. *Ibid.*

63. *Ibid.*, p. 144.

64. *Ibid.*, p. 137.

65. See, for example, Thomas Sowell, *Knowledge and Decisions* (New York: Basic Books, 1980), pp. 290–296.

66. *Louisville and Nashville Railroad Co. v. Barber Asphalt Paving Co.*, 197 U.S. 430, at 434.

67. *Ibid.*

68. *Baldwin et al. v. Missouri*, 281 U.S. 586, at 595.

69. *Nash v. United States*, 229 U.S. 373, at 378.

70. See, for example, Raoul Berger, *Government by Judiciary* (Cambridge, Mass.: Harvard University Press, 1977), p. 314; Thomas Paine, "The Rights of Man," *Selected Works of Tom Paine*, ed. Howard Fast (New York: The Modern Library, 1945), p. 99.

71. Alexander Bickel, *The Least Dangerous Branch* (Indianapolis: The Bobbs-Merrill Company, Inc., 1962), p. 110.

72. Chief Justice Earl Warren, *The Memoirs of Earl Warren* (New York: Doubleday and Company, Inc., 1977), p. 333.

73. Ronald Dworkin, *Taking Rights Seriously*, p. 260.

74. *Ibid.*, p. x.

75. *Ibid.*, p. 146.

76. *Ibid.*, p. 239.

77. F. A. Hayek, *The Counter-Revolution of Science: Studies on the Abuses of Reason* (Indianapolis: Liberty Press, 1979), pp. 162–163.

78. Edmund Burke, *Reflections on the Revolution in France*, p. 42.

79. Adam Smith, *An Inquiry into the Nature and Causes of the Wealth of Nations*, p. 423.

80. William Godwin, *Enquiry Concerning Political Justice*, Vol. I, p. vii.

81. *Ibid.*, p. 304.

82. *Ibid.*, p. 329.

83. *Ibid.*, p. 331.

84. *Ibid.*, p. 393.

85. *Ibid.*, p. 331.

86. "Duty is that mode of action on the part of the individual, which constitutes the best possible application of his capacity to the general benefit," *ibid.*, p. 156. See also *ibid.*, pp. 159, 161–162, 197–198; *ibid.*, Vol II, pp. 57, 415.

87. Edmund Burke, *Correspondence of Edmund Burke* (Chicago: University of Chicago Press, 1969), Vol. VIII, p. 138.

88. Joseph A. Schumpeter, *History of Economic Analysis* (New York: Oxford University Press, 1954), p. 43.

89. Alexander Bickel, *The Least Dangerous Branch*, p. 96.

90. *Ibid.*, p. 14.

91. Alexander Bickel, *The Morality of Consent* (New Haven: Yale University Press, 1975), p. 30.

92. William Godwin, *Enquiry Concerning Political Justice*, Vol. II, p. 341.

93. See, for example, *ibid.*, Vol. I, pp. xi, 302; *ibid.*, Vol. II, pp. 112–113.

94. V. I. Lenin, "What Is To Be Done?" *Selected Works* (Moscow: Foreign Languages Publishing Office, 1952), Vol. I, Part I, pp. 233, 237, 242.

95. *Ibid.*, p. 317.

96. Alexander Hamilton et al., *The Federalist Papers*, p. 57.

97. Adam Smith, *The Theory of Moral Sentiments*, pp. 243–244.

98. *Ibid.*, p. 529.

99. Keith Michael Baker, ed., *Condorcet: Selected Writings*, pp. 5–6.

100. William Godwin, *Enquiry Concerning Political Justice*, Vol. I, p. 100.

101. *Ibid.*, p. 47.

102. William Godwin, *The Enquirer: Reflections on Education, Manners, and Literature* (London: G. G. and J. Robinson, 1797), p. 70.

103. *Ibid.*, pp. 66–72.

104. *Ibid.*, p. 11.

105. For example, Thomas Hobbes, *Leviathan*, pp. 10, 11, 22, 35, 63.

106. Edmund Burke, *Speeches and Letters on American Affairs*, p. 203.

107. Quoted in Russell Kirk, *John Randolph of Roanoke* (Indianapolis: Liberty Press, 1951), p. 442.

108. Antoine-Nicolas de Condorcet, *Sketch for a Historical Picture of the Progress of the Human Mind*, p. 180.

109. William Godwin, *Enquiry Concerning Political Justice*, Vol. I, p. 315.

110. *Ibid.*, p. 385.

111. Edmund Burke, *Reflections on the Revolution in France*, p. 88.

112. *Ibid.*, p. 83.

113. Edmund Burke, *The Correspondence of Edmund Burke*, Vol. VI, p. 211.

114. Alexander Hamilton, *Selected Writings and Speeches of Alexander Hamilton*, p. 343.

115. *Ibid.*, p. 481. See also p. 74.

116. *Ibid.*, p. 223.

117. Thomas Hobbes, *Leviathan*, p. 16.

118. F. A. Hayek, *Law, Legislation and Liberty*, Vol. I, p. 99.

119. F. A. Hayek, *The Constitution of Liberty*, p. 30.

120. *Ibid.*, p. 377.

121. Thomas Hobbes, *Leviathan*, p. 63.

122. *Ibid.*, p. 40. See also p. 4.

123. *Ibid.*, p. 35.

124. *Ibid.*, p. 23.

125. Edmund Burke, *Reflections on the Revolution in France*, pp. 84–85, 92, 104, 107, 166–167, 168.

126. *Ibid.*, p. 200.

127. Thomas Hobbes, *Leviathan*, p. 89.

128. Alexander Hamilton, *Selected Writings and Speeches of Alexander Hamilton*, p. 392.

129. Russell Kirk, *John Randolph of Roanoke*, pp. 69–70.

130. William Godwin, *Enquiry Concerning Political Justice*, Vol. II, p. 538.

131. Keith Michael Baker, ed., *Condorcet: Selected Writings*, p. 111.

Chapter 4: VISIONS OF SOCIAL PROCESSES

1. F. A. Hayek, *Law, Legislation and Liberty* (Chicago: University of Chicago Press, 1973), Vol. I, p. 19. See also Richard Posner, *The Economics of Justice* (Cambridge, Mass.: Harvard University Press, 1981), pp. 44–45.

2. F. A. Hayek, *Law, Legislation and Liberty*, Vol. I, pp. 74–76.

3. Edmund Burke, *Reflections on the Revolution in France* (New York: Everyman's Library, 1967), pp. 19–20.

4. *Ibid.*, p. 162.

5. *Ibid.*, pp. 165–166.

6. F. A. Hayek, *Law, Legislation and Liberty*, Vol. III, p. 166.

7. *Ibid.*, pp. 154–158, 165–169.

8. See, for example, F. A. Hayek, *The Counter-Revolution of Science* (Indianapolis: Liberty Press, 1952), pp. 165–211.

9. See, for example, John Kenneth Galbraith, *The New Industrial State* (Boston: Houghton Mifflin Company, 1967); Thorstein Veblen, *The Theory of Business Enterprise* (New York: New American Library, 1958).

10. Hubert Humphrey in *National Planning: Right or Wrong for the U.S.?* (Washington, D.C.: American Enterprise Institute, 1976), p. 37.

11. Wassily Leontief in *ibid.*, pp. 14–15.

12. William Godwin, *Enquiry Concerning Political Justice* (Toronto: University of Toronto Press, 1969), Vol. I, p. 297.

13. *Ibid.*, p. 439.

14. *Ibid.*, p. 428.

15. Bernard Shaw, *The Intelligent Woman's Guide to Socialism and Capitalism* (New York: Brentano's Publishers, 1928), p. 127.

16. *Ibid.*, p. 154.

17. G. Bernard Shaw, "Economic," *Fabian Essays in Socialism*, ed. G. Bernard Shaw (Garden City, N.Y.: Doubleday, no date), p. 113.

18. *Ibid.*, p. 223.

19. Edward Bellamy *Looking Backward: 2000–1887* (Boston: Houghton Mifflin Company, 1926), p. 49.

20. *Ibid.*, p. 56.

21. *Ibid.*, p. 58.

22. *Ibid.*, p. 104.

23. *Ibid.*, p. 141.

24. *Ibid.*, p. 91.

25. *Ibid.*, pp. 100, 227–229, 315.

26. *Ibid.*, pp. 13, 49.

27. *Ibid.*, pp. 56, 231, 315, 329.

28. *Ibid.*, pp. 58, 140–145, 181–185.

29. Robert A. Dahl and Charles E. Lindblom, *Politics, Economics and Welfare* (Chicago: University of Chicago Press, 1967), p. 73.

30. *Ibid.*, pp. 387–388.

31. *Ibid.*, p. 401.

32. *Ibid.*, p. 79.

33. Antoine-Nicolas de Condorcet, *Sketch for a Historical Picture of the Progress of the Human Mind* (Westport, Conn.: Hyperion Press, Inc., 1955), p. 164.

34. *Ibid.*, p. 68.

35. *Ibid.*, pp. 162, 181, 190.

36. John Kenneth Galbraith, *The Affluent Society* (Boston: Houghton Mifflin Company, 1958), Chapter II.

37. William Godwin, *Enquiry Concerning Political Justice*, Vol. I, p. 245.

38. *Ibid.*, p. 191.

39. *Ibid.*, pp. 198–199.

40. *Ibid.*, Vol. II, p. 264.

41. *Ibid.*, Vol I, p. 199.

42. *Ibid.*, pp. 128–129.

43. *Ibid.*, pp. 129, 131, 173, 202, 214, 249, 264; Vol. II, pp. 264, 351, 507–514.

44. *Ibid.*, Vol. I, p. 215.

45. *Ibid.*, Vol. II, pp. 351–352.

46. Edmund Burke, *Reflections on the Revolution in France*, p. 83.

47. See, for example, F. A. Hayek, *The Counter-Revolution of Science: Studies on the Abuse of Reason* (Indianapolis: Liberty Press, 1979), *passim*.

48. Edmund Burke, *Reflections on the Revolution in France*, p. 58.

49. *Ibid.*, p. 52.

50. *Ibid.*, pp. 92–93.

51. F. A. Hayek, *Law, Legislation and Liberty*, Vol. I, p. 87.

52. Cited in Ronald Dworkin, *Taking Rights Seriously* (Cambridge, Mass.: Harvard University Press, 1980), p. 24.

53. Adam Smith, *The Theory of Moral Sentiments* (Indianapolis: Liberty Classics, 1976), p. 369.

54. F. A. Hayek, *Law, Legislation and Liberty*, Vol. I, p. 11.

55. *Ibid.*, p. 12.

56. *Ibid.*, p. 13.

57. *Ibid.*, p. 14.

58. *Ibid.*

59. Edmund Burke, *Reflections on the Revolution in France*, p. 42.

60. Alexander Hamilton, *Selected Writings and Speeches of Alexander Hamilton*, ed. Morton J. Frisch (Washington, D.C.: American Enterprise Institute, 1985), p. 457.

61. F. A. Hayek, *Law, Legislation and Liberty*, Vol. I, p. 21.

62. Edmund Burke, *Reflections on the Revolution in France*, p. 93.

63. P. T. Bauer, *Reality and Rhetoric: Studies in the Economics of Development* (Cambridge, Mass.: Harvard University Press, 1984), p. 5.

64. Edmund Burke, *Reflections on the Revolution in France*, p. 44. See also p. 193.

65. Alexander Hamilton, *Selected Writings and Speeches of Alexander Hamilton*, p. 234.

66. William Godwin, *Enquiry Concerning Political Justice*, Vol. I, p. 296.

67. *Ibid.*, Vol. II, pp. 146–147.

68. Adam Smith, *The Theory of Moral Sentiments* (Indianapolis: Liberty Classics, 1976), p. 375.

69. Alexander Hamilton, *Selected Writings and Speeches of Alexander Hamilton*, p. 227.

70. John Maynard Keynes, *The General Theory of Employment, Interest and Money* (New York: Harcourt, Brace and Company, 1965), pp. 84, 210–212.

71. Thomas Sowell, *Knowledge and Decisions* (New York: Basic Books, Inc., 1980), pp. 127–128.

72. John Bartlett, *Bartlett's Familiar Quotations* (Boston: Little, Brown and Company, 1968), p. 802.

73. Robert A. Dahl and Charles E. Lindblom, *Politics, Economics and Welfare*, p. 49.

74. *Ibid.*, p. 425.

75. *Ibid.*, p. 518.

76. Thomas Hobbes, *Leviathan* (London: J. M. Dent & Sons, Ltd., 1970), p. 82.

77. William Godwin, *Enquiry Concerning Political Justice*, Vol. II, p. 404.

78. *Ibid.*, p. 324.

79. Thomas Hobbes, *Leviathan*, p. 110.

80. Friedrich A. Hayek, *The Road to Serfdom* (Chicago: University of Chicago Press, 1972), pp. 25–26.

81. Ramsey Clark, *Crime in America* (New York: Simon and Schuster, 1970), p. 60.

82. Robert A. Dahl and Charles E. Lindblom, *Politics, Economics and Welfare*, p. 518.

83. Cited in Friedrich A. Hayek, *The Road to Serfdom*, p. 26n.

Chapter 5: VARIETIES AND DYNAMICS OF VISIONS

1. William Godwin, *Enquiry Concerning Political Justice*, (Toronto: University of Toronto Press, 1969), Vol. II, pp. 516–518; Antoine-Nicolas de Condorcet, *Sketch for a Historical Picture of the Progress of the Human Mind* (Westport, Conn.: Hyperion Press, Inc., 1955), pp. 188–189.

2. See, for example, Milton Friedman, *Capitalism and Freedom* (Chicago: University of Chicago Press, 1962), pp. 133–136.

3. William Godwin, *Enquiry Concerning Political Justice*, Vol. I, pp. xviii, 255, 257, 301, 302.

4. G. Bernard Shaw, "Transition," in *Fabian Essays in Socialism*, ed. G. B. Shaw (Garden City, N.Y.: Doubleday, no date), pp. 224–225.

5. John Rawls, *A Theory of Justice* (Cambridge, Mass.: Harvard University Press, 1971), pp. 12, 17–22.

6. Adam Smith, *The Theory of Moral Sentiments* (Indianapolis: Liberty Classics, 1976), pp. 161–162, 211, 228–229, 247, 352, 370–371, 422.

7. See Thomas Sowell, *Marxism: Philosophy and Economics* (New York: William Morrow, 1985), pp. 55–59, 75–79.

8. Karl Marx and Frederick Engels, *Selected Correspondence*, translated by Dona Torr (New York: International Publishers, 1942), p. 58.

9. Karl Marx and Frederick Engels, *Basic Writings on Politics and Philosophy*, ed. Lewis S. Feuer (New York: Anchor Books, 1959), p. 119.

10. *Ibid.*, p. 109.

11. *Ibid.*, p. 399.

12. See, for example, Karl Marx, *Capital* (Chicago: Charles H. Kerr and Company, 1906), Vol. I, p. 15; Friedrich Engels, "Ludwig Feuerbach and the End of Classical German Philosophy," in Karl Marx and Friedrich Engels, *Basic Writings on Politics and Philosophy*, p. 230; Karl Marx and Frederick Engels, *Selected Correspondence*, p. 476.

13. Karl Marx, "Wage Labour and Capital," Karl Marx and Frederick Engels, *Selected Works* (Moscow: Foreign Languages Publishing House, 1955), Vol. I, pp. 99–101.

14. Karl Marx, *Theories of Surplus Value* (New York: International Publishers, 1952), p. 380.

15. Karl Marx, "The Eighteenth Brumaire of Louis Bonaparte," in Karl Marx and Frederick Engels, *Selected Works*, Vol. I, p. 288.

16. Frederick Engels, *Herr Eugen Dühring's Revolution in Science* (New York: International Publishers, 1939), p. 200; Karl Marx and Frederick Engels, *Selected Works*, Vol. II, p. 199n.

17. Frederick Engels, *Herr Eugen Dühring's Revolution in Science*, p. 306.

18. Karl Marx and Frederick Engels, *The German Ideology* (New York: International Publishers, 1947), p. 74.

19. K. Marx and F. Engels, *The Holy Family* (Moscow: Foreign Languages Publishing House, 1956), p. 227.

20. Karl Marx, *Capital*, Vol. I, p. 836.

21. *Ibid.*, p. 297.

22. See Thomas Sowell, *Marxism: Philosophy and Economics* (New York: William Morrow, 1985), Chapter 4.

23. See John Stuart Mill, *Collected Works* (Toronto: University of Toronto Press, 1969), Vol. X, pp. 86–87.

24. In Mill's words, "Bentham's idea of the world is that of a collection of persons pursuing each his separate interest or pleasure." *Ibid.*, p. 97.

25. Jeremy Bentham, *The Principles of Morals and Legislation* (New York: Hafner Publishing Company, 1948), p. 70.

26. The "extreme tidiness of his mind and the austere discipline of his mental processes" are noted in W. Stark, "Introduction," *Jeremy Bentham's Economic Writings* (London: George Allen & Unwin, Ltd., 1952), Vol. I, p. 17.

27. Jeremy Bentham, *Jeremy Bentham's Economic Writings*, ed. W. Stark, Vol. I, pp. 14, 123–207.

28. *Ibid.*, p. 129.

29. *Ibid.*, pp. 115–116.

30. John Stuart Mill, *Collected Works*, Vol. X, pp. 209n–210n.

31. *Ibid.*, pp. 5–18, 75–115.

32. *Ibid.*, pp. 117–163.

33. *Ibid.*, p. 91.

34. John Stuart Mill, *Essays on Some Unsettled Questions of Political Economy* (London: John W. Parker, 1844), p. 50.

35. John Stuart Mill, *Collected Works*, Vol. X, p. 15.

36. *Ibid.*, Vol. II, pp. 199–200.

37. *Ibid.*, p. 200.

38. Thomas Sowell, *Say's Law: An Historical Analysis* (Princeton: Princeton University Press, 1972), Chapter 5.

39. William Godwin, *Enquiry Concerning Political Justice*, Vol. I, pp. 158–162, 195; *ibid.*, Vol. II, p. 57.

40. *Ibid.*, Vol. I, pp. 168–169, 206.

41. Adam Smith, *An Inquiry into the Nature and Causes of the Wealth of Nations* (New York: Modery Library, 1937), p. 308.

42. *Buck v. Bell, Superintendent*, 274 U.S. 200, at 207.

Chapter 6: VISIONS OF EQUALITY

1. Edmund Burke, *Reflections on the Revolution in France* (New York: Everyman's Library, 1967), p. 56.

2. Alexander Hamilton et al., *The Federalist Papers* (New York: New American Library, 1961), p. 21.

3. *Ibid.*, p. 117.

4. F. A. Hayek, *Law, Legislation and Liberty* (Chicago: University of Chicago Press, 1973), Vol. I, p. 141.

5. *Ibid.*, Vol. II, p. 88.

6. *Ibid.*, Vol. I, p. 12.

7. Milton and Rose Friedman, *Free to Choose* (New York: Harcourt Brace Jovanovich, 1980), p. 148.

8. William Godwin, *Enquiry Concerning Political Justice* (Toronto: University of Toronto Press, 1969), Vol. II, p. 109.

9. *Ibid.*, p. 114.

10. *Ibid.*, p. 110.

11. Antoine-Nicolas de Condorcet, *Sketch for a Historical Picture of the Progress of the Human Mind* (Westport, Conn.: Hyperion Press, Inc., 1955), p. 174.

12. Bernard Shaw, *The intelligent Woman's Guide to Socialism and Capitalism* (New York: Brentano's Publishers, 1928), p. 94.

13. *Regents of the University of California v. Allan Bakke*, 438 U.S. 265, at 297.

14. *Ibid.*, at 387–394.

15. William Godwin, *Enquiry Concerning Political Justice*, Vol. I, p. 15.

16. Bernard Shaw, *The intelligent Woman's Guide to Socialism and Capitalism*, p. 22.

17. *Ibid.*, p. 126.

18. *Ibid.*, p. 137.

19. William Godwin, *Enquiry Concerning Political Justice*, Vol. II, p. 429.

20. Bernard Shaw, *The Intelligent Woman's Guide to Socialism and Capitalism*, p. 146.

21. Edward Bellamy, *Looking Backward: 2000–1887* (Boston: Houghton Mifflin Company, 1926), p. 136.

22. William Godwin, *Enquiry Concerning Political Justice*, Vol. I, p. 17.

23. Adam Smith, *The Theory of Moral Sentiments* (Indianapolis: Liberty Classics, 1976), 113ff; Milton and Rose Friedman, *Free to Choose*, p. 146.

24. Milton and Rose Friedman, *Free to Choose*, p. 146.

25. Adam Smith, *The Wealth of Nations* (New York: Modern Library, 1937), pp. 683, 736; Milton Friedman, *Capitalism and Freedom* (Chicago: University of Chicago Press, 1962), Chapter XII.

26. Milton and Rose Friedman, *Free to Choose*, p. 146.

27. *Ibid.*, p. 147.

28. Friedrich A. Hayek, *The Road to Serfdom* (Chicago: University of Chicago Press, 1972), p. 31.

29. *Ibid.*, p. 137.

30. See Friedrich A. Hayek, *The Road to Serfdom*, especially Chapter X. According to Hayek, "socialism can be put into practice only by methods which most socialists disapprove." Friedrich A. Hayek, *The Road to Serfdom*, p. 137. The phrase "the mirage of social justice" is the subtitle of the second volume of his later elaboration of his thesis in *Law, Legislation and Liberty*.

31. F. A. Hayek, *Law, Legislation and Liberty*, Vol. II, p. 20.

32. *Ibid.*, p. 22.

33. *Ibid.*, p. 33.

34. *Ibid.*, p. 2.

35. *Ibid.*, p. 39.

36. *Ibid.*, p. 65.

37. *Ibid.*, p. 64.

38. *Ibid.*, p. 64.

39. William Godwin, *Enquiry Concerning Political Justice*, Vol. I, p. 17.

40. *Ibid.*, Vol. II, p. 15.

41. *Ibid.*, p. 18.

42. *Ibid.*, p. 102.

43. *Ibid.*, p. 419.

44. Bernard Shaw, *The Intelligent Woman's Guide to Socialism and Capitalism*, p. 254.

45. *Ibid.*, p. 169.

46. F. A. Hayek, *Law, Legislation and Liberty*, Vol. II, p. 74.

47. *Ibid.*

48. Milton and Rose Friedman, *Free to Choose*, p. 146; Ronald Dworkin, *Taking Rights Seriously* (Cambridge, Mass.: Harvard University Press, 1980).

49. See, for example, Milton Friedman, *Capitalism and Freedom*, Chapter I.

50. Adam Smith, *The Wealth of Nations*, p. 16.

51. *Ibid.*, pp. 15–16.

52. Adam Smith, *The Theory of Moral Sentiments*, p. 337.

53. Adam Smith, *The Wealth of Nations*, pp. 80–81, 365.

54. Adam Smith, *The Theory of Moral Sentiments*, pp. 126–127.

55. *Ibid.*, p. 129.

56. *Ibid.*, p. 120.

57. Jacob Viner, "Adam Smith and Laissez-Faire," *Journal of Political Economy*, April 1927, p. 215.

58. Alexander Hamilton, *Selected Speeches and Writings of Alexander Hamilton*, p. 210.

59. William Godwin, *Enquiry Concerning Political Justice*, Vol. I, p. 143; ibid., Vol. II, pp. 98, 137.

60. *Ibid.*, Vol. II, pp. 101, 110.

61. *Ibid.*, Vol. I, pp. 18–19; ibid., Vol. II, p. 15.

62. *Ibid.*, Vol. I, pp. 257, 267–268, 302; ibid., Vol. II, pp. 531–532, 539, 543.

63. Thomas Hobbes, *Leviathan* (New York: E. P. Dutton and Company, 1970), pp. 35, 40.

64. William Godwin, *Enquiry Concerning Political Justice*, Vol. I, p. 446.

65. Jean-Jacques Rousseau, *The Social Contract* (New York: Penguin Books, 1968), p. 89.

66. Antoine Nicolas de Condorcet, *Sketch for a Historical Picture of the Progress of the Human Mind*, p. 114.

67. Bernard Shaw, *The Intelligent Woman's Guide to Socialism and Capitalism*, p. 456.

68. P. T. Bauer, *Reality and Rhetoric: Studies in the Economics of Development* (Cambridge, Mass.: Harvard University Press, 1984), pp. 1–18, 24; Theodore W. Schultz, *Investing in People: The Economics of Population Quality* (Berkeley: University of California Press, 1981), pp. 8–9, 25–26.

69. Gunnar Myrdal, *Asian Drama*, abridged by Seth S. King (New York: Vintage Books, 1972), pp. 44, 45, 53, 55, 68–69.

70. Gerald W. Chapman, *Edmund Burke: The Practical Imagination* (Cambridge, Mass.: Harvard University Press, 1967), pp. 134–135. See also Edmund Burke, *The Correspondence of Edmund Burke*, Vol. VIII, p. 343; ibid., Vol. IX, pp. 89, 315.

71. Edmund Burke, *Reflections on the Revolution in France*, p. 42.

72. Ronald Dworkin, *Taking Rights Seriously*, p. 239.

Chapter 7: VISIONS OF POWER

1. William Godwin, *Enquiry Concerning Political Justice* (Toronto: University of Toronto Press, 1969), Vol. II, p. 143.

2. Alexander Hamilton et al., *The Federalist Papers* (New York: New American Library, 1961), p. 46.

3. *Ibid.*, p. 58.

4. *Ibid.*, p. 60.

5. *Ibid.*, p. 87.

6. William Godwin, *Enquiry Concerning Political Justice*, Vol. II, pp. 144–145.

7. *Ibid.*, pp. 144–145, 155, 173.

8. *Ibid.*, pp. 164, 173.

9. *Ibid.*, p. 180.

10. *Ibid.*, p. 146.

11. *Ibid.*, pp. 167–168, 169.

12. Adam Smith, *The Theory of Moral Sentiments* (Indianapolis: Liberty Classics, 1976), p. 390.

13. *Ibid.*, p. 256.

14. *Ibid.*, pp. 373–374.

15. Antoine-Nicolas de Condorcet, *Sketch for a Historical Picture of the Progress of the Human Mind* (Westport, Conn.: Hyperion Press, Inc., 1955), p. 193.

16. William Godwin, *Enquiry Concerning Political Justice*, Vol. I, p. 276.

17. Ramsey Clark, *Crime in America* (New York: Simon and Schuster, 1970), p. 220.

18. *Ibid.*, p. 43.

19. *Ibid.*, p. 29.

20. *Ibid.*, p. 36.

21. *Ibid.*, p. 17.

22. *Ibid.*

23. Adam Smith, *The Theory of Moral Sentiments*, p. 170.

24. Ramsey Clark, *Crime in America*, p. 219.

25. William Godwin, *Enquiry Concerning Political Justice*, Vol. II, p. 355.

26. *Ibid.*, p. 380.

27. *Ibid.*, p. 381.

28. *Ibid.*, p. 382.

29. *Ibid.*, p. 532.

30. *Ibid.*, p. 380.

31. Ramsey Clark, *Crime in America*, p. 220.

32. John Stuart Mill, *Collected Works* (Toronto: University of Toronto Press, 1977), Vol. XVIII, p. 241.

33. *Ibid.*, p. 269.

34. Ronald Dworkin, *Taking Rights Seriously* (Cambridge, Mass.: Harvard University Press, 1980), pp. 200–222.

35. Milton and Rose Friedman, *Free to Choose* (New York: Harcourt Brace Jovanovich, 1980), p. 17.

36. *Ibid.*, p. 18.

37. Adolf A. Berle, *Power* (New York: Harcourt Brace and World, Inc., 1969), p. 200.

38. *Ibid.*, p. 208.

39. John Kenneth Galbraith, *The New Industrial State* (Boston: Houghton Mifflin Company, 1967), p. 58.

40. John Kenneth Galbraith, *The Affluent Society* (Boston: Houghton Mifflin Company, 1958), pp. 110–11; George J. Stigler, *The*

Economist as Preacher (Chicago: University of Chicago Press, 1982), p. 57.

41. Harry G. Johnson, *On Economics and Society* (Chicago: University of Chicago Press, 1975), p. 202.

42. Gunnar Myrdal, *Asian Drama*, abridged by Seth S. King (New York: Vintage Books, 1972), p. 11.

43. P. T. Bauer, *Dissent on Development*, (Cambridge, Mass.: Harvard University Press, 1979), p. 25.

44. Gunnar Myrdal, *Asian Drama*, p. 131.

45. *Ibid.*, p. 142.

46. P. T. Bauer, *Reality and Rhetoric: Studies in Economics of Development* (Cambridge, Mass.: Harvard University Press, 1984), p. 36.

47. Gunnar Myrdal, *Asian Drama*, pp. 3, 106, 131–145.

48. *Ibid.*, pp. 18, 25, 55.

49. Gunnar Myrdal, *Asian Drama*, p. 150.

50. *Ibid.*, p. 181.

51. *Ibid.*, p. 43.

52. *Ibid.*, p. 53.

53. *Ibid.*, pp. 68–69.

54. *Ibid.*, p. 4.

55. P. T. Bauer, *Reality and Rhetoric*, pp. 2–3, 6, 30–31.

56. P. T. Bauer, *Equality, the Third World, and Economic Delusion* (Cambridge, Mass.: Harvard University Press, 1981), p. 80.

57. P. T. Bauer, *Dissent on Development*, p. 162.

58. P. T. Bauer, *Equality, the Third World, and Economic Delusion*, p. 83.

59. *Ibid.*, p. 84.

60. P. T. Bauer, *Dissent on Development*, p. 44.

61. P. T. Bauer, *Equality, the Third World, and Economic Delusion*, p. 49.

62. P. T. Bauer, *Dissent on Development*, pp. 205–206.

63. P. T. Bauer, *Reality and Rhetoric*, p. 35.

64. P. T. Bauer, *Dissent on Development*, p. 221.

65. Gunnar Myrdal, *Asian Drama*, p. 63.

66. *Ibid.*, p. 79.

67. *Ibid.*, p. 82.

68. *Ibid.*, p. 143.

69. P. T. Bauer, *Reality and Rhetoric*, p. 25.

70. John Kenneth Galbraith, *The Anatomy of Power* (Boston: Houghton Mifflin Company, 1983), p. 7.

71. Robert A. Dahl and Charles E. Lindblom, *Politics, Economics and Welfare* (Chicago: University of Chicago Press, 1967), p. 94.

72. John Kenneth Galbraith, *The Anatomy of Power*, p. 14.

73. One of the noted contemporary advocates of the concept of "economic power" defines it as the "capacity to cause or to refuse production, purchase, sale, or delivery of goods, or to cause or prevent the rendering of service (including labor)." Adolf A. Berle, *Power*, p. 143.

74. John Dewey, *Intelligence in the Modern World* (New York: Random House, 1939), p. 448.

75. *Superior Oil Company v. State of Mississippi, ex rel. Knox, Attorney General*, 280 U.S. 390, at 395–296.

76. Oliver Wendell Holmes, *Collected Legal Papers* (New York: Peter Smith, 1952), p. 208.

77. *Erie Railroad Co. v. Board of Public Utility Commissioners et al.*, 254 U.S. 394, at 411.

78. *Otis v. Parker*, 187 U.S. 606, at 608.

79. *Brown v. United States*, 256 U.S. 335, at 343.

80. Ronald Dworkin, *Taking Rights Seriously*, p. 137.

81. *Ibid.*, p. 139.

82. *Ibid.*, p. 277.

83. *Ibid.*, pp. 265, 265.

84. Laurence H. Tribe, *Constitutional Choices* (Cambridge, Mass.: Harvard University Press, 1985), p. 22.

85. *Ibid.*, p. 227.

86. Ronald Dworkin, *Taking Rights Seriously*, p. 149.

87. Laurence H. Tribe, *Constitutional Choices*, p. 28.

88. *Ibid.*, p. 165.

89. *Ibid.*, p. 171.

90. *Ibid.*, p. 179.

91. *Ibid.*, p. 187.

92. Ronald Coase, "The Problem of Social Cost," *Journal of Law Economics*, October 1960, p. 16.

93. Erik G. Furuboth and Svetozar Pejovich, "Property Rights and Economic Theory: A Survey of the Literature," *Journal of Economic Literature*, December 1972, p. 1137.

94. Laurence H. Tribe, *Constitutional Choices*, p. 189.

95. *Ibid.*, p. 193.

96. *Ibid.*, p. 220.

97. *Ibid.*, p. 197.

98. *Ibid.*, p. 193.

99. Armen A. Achian and Harold Demsetz, "Production, Information Costs, and Economic Organization," *American Economic Review*, December 1972, pp. 777, 788.

100. *Ibid.*, p. 777.

101. Laurence H. Tribe, *Constitutional Choices*, p. 243.

102. See, for example, *Food Employees Local Union v. Logan Valley Plaza*, 391 U.S. 308, and *Lloyd Corp., Ltd., v. Tanner*, 407 U.S. 551.

103. Laurence H. Tribe, *Constitutional Choices*, p. 255.

104. *Ibid.*, p. 247.

105. *Peterson et al. v. City of Greenville*, 373 U.S. 244, at 250.

Chapter 8: VISIONS OF JUSTICE

1. John Rawls, *A Theory of Justice* (Cambridge, Mass.: Harvard University Press, 1971), pp. 3–4.

2. Ronald Dworkin, *Taking Rights Seriously* (Cambridge, Mass.: Harvard University Press, 1980), p. xi; Laurence H. Tribe, *Constitutional Choices* (Cambridge, Massachusetts: Harvard University Press, 1985), p. 5.

3. William Godwin, *Enquiry Concerning Social Justice* (Toronto: University of Toronto Press, 1969), Vol. I, p. 166.

4. Godwin, for example, was averse to government's redressing inequalities in the distribution of property, though he regarded these inequalities as moral inequities. *Ibid.*, Vol. II, pp. 433–434.

5. Adam Smith, *The Theory of Moral Sentiments* (Indianapolis: Liberty Classics, 1976), p. 169.

6. *Ibid.*, p. 167.

7. *Ibid.*, pp. 167–168.

8. *Ibid.*, p. 166.

9. Oliver Wendell Holmes, Jr., *The Common Law* (Boston: Little, Brown and Company, 1923), p. 108.

10. *Ibid.*, p. 48.

11. Oliver Wendell Holmes, Jr., *Collected Legal Papers* (New York: Peter Smith, 1952), p. 179.

12. Oliver Wendell Holmes, Jr., *The Common Law*, p. 48.

13. *Buck v. Bell, Superintendent*, 274 U.S. 200, at 207.

14. Oliver Wendell Holmes, Jr., *The Common Law*, p. 1.

15. Oliver Wendell Holmes, Jr., *Collected Legal Papers*, p. 194.

16. *Ibid.*

17. William Blackstone, *Commentaries on the Laws of England* (Chicago: University of Chicago Press, 1979), Vol. I, p. 62.

18. *Ibid.*, p. 41.

19. *Ibid.*, p. 70.

20. *Ibid.*, p. 68.

21. *Ibid.*, pp. 59, 60, 61, *passim*.

22. *Ibid.*, p. 70.

23. Edmund Burke, *Reflections on the Revolution in France* (New York: Everyman's Library, 1967), p. 92.

24. F. A. Hayek, *Legislation and Liberty* (Chicago: University of Chicago Press, 1973), Vol. I, p. 100.

25. Adam Smith, *The Theory of Moral Sentiments* (Indianapolis: Liberty Classics, 1976), p. 142.

26. *Ibid.*, p. 156.

27. Oliver Wendell Holmes, Jr., *The Common Law*, p. 2.

28. William Godwin, *Enquiry Concerning Social Justice*, Vol. II, p. 347.

29. *Ibid.*, p. 400.

30. *Ibid.*, p. 404.

31. John Dewey, *Human Nature and Conduct* (New York: Random House, 1957), p. 46.

32. William Godwin, *Enquiry Concerning Social Justice*, Vol. I, p. 171.

33. *Ibid.*, p. 173.

34. Deterrence versus rehabilitation approaches to crime control, for example.

35. Antoine-Nicolas de Condorcet, *Sketch for a Historical Picture of the Progress of the Human Mind* (Westport, Conn.: Hyperion Press, Inc., 1955), p. 192.

36. William Godwin, *Enquiry Concerning Social Justice*, Vol. I, pp. 437–438.

37. *Ibid.*, 171 ff.

38. Antoine-Nicolas de Condorcet, *Sketch for a Historical Picture of the Progress of the Human Mind*, p. 112.

39. *Ibid.*, p. 31.

40. Laurence H. Tribe, *Constitutional Choices* (Cambridge, Mass.: Harvard University Press, 1985), p. ix.

41. *Ibid.*, p. viii.

42. *Ibid.*, p. 4.

43. *Ibid.*, p. 5.

44. *Ibid.*, p. 268.

45. *Ibid.*, p. 11.

46. *Ibid.*, p. 13.

47. *Ibid.*, p. 26.

48. *Ibid.*, p. 239.

49. *Ibid.*, pp. 241–242.

50. Ronald Dworkin, *Taking Rights Seriously*, p. 147.

51. See, for example, Richard Posner, *Economic Analysis of Law* (Boston: Little, Brown, and Company, 1972), Chapter 2.

52. *Ibid.*, pp. 12–13, 18. See also *idem.*, *The Economics of Justice* (Cambridge, Mass.: Harvard University Press, 1981), pp. 70–71, 180–182.

53. Milton Friedman *Capitalism and Freedom*, Chapter 1.

54. 250 U.S. 616 (1919), at 659; *Abrams et al. v. United States*, 250 U.S. 616, at 630.

55. *Ibid.* Holmes also said, in this dissent: "I do not doubt for a moment that by the same reasoning that would justify punishing persuasion to murder, the United States constitutionally may punish speech that produces or is intended to produce a clear and imminent danger that it will bring about forthwith certain substantive evils that the United States constitutionally may seek to prevent." *Ibid.*, at 627.

56. Ronald Dworkin, *Taking Rights Seriously*, p. 264.

57. Laurence H. Tribe, *Constitutional Choices*, p. 165.

58. *Ibid.*, p. 169.

59. *Ibid.*, p. 165.

60. *Ibid.*, p. 11.

61. *Ibid.*, p. 189.

62. *Ibid.*, p. 197.

63. *Ibid.*, p. 188.

64. *Ibid.*, p. 220.

65. See, for example, *Marsh v. Alabama*, 326 U.S. 501; *Food Employees Union v. Logan Valley Plaza*, 391 U.S. 308.

66. Laurence H. Tribe, *Constitutional Choices*, p. 258.

67. William Godwin, *Enquiry Concerning Social Justice*, Vol. II, p. 57.

68. *Ibid.*, Vol. I, pp. 161, 162.

69. *Ibid.*, pp. 168–169, 206; *ibid.*, Vol. II, pp. 432, 439–445; Antoine-Nicolas de Condorcet, *Sketch for a Historical Picture of the Progress of the Human Mind*, pp. 130–131, 180.

70. F. A. Hayek, *Law, Legislation and Liberty* (Chicago: University of Chicago Press, 1976), Vol. II, p. 64.

71. See subtitle, *ibid.*, title page.

72. F. A. Hayek, *Law, Legislation and Liberty*, Vol. II, p. xii.

73. *Ibid.*, p. 66.

74. *Ibid.*, p. 78.

75. Adam Smith, *The Wealth of Nations*, pp. 683, 734–738; John Rae, *Life of Adam Smith* (New York: Augustus M. Kelley, 1965), p. 437.

76. Michael St. John Packe, *The Life of John Stuart Mill* (New York: The Macmillan Company, 1954), pp. 56–59, 457–462, 484.

77. Edmund Burke, *The Correspondence of Edmund Burke* (Chicago: University of Chicago Press, 1968), Vol. VII, pp. 124–125; Adam Smith, *The Theory of Moral Sentiments*, p. 337; Adam Smith, *The Wealth of Nations*, pp. 365–366; William Godwin, *Enquiry Concerning Political Justice*, pp. 443–444; Antoine Nicolas de Condorcet, *Sketch for a Historical Picture of the Progress of the Human Mind*, p. 114.

78. Milton Friedman, *Capitalism and Freedom*, pp. 191–193; Bernard Shaw, *The Intelligent Woman's Guide to Socialism and Capitalism* (New York: Brentano's Publishers, 1928), pp. 112–117.

79. William Godwin, *Enquiry Concerning Social Justice*, Vol. II, pp. 439–430.

80. Bernard Shaw, *The Intelligent Woman's Guide to Socialism and Capitalism*, pp. 95–96.

81. F. A. Hayek, *Law, Legislation and Liberty*, Vol. II, p. 75.

82. *Ibid.*, p. 67.

83. F. A. Hayek, *Studies in Philosophy, Politics and Economics* (New York: Simon and Schuster, 1969), p. 238.

84. F. A. Hayek, *Law, Legislation and Liberty*, Vol. II, p. xii.

85. *Ibid.*, p. xi.

86. *Ibid.*, p. 80.

87. *Ibid.*, p. 97.

88. *Ibid.*, p. 130.

89. Friedrich A. Hayek, *The Road to Serfdom* (Chicago: University of Chicago Press, 1972), p. 79.

90. F. A. Hayek, *Law, Legislation and Liberty*, Vol. II, pp. 62–63.

91. *Ibid.*, p. 33.

92. *Ibid.*, p. 70.

93. *Ibid.*, p. 64.

94. F. A. Hayek, *Studies in Philosophy, Politics and Economics*, p. 240.

95. *Ibid.*, p. 243.

96. F. A. Hayek, *Law, Legislation and Liberty*, Vol. II, p. 36.

97. See, for example, Milton Friedman, *Capitalism and Freedom* (Chicago: University of Chicago Press, 1962), pp. 133–136, 161–177.

98. Richard Posner, *The Economics of Justice* (Cambridge, Mass.: Harvard University Press, 1981).

99. Friedrich A. Hayek, *The Road to Serfdom*, p. 167.

100. *Ibid.*, Chapter XII.

101. F. A. Hayek, *Law, Legislation and Liberty*, Vol. II, p. 86.

102. *Ibid.*, p. 86.

103. Ronald Dworkin, *Taking Rights Seriously*, pp. 184–205.

104. Antoine-Nicholas de Condorcet, *Sketch for a Historical Picture of the Progress of the Human Mind*, p. 174.

105. *Regents of the University of California v. Allan Bakke*, 438 U.S. 265, at 294n.

Chapter 9: Visions, Values, and Paradigms

1. Thomas Kuhn, *The Structure of Scientific Revolutions* (Chicago: University of Chicago Press, 1970), pp. viii, 10, 23–34.

2. *Ibid.*, p. 10.

3. *Ibid.*, p. 17.

4. Thomas Robert Malthus, *Population: The First Essay* (Ann Arbor: University of Michigan Press, 1959), pp. 3, 50–105.

5. *Ibid.*, p. 4.

6. Though implicit, diminishing returns did not become explicit until seventeen years later, when Malthus and Sir Edward West simultaneously published pamphlets which made them the accredited co-discoverers of this economic principle. Thomas Robert Malthus, *An Inquiry into the Nature and Progress of Rent* (Baltimore: Johns Hopkins University Press, 1903); [Sir Edward West], *An Essay on the Application of Capital to Land* (London: P. Underwood, 1815). See also Thomas Sowell, *Classical Economics Reconsidered* (Princeton: Princeton University Press, 1974), pp. 75–77.

7. Thomas Robert Malthus, *Population*, p. 20.

8. Thomas Robert Malthus, *Principles of Political Economy*, 2nd edition (London: John Murray, 1836), p. 226.

9. Thomas Robert Malthus, *Population*, p. 34.

10. *Ibid.*, p. 57.

11. *Ibid.*, p. 67.

12. *Ibid.*, p. 95.

13. See Thomas Sowell, "Adam Smith in Theory and Practice," *Adam Smith and Modern Political Economy*, ed. Gerald P. O'Driscoll (Ames, Iowa: Iowa State University Press, 1979), pp. 11–13.

14. Richard A. Lester, "Shortcomings of Marginal Analysis for Wage-Employment Problems," *American Economic Review*, March 1946, pp. 63–82.

15. Herbert G. Gutman, *The Black Family in Slavery and Freedom, 1750–1925* (New York: Vintage Books, 1976).

16. Friedrich A. Hayek, *The Road to Serfdom* (Chicago: University of Chicago Press, 1972), pp. 103–105.

17. Adam Smith, *The Wealth of Nations*, p. 250.

18. *Ibid.*, p. 438.

19. *Ibid.*, p. 128.

20. *Ibid.*, p. 401.

21. Milton and Rose Friedman, *Tyranny of the Status Quo* (New York: Harcourt Brace Jovanovich, 1984), pp. 35–39, 46, 52–53, 119; F. A. Hayek, *Studies in Philosophy, Politics and Economics* (New York: Simon and Schuster, 1967), p. 192.

22. William Godwin, *Enquiry Concerning Political Justice* (Toronto: University of Toronto Press, 1969), Vol. I, p. 21; *ibid.*, Vol. II, p. 454; Bernard Shaw, *The Intelligent Woman's Guide to Socialism and Capitalism* (New York: Brentano's Publishers, 1928), pp. 386–391; John Ken-

neth Galbraith, *The Anatomy of Power* (Boston: Houghton Mifflin Company, 1983), pp. 138–140.

23. Adam Smith, *The Wealth of Nations*, p. 718ff.

24. Joseph A. Schumpeter was one of the rare exceptions, but he was only briefly a businessman—and unsuccessfully so.

25. Thomas Robert Malthus, *Population*, p. 3.

26. William Godwin, *Of Population* (London: Longman, Hurst, Rees, Orme, and Brown, 1820), p. 520.

27. *Ibid.*, p. 554.

28. *Ibid.*, p. 550.

29. *Ibid.*, p. 565.

30. See, for example, Friedrich A. Hayek, *The Road to Serfdom*, pp. iv-v.

31. *Ibid.*, p. 55.

32. *Ibid.*, p. 185.

33. See, for example, J. A. Schumpeter, "Science and Ideology," *American Economic Review*, March 1949, pp. 345–359.

34. Thomas Sowell, *Knowledge and Decisions* (New York: Basic Books, 1980), pp. 147–149.

INDEX